ALSO BY KRISTEN R. GHODSEE

Why Women Have Better Sex Under Socialism:
And Other Arguments for Economic Independence

Red Valkyries: Feminist Lessons from Five Revolutionary Women

Everyday Utopia

What 2,000 Years of Wild Experiments
Can Teach Us About the Good Life

Kristen R. Ghodsee

SIMON & SCHUSTER

NEW YORK   LONDON   TORONTO   SYDNEY   NEW DELHI

Simon & Schuster
1230 Avenue of the Americas
New York, NY 10020

First Simon & Schuster hardcover edition May 2023

SIMON & SCHUSTER and colophon are registered trademarks of Simon & Schuster, Inc.

For information about special discounts for bulk purchases, please contact Simon & Schuster Special Sales at 1-866-506-1949 or business@simonandschuster.com.

The Simon & Schuster Speakers Bureau can bring authors to your live event. For more information or to book an event, contact the Simon & Schuster Speakers Bureau at 1-866-248-3049 or visit our website at www.simonspeakers.com.

Interior design by Carly Loman

Manufactured in the United States of America

10 9 8 7 6 5 4 3 2 1

Library of Congress Cataloging-in-Publication Data

Names: Ghodsee, Kristen Rogheh, 1970– author.
Title: Everyday utopia : what 2,000 years of wild experiments can teach us about the good life / Kristen R. Ghodsee.
Description: First Simon and Schuster hardcover edition. | New York : Simon & Schuster, [2023] | Includes bibliographical references and index.
Identifiers: LCCN 2022027753 (print) | LCCN 2022027754 (ebook) | ISBN 9781982190217 (hardcover) | ISBN 9781982190231 (ebook)
Subjects: LCSH: Utopian socialism—History. | Utopias—History. | Communal living—History.
Classification: LCC HX630 .G46 2023 (print) | LCC HX630 (ebook) | DDC 335/.02—dc23 eng/20220804
LC record available at https://lccn.loc.gov/2022027753
LC ebook record available at https://lccn.loc.gov/2022027754

ISBN 978-1-9821-9021-7
ISBN 978-1-9821-9023-1 (ebook)

For Tom and Betty

Contents

Author's Note

In what is now the southern Italian region of Calabria, in the seaside village of Kroton (today called Crotone), an ancient Greek philosopher named Pythagoras founded a colony for his followers in the sixth century BC or BCE (Before the Common Era), about two thousand and five hundred years ago. Although most of us know Pythagoras for his famous theorem—that in a right-angled triangle, the square of its longest side is equal to the sum of the squares of the other two sides—Pythagoras was also a great-grandfather of utopian thinking. While the daily lives of the inhabitants of Kroton are obscured by the passage of time, the evidence suggests that the people there lived a uniquely collaborative lifestyle as they dedicated themselves to the study of mathematics and the mysteries of the universe.

In his third century AD or CE (Common Era) text on the *Life of Pythagoras*, the philosopher Iamblichus reports of Pythagoras that, "For all things [with his disciples] were common and the same to all, and no one possessed any thing private."[1] By sharing all of their property, Iamblichus tells us that the followers of Pythagoras avoided "sedition and tumult" in their community and sought to enjoy more harmonious and cooperative lives than their contemporaries. Pythagoras may also have been a proto-feminist. Theano, the world's first-known woman mathematician, whom Iamblichus describes as "a woman of a wise and excellent soul," assumed the leadership of the colony after Pythagoras's death around 490 BCE, and Iamblichus suggests that the Pythagoreans viewed women and men as intellectual and spiritual equals at a time when most Greek women were considered little more than vessels for making babies. Iamblichus also tells us that the Pythagorean principle, that all things should be shared in common among friends, female and male, influenced the philosopher Plato, the author of the *Republic*. He not only included the idea of collective property in his description of the ideal city of Kallipolis—a Kroton on a larger scale—but also asserted that men and women were equally suited to be the Guardians of his Republic.

These two key ideas (of sharing property and treating women as equals), together with others that I will explore in these pages, have infused visions for rethinking the way we live out our private lives for over two and a half millennia. For generations, stretching all the way back to antiquity, different communities, both spiritual and secular, have experimented with ways to render these ideals a reality. How is it then that in the year 2023 our domestic lives—what we do inside our homes, with our families, and in our interactions with friends, neighbors, and members of our wider communities—are still very much shaped by decidedly inegalitarian and sexist traditions?

When I began writing this book a few months into the coronavirus pandemic, the sudden school shutdowns revealed how much we rely on unpaid labor in the home to keep our nations functioning. Parents—especially mothers—were overwhelmed and exhausted. Women around the globe woke up and realized that decades of feminism had done little to reverse the social expectation that mothers, sisters, wives, and daughters should provide care for young children, elderly parents, and sick relatives, as well as perform the emotional labors that hold families together in times of crisis: planning Zoom birthday parties, organizing virtual funerals, or lending a sympathetic ear to support the psychological health of loved ones far and near. I wondered: How many women with "wise and excellent" souls were crushed under the avalanche of nurturing suddenly required of them?

In the first six months of the pandemic, all statistics pointed to a female jobs apocalypse. By September 2020, four times as many American women as men had left the labor market as COVID-19 forced remote learning to continue for the new school year. Not all departures were voluntary. C. Nicole Mason of the Institute for Women's Policy Research coined the term "shecession" to describe the wave of unemployment that hit mothers the hardest.[2] A July 24 article in the *Guardian* ran with the headline that "UK Working Mothers Are the 'Sacrificial Lambs' in the Coronavirus Childcare Crisis."[3] In the same month, the British Office for National Statistics reported that women performed two-thirds of households' additional childcare duties, and that most of these duties compromised "non-developmental care," meaning that while fathers played with their children, mothers did the cooking, cleaning, nappy changing, and washing up.[4] In households with kids under the age of five, women did on average about *80 percent* more caring than men.

Even in the best of times, women give up their own dreams, ambitions, and interests to provide unpaid care, producing for free the next generation of workers, taxpayers, and consumers necessary for our economies to function. This at-home labor allows states to cut or reduce public expenditures for the provision of childcare, elder care, health care, and education, thereby lightening tax burdens, often for the wealthy. When a crisis hits, social expectations about their "inherently" nurturing dispositions mean that women's self-sacrifice is the ultimate backup plan.

It didn't have to be this way. For over two millennia, people have dreamed of building societies that reimagined the role of the family—not just for the benefit of women but for men, too. These utopian thinkers envisioned communities bonded by friendship, love, and a desire for mutual aid, that joined together to support the many essential labors typically performed behind closed doors: sharing chores, homes, sometimes possessions, and often the responsibility for raising the next generation. As the pandemic created more chaos and upheaval in the world of work and expanded the role of governments in protecting public health, I began to wonder what kinds of changes would reshape our private lives, and how these new ways of living might draw inspiration from earlier utopian experiments.

Rather than an exhaustive survey, I wrote this book as an accessible introduction to a wide variety of ideas from a broad scope of intellectual traditions that might help us think our way into a different future. Although I occasionally mention utopian visions in literature, film, television, and other sorts of popular culture, I chose to focus on political, philosophical, and theological texts, as well as existing historical and contemporary communities. Everywhere you look today, people are exploring new and different ways of organizing their personal lives, from the successful cohousing movement in Denmark; the flourishing ecovillages of Colombia and Portugal; or the new vision of schooling once proposed by the "Education for Self-Reliance" program in Tanzania. The inclusion of true-life examples highlights that even the most outlandish ideas can have real impacts on the way we shape our private relationships. It is silly to be dismissive of radical social dreams when there are so many people already showing us how to turn these dreams into practical realities.

I use the term "utopian" quite broadly in this book, following the work of the German sociologist Karl Mannheim, and realize that many activists or members of specific religious communities might bristle at the application of this term to their worldview. But today, too many people use the words "utopian" and "unrealistic" synonymously and I want to challenge this equivalence. "Utopian" as I use it simply denotes thinkers and movements that attempted to rearrange the domestic sphere in ways significantly out of keeping with the prevailing traditions of their societies for the purpose of living together in greater harmony in pursuit of either secular or spiritual goals. By including utopian communities of faith, I want to show that social dreaming spans the political spectrum, just as it crosses cultures and transverses historical epochs.

I realize that many of my academic colleagues may frown at my attempt to make these ideas accessible to a general audience when literally centuries worth of nuanced scholarship and theoretical writing already exists. But there are always more things than can be encompassed in any book, and I had to make tough editorial decisions about where to go deep and where to pull back. I hope that interested readers will be inspired to further explore these ideas by consulting the many works listed in the endnotes or checking out my selected suggestions for further reading. And because I wanted to make this book as international as possible, I chose not to include a disproportionate number of examples from the United States—not to dwell, for instance, too long on the "hippie communes" of the 1960s, which have been discussed at length elsewhere. Instead, I highlight different experiments that have received relatively less attention.

Since I am dealing with many historical texts and cross-cultural analyses, I've also had to think carefully about how words change their meanings over time. In this book, I use the terms "woman," "mother," and "female" to refer to what many English language speakers would call "cisgendered women." I am particularly interested in utopian visions that seek to improve the lives of women, since the burden of work inside the home, or what is often called "care work" (the cooking, cleaning, cuddling, and caressing necessary for the making and raising of children, as well as the domestic labors that underpin the health and well-being of all family members), so often falls disproportionately on them. But I have no intention of excluding the concerns of other genders from the discussion of a more utopian future. I hope that all readers will find compelling reasons to think beyond the rigid gender roles that have been upheld and perpetuated by a specific set of historically contingent social and economic customs. I believe the ideas discussed in these pages can benefit everyone, including men who struggle with societal expectations that they must be financial providers.

In 1891, Oscar Wilde wrote: "A map of the world that does not include Utopia is not worth even glancing at." This book is my attempt to revisit some of the social dreams of earlier utopian thinkers in different historical and cultural contexts. I recognize that many of these visions contain flaws and that some may seem far-fetched, and my discussion of different visions does not imply a blanket endorsement of their worldviews or some kind of retrospective absolution for their failures. But taken together as a panorama of different ideas combined with some reflections on the communities adapting those visions to the real world today, I think they can help us consider different ways of organizing our lives to deal with a number of contemporary issues we face in the twenty-first century.

By studying the history of social dreams, we can reject the bad bits and keep the good: challenging ourselves to explore alternatives for how we live, love, own our things, choose our families, and raise children. By making change in our private lives, we can help to decrease loneliness and isolation, reduce our carbon footprints to save the planet, tackle inequality and social injustice, treat the epidemic levels of stress, depression, and anxiety permeating our societies, and help to nurture and nourish the dreams and aspirations of the next generation. We need to think big, with more expansive visions of building stronger communities. As the mathematicians of Kroton knew two and a half millennia ago, utopian thinking is an essential ingredient of progress—whether unraveling the mysteries of the universe or ensuring that the burden of care work doesn't always fall disproportionately on anyone's shoulders. It's time to let our imaginations run wild.

CHAPTER 1

To Boldly Know Where No One Has Known Before

How Blue Sky Thinking Can Set Us Free

O ne of my earliest memories is swaying back and forth on the swing set in front of the massive screen of the old drive-in theater on Bella Pacific Row in San Diego in the summer of 1977. My dad had heard about a new movie with the actor Alec Guinness and packed our whole family into the burnt-red Chevy Impala for an evening out. The opening music and scroll of words giving way to the violent boarding of the Rebel ship froze my mouth open in midair. And when Leia first stepped out of the shadows to blast a stormtrooper and then jutted her chin out at Lord Vader to assert that she was "a member of the Imperial Senate on a diplomatic mission to Alderaan," I felt that sudden swoosh of preadolescent hero worship. I spent the rest of the film lying on the hood of the car, staring up into a distant galaxy where rescued princesses weren't damsels in distress, but sassy politicians with their own insurgent armies.

My obsession with Princess Leia followed hard upon a fascination with Lynda Carter's TV portrayal of Wonder Woman. The pilot had aired in November of 1975 when I was five and a half, and for my sixth birthday the next year, they released two more episodes. My mother tells me that I once had a metal Wonder Woman lunch box (with a matching thermos) and wore cotton Wonder Woman Underoos beneath my clothes to elementary school—an Amazon warrior of addition and subtraction.

I thus spent much of my early childhood imagining myself alternatively in an eagle-encrusted bustier with satin tights or in flowing white robes with cinnamon buns attached to either side of my head. Themiscyra (Pontus) was an ancient town on the southern coast of the Black Sea and the supposed capital city of the female warriors called the Amazons in Greek mythology. In the Detective Comics (DC) universe, creator William Moulton Marston reimagined "Themyscira" as an island city-state of independent women, a kind of feminist utopia where the Amazons enjoyed their immortal lives in peace. Queen Hippolyta is mother to Princess Diana (Wonder Woman), who leaves Paradise Island to help fight the Axis powers in World War II.[1] In the galaxy built by George Lucas, Leia Organa inhabited an alternate reality where princesses could be tough and bossy without being bitches. Motivated by her political convictions, rather than being driven by romantic love or a desire to protect her family, Leia believed in a righteous cause and was willing to die for it. Within the power hierarchy of the Rebel Alliance, it seemed perfectly normal that a middle-aged woman (Mon Mothma) would lead the scrappy resistance against the warmongering space Nazis of the Empire.

Young as I was, I understood that Wonder Woman and Princess Leia were allowed to be the heroes of their own stories because *they didn't live in my world*. I grew up in the military-dominated milieu of 1970s San Diego, which still reified traditional gender roles. Ivy League colleges like Harvard and Yale had just started admitting female undergraduates, and Title IX, the federal law that states that "no person in the United States shall, on the basis of sex, be excluded from participation in, be denied the benefits of, or be subjected to discrimination under any education program or activity receiving Federal financial assistance," had only passed in 1972. Although the Equal Rights Amendment—an amendment to the US Constitution that would have guaranteed equality between all citizens regardless of sex—received congressional approval that same year, it failed to win subsequent ratification. Spunky girls my age had few real-life role models. And so, in my daydreams, my adventures took place in fictional worlds. Armed with my make-believe blaster or bullet-bouncing bracelets, I fantasized my way into an uncertain future.

When faced with bullies, insecurities, fierce family conflicts, or just the basic tediousness of elementary school, I found comfort in my imagination, as so many children do. And then somewhere around mid-adolescence, I watched with curiosity as most of my peers abandoned their make-believe places to concentrate on grades, sports, jobs, college applications, and the dramas of dating. I found myself an outlier among my friends for whom the looming end of high school meant the end of daydreaming. But as a certified Model United Nations dork (I was secretary-general of my club), make-believe was an official extracurricular activity. Rather than embrace the hegemonic realpolitik and greed-lionizing sensibilities of the 1980s, I carried on imagining the possibility of different worlds. I discovered that learning about other political and economic systems opened my mind to the possibility that the reality in which I lived was not the only one available. Once I started thinking about the world not as it was but as it might be, I could more clearly diagnose the problems with my own time and place—and mentally play with possible solutions.

The Upside of Upheaval

I don't think it was a coincidence that my first lessons in utopian thinking came when they did: in the midst of the Cold War and in the aftermath of the turbulent 1960s. Historically, moments of political uncertainty often give birth to utopian dreaming, which is one reason why it is enjoying such a renaissance today. For millennia, new ways of organizing social relations have emerged when philosophers, theologians, reformers, writers, and other visionaries imagine them *elsewhere*, in some idealized world that serves as a mirror to reflect the deficiencies of the accepted state of things. Perhaps the most influential early rendering of an ideal society is Plato's *Republic*, written about 2,350 years before Princess Leia captured my imagination. The *Republic* was produced in the aftermath of the Peloponnesian War, a conflict the historian Thucydides memorialized as "the greatest war of all."[2] This conflagration had engulfed the entire Greek world and precipitated the demise of its relatively peaceful and prosperous golden age after the Persian wars. Among the many casualties was Athenian democracy. Plato's childhood coincided with the violent reign of the oligarchic "Thirty Tyrants," who seized power after Athens's catastrophic defeat. He witnessed the economic devastation and plague that ravaged his once prosperous home. Plato published his famous outline for a perfect society following these world-changing events.

Centuries after Plato, the English humanist and statesman Sir Thomas More coined the word "Utopia" for his 1516 treatise: *Libellus vere aureus, nec minus salutaris quam festivus, de optimo rei publicae statu deque nova insula Utopia* (*A Little, True Book, Not Less Beneficial Than Enjoyable, on the Best State of a Republic and on the New Island of Utopia*). The word "Utopia" derives from the Greek roots for "not" and "place," which means that "Utopia" references a "no place" or nowhere, although it is also a homonym for the word "Eutopia," which means "good place." This ambiguity was intentional. More published his book in Latin and it never saw an English translation until after Henry VIII had him executed, probably because More understood that Henry would consider the book's contents subversive and might have beheaded him sooner.

Sir Thomas More wrote *Utopia* within thirty years of the journeys of Christopher Columbus and Amerigo Vespucci. Their "discoveries" filled his contemporaries' minds with dreams of new worlds and provoked profound debates about the supposed universality of institutions once taken for granted. The old world of Europe, with its rigid social customs of squabbling hereditary landowners lording over toiling serfs and the often-corrupt dominance of the Roman Catholic Church, suddenly faced the reality of its own ignorance. If there were entirely unexplored continents to the west, perhaps there were also newer and better ways to organize society to maximize human flourishing.

In the wake of these profound cartographic and theological uncertainties, More conjured a protagonist, a man named Raphael Hythloday, who claims to have traveled with Vespucci on his voyage to what is now Brazil before settling down to live among the Utopians for five years. Hythloday's narrative of life in Utopia challenged educated men to consider the possibility of a more equitable and just society, not only for different social classes, but also for the "weaker sex." Although not as proto-feminist as his acknowledged historical inspiration—Plato, who believed men and women were equally capable of becoming ruling warriors and philosophers—Thomas More imagined greater freedoms for women and girls than existed in European societies in the early sixteenth century.

Figure 1.1. A map of Thomas More's Utopia.

The Italian philosopher Tommaso Campanella also wrote his own vision of utopia, *La città del Sole* (*The City of the Sun*), following the stunning revelations of the Polish astronomer Copernicus in his 1543 publication, *De revolutionibus orbium coelestium libri vi* (*Six Books Concerning the Revolutions of the Heavenly Orbs*). After Martin Luther launched the Protestant Reformation, Copernicus dropped the idea of heliocentrism on the Western world like a bomb. Campanella knew and supported one of heliocentrism's greatest defenders, Galileo Galilei. Although Campanella largely rejected the idea that the earth revolved around the sun (because he preferred the cosmology of the Italian natural philosopher Bernardino Telesio), Campanella did pub-

Figure 1.2. Portrait of Thomas More.

lish an exceptionally brave defense of his Italian compatriot (*Apologia per Galileo*) and was generally a proponent of allowing the truth of the natural world to reveal itself: an idea for which, among other charges brought against him by the Inquisition, Campanella would spend almost twenty-seven years in prison.

Contacts with the Indigenous peoples of the Americas and a new understanding of the movements of the heavenly bodies helped to fuel the European Enlightenment. Ossified ideas like the divine right of kings and the rigid hierarchies of feudalism began to crumble in the face of reason and science, culminating in the massive convulsion of the French Revolution. Aristocrats lost their heads while citizens de-

Figure 1.3. Portrait of Tommaso Campanella.

manded liberty, equality, and brotherhood. Not surprisingly, a slew of new utopian writings appeared after the momentous upheaval of 1789. In that plastic moment of rapid social change, where all the old rules seemed negotiable, a Frenchman named Charles Fourier began dreaming up a new theory of "passionate attraction." His detailed writings contributed to the foundation for what later became known as utopian socialism, which inspired intentional communities around the globe (voluntary residential communities where members organize their lives in accord with a shared social, political, or spiritual intention). These include the Social Palace in Guise, France, an experiment in collective living that lasted for more than a hundred years, and which will be discussed in the next chapter.

The tumultuous events of the late eighteenth and nineteenth centuries also inspired other thinkers and writers to dream of new ways of organizing production and reproduction, including Fourier's fellow utopian socialists: Robert Owen and Henri de Saint-Simon. The Peruvian-French Flora Tristan also argued that the emancipation of workers could not be accomplished without the concomitant emancipation of women. She was the first to assert that the domestic relationship between husband and wife mirrored the oppression found in the relationship between the bourgeoisie and the working class. Over in Tsarist Russia, the emancipation of the serfs in 1861 and the onset of new industrial forms of production immediately preceded Nikolai Chernyshevsky's 1863 *What Is to Be Done?*, a work that profoundly influenced later Russian Bolsheviks, including a young Vladimir Ilyich Ulyanov (also known as Lenin). In his protagonist Vera Pavlovna's third dream sequence, Chernyshevsky outlined a utopian vision where women are emancipated and workers would finally enjoy the fruits of their own labor. "Tell everyone that the future will be radiant and beautiful," Chernyshevsky wrote. "Love it, strive toward it, work for it, bring it nearer, transfer into the present as much as you can from it."[3]

By the end of the nineteenth century, socialists, social democrats, nihilists, communists, and anarchists began challenging the social and ideological structures that underpinned early industrial capitalism, with its grueling fourteen-hour workdays and voracious appetite for cheap child labor. In 1892, the Russian Peter Kropotkin published *The Conquest of Bread*, a foundational treatise that proposed an idealistic decentralized economic system based on the innate human tendencies toward voluntary cooperation and mutual aid. "Struggle so that all may live this rich, overflowing life," he wrote in 1897. "And be sure that in this struggle you will find a joy greater than anything else can give."[4] In 1908, V. I. Lenin's Bolshevik rival, the physician, philosopher, and science fiction writer Alexander Bogdanov, published *Red Star*, about an advanced society where men and women worked side by side to maintain a utopia on Mars.

On the left side of the Atlantic, the tumultuous events of the late 1960s—student protests, the sexual revolution, the civil rights movement, and widespread anti–Vietnam War activism—also inspired a new generation of explicitly utopian fiction as Americans experimented with alternative ways of living and thinking about the world. In 1974, Ursula K. Le Guin tore a page from Bogdanov's *Red Star* and published *The Dispossessed: An Ambiguous Utopia*, about a sexually liberated, anarchist community on a planet called Anarres. In the midst of the Cold War, Le Guin found inspiration in the works of Kropotkin and used the fictional journey of a brilliant physicist, Shevek, back to the mother planet of Urras to reflect on the many deficiencies of both Western capitalism and Eastern Bloc communism. Ernest Callenbach's 1975 cult novel, *Ecotopia: The Notebooks and Reports of William Weston*, features one of the first environmental utopias. Callenbach imagined a breakaway country formed from the previous U.S. states of Washington, Oregon, and Northern California. This new country prioritized ecological sustainability and the full equality of women and conjured things like public recycling bins and communal bicycles. Callenbach saw the novel as a possible blueprint for the future, inspiring many green activists. This same decade also gave Wonder Woman her own TV show in 1975 and George Lucas a hit film in 1977. Lucas himself admits that the North Vietnamese communists served as an inspiration for his Rebel Alliance.[5]

Dreamers Have Always Had Haters

As a Generation X scholar of global women's movements, I've spent twenty-five years researching, writing, and teaching about different ways of organizing social relations to free women from their traditional roles as unpaid caregivers and to free men from their expected duties as financial providers. Across a wide variety of university courses, I've explored the alternative visions of American transcendentalists and spiritual perfectionists, British and French utopian socialists, and German and East European communists and anarchists. As a mother and a mentor, I've also witnessed the growing frustration of younger generations who feel suffocated by the persistence of sclerotic gender roles and outmoded ideals of living a "successful life."

Back in 2017 and 2018, I wrote a book called *Why Women Have Better Sex Under Socialism: And Other Arguments for Economic Independence*. It surveyed the available empirical evidence to support the idea that various historical experiments with socialism had more successfully improved the material conditions of women's lives than their capitalist counterparts. I focused on work, motherhood, leadership, intimacy, and citizenship and suggested that adopting some socialist policies could more effectively promote women's autonomy and happiness in the twenty-first century. By increasing public support for childcare, education, elder care, health care, and social programs, policies that redistribute the state's resources to expand these social safety nets also improve the quality of life for everyone, including those traditionally expected to fill the role of the private breadwinner.

For many readers, it was the first time they had considered what an alternative to capitalism might look like and how it would impact their personal lives. Young people especially reacted with enthusiasm, and their collective excitement caused that book to find a wider international audience with fifteen foreign editions in languages as diverse as Portuguese, Japanese, Indonesian, Albanian, Polish, and Thai. But I also received a lot of pushback. One of the most common responses to my investigation of socialism in Europe was that any move toward more state social guarantees would lead to breadlines and gulags. In the conversations I've shared with readers over the last five years, I learned that while many ordinary citizens admit that our current economic system contains serious flaws, they instinctively dismiss alternatives as not feasible "in the real world." I discovered a persistent and profound suspicion of political imagination; readers avoid even thinking about visions labeled or derided as "utopian."

I am, of course, not the first to run into such resistance: skeptics and haters have always scoffed at visions of a better world, especially if they might benefit women. Plato's description of an ideal communal society may have been a response to Aristophanes's earlier derision of such a community in his play, *A Parliament of Women*. In this comedy, written around 391 BCE, the protagonist, a housewife named Praxagora (whose name means something like "public spirited") convinces the women of Athens to seize political power and institute an egalitarian society. "Let everyone have everything there is and share in common," Praxagora explains. "Let everyone enjoy an equal living; no more rich men here, poor men there; no more farmer with a huge extensive farm and some impoverished farmer with absolutely nothing, not even a patch to bury his body in. . . ."[6] As the people of Athens prepare to donate their property to the new communal fund, Aristophanes introduces a character called simply "Mean Man" (sometimes translated as "Selfish Man"), who gives nothing but still expects his share of the redistributed wealth, the so-called free rider problem. Today, as in ancient Greece, the fear of moochers and shirkers who refuse to do their "fair share" continues to undermine attempts to do things more communally. The cynical idea that "one bad apple spoils the barrel" goes back thousands of years.

Doubters can mount a stiff resistance, but in every generation from Aristophanes on down, the dreamers persist. "Every daring attempt to make a great change in existing conditions, every lofty vision of new possibilities for the human race, has been labeled Utopian," noted the Russian-American anarchist Emma Goldman in 1911."[7] The German sociologist Karl Mannheim argued that utopia was a necessary antidote to what he considered the normative role of "ideology," a term he specifically defined as the unseen but omnipresent social, cultural, and philosophical structure that upholds a particular "order of things" and protects those who wield political and economic power. "The representatives of a given order will label as utopian all conceptions of existence which *from their point of view* can in principle never be realized," Mannheim wrote in 1929.[8] Those who benefit from the way things are have a strong motive for labeling as "utopian" any ideas that threaten the status quo. But even beyond that, those steeped in the ideology of their current existence cannot imagine an alternative to it. And most of us follow along.

We accept the way things are because we've never known them to be different. Behavioral economists call this the "status quo bias." People prefer things to stay the same so they don't have to take responsibility for decisions that might potentially change things for the worse.[9] The psychologists Daniel Kahneman and Amos Tversky famously found that people want to avoid feeling regret, and that they are more likely to feel regret about a bad outcome resulting from a decision they made compared to a bad outcome that came from inaction. It's just so much easier to do nothing. Accepting the status quo—even if we hate it—means the potential for fewer regrets.[10] We might not want to admit it, but many of us are too scared, too tired, or too lazy to dream. Thinking outside the box requires courage.

This is why utopian visions of how to build a different future often follow moments of great social upheaval. Ordinary people find themselves unmoored from the realities they once believed to be fixed and immutable—the "order of things" is disturbed. Certain events—wars, pandemics, natural disasters, scientific breakthroughs—disrupt the smooth functioning of the ideologies that bring coherence to the world in which we live. Like Jim Carrey's character in *The Truman Show*, who does not realize his whole life is on TV, or Keanu Reeves's in *The Matrix*, whose initial world is a computer-generated simulation, sudden change forces us to question our perception of reality and consider new possibilities that may have previously seemed unthinkable. "It is so hard to imagine anything fundamentally different from what we have now," *Ecotopia* author Ernest Callenbach told the *New York Times* in 2008. "But without these alternate visions, we get stuck on dead center."[11]

We have to fight against our own deeply ingrained status quo bias and control the normal defense mechanisms of cynicism and apathy because without social dreaming, progress becomes impossible. Before the pandemic, people said that a universal basic income was impossible. "The government can't just give money away!" But then in 2020, governments around the world did exactly this. "The disappearance of utopia," Mannheim warns, "brings about a static state of affairs in which man himself becomes no more than a thing . . . a mere creature of impulses."[12]

And although it cannot be denied that many past utopian experiments have failed, we must remember that such experiments typically faced fierce and continued resistance from mainstream societal forces. Status quo bias is powerful. Those who challenge long-standing traditions often meet with violent opposition, from angry villagers with pitchforks to the Catholic Inquisition. Many of the social dreamers profiled in these pages were ridiculed, humiliated, persecuted, exiled, excommunicated, imprisoned, or murdered. Detractors like to claim that the relative brevity of so many utopian experiments resulted from their internal contradictions, but if these various communities were destined to implode anyway, why have those in power always fought so hard against them?

Rather than endorsing any one particular utopian vision from the past, or championing specific experiments, I want to remind you of their dogged reappearance time and time again. Depending on what is going on in the world, humanity has always looked to utopias for inspiration, and many are still willing to throw themselves into new experiments. No matter the risk, no matter how long the record of disappointment and failure, and no matter the constant refrain warning us that utopianism is "dangerous," people still keep dreaming of different ways to organize their lives. Given the sudden social upheavals of the pandemic, the destabilizing effects of the climate crisis, and the growing prevalence of isolation and despair in communities across the globe, we are once again at a moment when utopian dreaming feels appropriate. It may even be necessary for our collective survival.

Asteroid Miners and Aspiring Immortals

In the last decade, a growing number of future-positive books have suggested political and economic changes that might seem far-fetched, but are increasingly debated as real possibilities. The French economist Thomas Piketty has called for a progressive supranational wealth tax to combat income inequality.[13] The Dutch journalist Rutger Bregman has promoted several utopian visions "for realists," including open borders and a fifteen-hour workweek.[14] In *Abundance: The Future is Better Than You Think*, Greek-American engineer Peter Diamandis (founder of XPRIZE, which rewards inventors for technological developments that benefit humanity) and science journalist Steven Kotler look to the wonders of artificial intelligence and advances in robotics to propose technological solutions to problems like food scarcity, aging populations, and climate change. And in *Fully Automated Luxury Communism*, British author Aaron Bastani argues that technologies like cheap solar energy, asteroid mining, and CRISPR gene-editing will lead us into a world of post-scarcity universal health and leisure.

For me, one of the most interesting aspects of this popular neo-utopianism lies in its primary focus on the public sphere. Today's future-positive writers critique our economies while largely seeming to ignore that anything might be amiss in our private lives. But where we reside, how we raise and educate our children, our personal relationship to things, and the quality of our connections to friends, families, and partners impact us as much as tax policies, the price of energy, or the way we organize formal employment. How can you challenge or change political and economic systems when both are directly dependent on the primary institution in society responsible for the production and care of the next generation? Since political and economic systems accrue and distribute power and wealth among people, those *people* are essential inputs to those systems. For thinkers like Plato, Thomas More, and Charles Fourier, political reforms or revolutions will fail unless they also rethink how we create and sustain our families and communities. In the chapters that follow, I explore how past utopians believed that changes in our intimate worlds would help us forge stronger and more harmonious societies.

And yet resistance to new ways of thinking may be most extreme when it concerns how we structure our private lives. I've thought a lot about how and why so many people today fear these types of changes. According to the anthropologist Wade Davis, "the world into which you were born does not exist in an absolute sense but is just one model of reality—the consequence of one particular set of intellectual and adaptive choices that your own ancestors made, however successfully, many generations ago."[15] As individuals going about our daily lives, it is often hard to step out of the flow of history and consider how things might have been different if our ancestors had made an alternative set of "intellectual and adaptive choices" and to imagine what those choices might look like in practice. When we lose sight of the past, we lose sight of the idea that there were other pathways forward, other roads not taken. We begin to feel our present reality as static and inflexible. We convince ourselves that things cannot change, and that if they do, they will change for the worse.

At the same time, profit-seeking corporations and think tanks often encourage brainstorming sessions open to all ideas regardless of practical constraints: so-called blue sky thinking. Conjuring up new technologies, products, or marketing slogans to increase profits distinguishes the entrepreneurial mastermind from the mere corporate flunky. We accept that this is a good approach for solving economic issues and scientific problems. Yet at the same time, dreaming of different ways of organizing our lives is dangerous and discouraged.

Apple Computer provides one paradigmatic case. After their runaway success in the 1980s, Apple fell into a rut and brought back its cofounder Steve Jobs to reinvigorate its product line. The return of Jobs coincided with the 1997 to 2002 Apple advertising slogan "Think Different," which epitomized the spirit of blue sky thinking. The now iconic television advertisement included Steve Jobs's own narration over a series of black-and-white images of people like Mahatma Gandhi, Martha Graham, Martin Luther King Jr., Frank Lloyd Wright, Alfred Hitchcock, Maria Callas, and John Lennon with Yoko Ono. "Here's to the crazy ones. The misfits. The rebels, the troublemakers. The round pegs in the square holes. The ones who see things differently," Jobs tells us, celebrating the idea that those who "have no respect for the status quo" inevitably become the ones who "push the human race forward." At the end of the ad, Jobs explains, "While some may see them as the crazy ones, we see genius. Because the people who are crazy enough to think they can change the world, are the ones who do."[16] It was an explicitly optimistic commercial message about the transformative power of utopian thinking. . . . So why limit such thinking to designing better Apple products?

In academia, blue sky thinking underpins the discipline of geoengineering—scientists who hope to hack the earth's weather systems in order to prevent the deleterious effects of climate change.[17] The Cambridge University Center for Climate Repair suggests ocean greening, recycling CO2, refreezing the polar ice caps, and spraying aerosols of sulphate particles into the stratosphere to prevent solar radiation from reaching the planet.[18] In Silicon Valley, a new breed of extreme dreamers, such as the Coalition for Radical Life Extension, is experimenting with ways to achieve human immortality.[19] And those who study artificial life (in its hard, soft, and wet forms) push the boundaries of their imaginations to understand how sentience might evolve from complex systems.[20] In the technology sector, entrepreneurs reap rewards when they "move fast and break things," no matter what the costs to society as a whole. We can break democracy as long as we don't challenge the social and economic systems, which ensure that the billions generated by new innovations accrue to a smaller and smaller handful of people.

To be sure, we need to think critically about which sorts of visions are realistic and which are not. The twentieth century gave us examples of utopian dreams that went badly awry. But the lesson should not be to stop dreaming—to suck it up and get on with the status quo. There are those for whom our present arrangements work out quite nicely: mostly men, mostly white, and all wealthy. These people have every reason to inculcate a collective fear of political blue sky thinking, a fear that immobilizes and prevents us from even considering new ideas that might lessen the pressures we place on individual households and families. Don't let them. By experimenting with old ideas in new ways—forms of collective living and child-rearing, for instance—we can not only reduce the burdens on women but also build more robust and flourishing communities that benefit everyone.

Unlike my previous book, where I focused specifically on state-sponsored solutions arising from secular projects to build a better economic system, in this book I expand out to include autonomous and community-based experiments inspired by a wide variety of ideological frameworks, including those that are explicitly religious in orientation. By investigating a long history and amazing diversity of utopian traditions regarding the private sphere, I hope to highlight the historical tenacity of these visions. It turns out that pagans, Christians, Jews, Hindus, Buddhists, anarchists, pacifists, socialists, feminists, and environmentalists have all shared similar ideas about how we can better organize our homes and communities. The justifications may be different, but the fundamental proscriptions remained the same for two and a half millennia.

Two Very Important P-Words

To make sense of utopian visions for rearranging our domestic lives, it's essential to understand the ruling ideology that many hoped to undo: the institution of patriarchy. A Greek word that means "the rule of the father," patriarchy has long worked to oppress all people who lack the social position or necessary requirements to become patriarchs (such as being a first-born son or having independent means). It shapes our public worlds as workers and consumers and regulates the most intimate details of our private experiences. But the "rule of the father" isn't something just asserted; it depends on specific social customs regarding the shape of our families. Patriarchy is partially rooted in the cultural and legal traditions of patrilineality (paternal descent) and patrilocality (where wives leave their natal kin to join a husband's family). These twin forces still operate in the daily lives of billions of people and maintain a distinct lingering influence even in contemporary cultures that see themselves as more "enlightened" with regards to the traditional family. We can't #SmashThePatriarchy without dealing first with these two less familiar P-words.

Patrilineality denotes a set of social customs that confer primacy on the father's family line. The best example of patrilineality comes from Genesis 5 and 11 in the Old Testament, the "begats" from Adam to Noah and from Shem to Abram, where we learn the names of each father and his firstborn son. Patrilineality is why fathers still "give the bride away" to the bridegroom during the traditional Western wedding ceremony, and it's why about 70 percent of American women in 2015 and 90 percent of British women in 2016 still took their husband's name after tying the knot.[21] It is also why the children of heterosexual couples generally take their father's name even though it is the mother who gestates them for nine months and labors to bring them into the world. One 2018 survey from the American website BabyCenter, found that only 4 percent of children have their mother's surname.[22] And in Belgium until 2014, a child born to a married couple was legally obligated to have its father's name.[23] When you receive a holiday card from "the Andersons," the whole family is identified by the last name of the father, which was his father's last name, and his grandfather's last name, and so on.

Historically, patrilineality meant that, upon marriage, rights over a woman's body were transferred from father to groom. Flora Tristan, for example, lived her life governed by the 1804 Napoleonic Code, a wide-ranging law that stipulated that married women must obey their husbands, reside with their husbands, follow their husbands whenever they changed domiciles, and give over all property and wages for their husbands to administer.[24] In 1816, the French state also re-outlawed divorce, further trapping women in indissoluble marriages no matter how abusive or reprehensible the husband. Flora Tristan only escaped her own nuptial chains after her husband repeatedly molested their daughter and then subsequently shot Tristan at point-blank range in broad daylight on the streets of Paris. With her husband imprisoned for life, Tristan became a prominent utopian socialist intellectual who understood that women's subjugation within the institution of monogamous marriage served to ensure women's fidelity so that they produced only "legitimate" heirs. In postrevolutionary France, the Napoleonic family code facilitated the transfer of private property from fathers to sons among a newly ascendant bourgeois class. Propertied men demanded strict wifely fidelity so that their wealth and privileges did not end up in the hands of some sneaky milkman's son.

Laws establishing a husband's legal rights over his wife can still be found across the globe and were only repealed in Western countries in the last 150 years. In the United Kingdom, the Married Women's Property Act granted wives the right to own, buy, and sell their own property in 1882. In the United States, the 1907 Expatriation Act meant that American women who married immigrant husbands automatically lost their citizenship and had to apply for naturalization when their foreign husbands became eligible.[25] The provisions of this act weren't fully repealed until 1940. In West Germany, married women could not work outside the home without their husbands' permission until 1957, and then only if their jobs did not interfere with their domestic responsibilities. This latter provision was not removed until 1977.[26]

Although American women won the right to vote in 1920, married women were legally obliged to vote under their husband's surname until 1975. Married women also had to fight for the right to maintain driver's licenses and passports in their maiden names if they preferred.[27] In Japan in July 2021, the Supreme Court upheld a law that required married couples to have the same surname. Although in theory it could be either spouse's name, in practice 96 percent of Japanese women took their husband's name.[28] To counter these pervasive patrilineal customs, countries such as Greece, as well as the province of Quebec in Canada, have rendered it illegal for a woman to take her husband's name after marriage even if she wants to.[29] In Canada as a whole, where white settlers once imposed patrilineal naming conventions on matrilineal Indigenous peoples to help "regulate [the] division of property among heirs in a way that conformed with European, not Indigenous, property laws," the 2008 to 2015 Truth and Reconciliation Commission allowed for the free restoration of Indigenous names, including mononyms (the ability not to have a surname at all).[30]

Patrilocality means that a new bride must leave her family and move into her husband's household, usually with or near his family (think of Elizabeth Bennet moving from Longbourn to Pemberley in *Pride and Prejudice*). In many societies in Asia and Africa, wives are still expected to reside with their in-laws and obey their authority. In Greece, it was only a 1983 Family Law reform that abolished the provision in the Civil Code that automatically established that a married woman's legal residence was that of her husband. Although new families in many industrialized nations prefer to form their own residences (called neolocality), our deeper history of patrilocality means that men are expected to be breadwinners because a patrilocal culture assumes that the father must be the head of the new household and therefore primarily responsible for its provisioning. A 2017 study found that 72 percent of American men and 71 percent of American women agreed that a man must be able to financially provide for his family in order to be considered a "good husband or partner."[31] This puts a lot of pressure on men, especially in weak economies with labor markets transformed by outsourcing and automation. Although the percentage of female breadwinners has grown in the last decades, about 71 percent of husbands still outearn their wives in households of heterosexual couples where both spouses work.[32]

Patrilocal traditions also explain why only in exceptional cases do men uproot their lives to relocate for the new job of a wife or girlfriend. In my own field of academia, for example, one 2008 study of 9,043 full-time faculty at thirteen leading American research universities found that 36 percent of faculty had a partner also employed in academia and another 36 percent had a partner working in a different industry—but women disproportionately felt the limiting effects of being in a dual-career couple. In contrast to men who prioritize their professional ambitions, the study noted that: "Women in academic couples report that their partner's employment status and opportunities are important to their own career decisions," with the number one reason women academics gave for refusing an external offer of employment being that their male partners "were not offered appropriate employment at the new location."[33] The availability of a job for their partners outweighed other key considerations such as salary, benefits, research funds, or opportunities for promotion. And since getting a decent raise in academia usually requires moving to a new university, women's relative immobility exacerbates the gender pay gap.

Whether it is in academia, in the military, or within the corporate world, women are more likely to follow their partners to a new city or country. When a couple needs to decide whether or not to take a job in a new place, it makes sense to invest in the career prospects of the partner with the higher salary. And because on average women more frequently leave their jobs to follow their partners than men do, employers may consider all women less reliable workers in the aggregate and pay them less than "more reliable" men. Finally, following a partner to a new city or country often separates women from their support networks: family, friends, and perhaps their pre-existing childcare arrangements. The resultant isolation makes it more difficult to restart careers in the new location.

Too many women, with higher degrees and years of work experience, simply give up because it is so hard to "have it all." Of those parents who did not work outside of the home in the United States in 2016, 78 percent of mothers reported they didn't work because they were taking care of their home and family.[34] For women, who generally earn less than men and who societies expect to provide more unpaid care work, it makes rational sense in economies with few social safety nets to embrace what social scientists call "hypergamy," or the desire to marry up and find a partner who can and will support them. This practice reinforces the traditions of patrilineality and patrilocality because the man remains the "head of household." And even in couples where wives outearn their husbands, women still bear a disproportionately larger share of household tasks, which is why so many pine for new domestic arrangements.[35]

Patrilocality is only one way of organizing domestic relations and human societies once displayed a diversity of traditions. But after centuries of Western colonialism that dispersed patriarchal family forms across the globe, fewer than thirty human societies remain matrilocal today. One community of Tibetan Buddhists called the Mosuo provides a fascinating example of a matrilocal society where neither spouse is expected to relocate. Among the Mosuo, grandmothers preside over large multigenerational families. Women own and inherit property through the maternal line and live with their mother's extended family. Men live in their maternal grandmother's household and practice a form of "walking marriage," whereby they visit their partner only at night. Both men and women can have as many companions as they desire, without stigma, and women often do not know who has fathered their children. The concept of "father" barely exists, and men have few paternal responsibilities. Being a good uncle is far more important, as men help raise the children of their sisters. Since there is no formal marriage, the only reason men and women form pairs is because they are attracted to each other or enjoy each other's company. When the attraction fades, romantic ties can be dissolved without negative financial consequences or social impacts on the children. How very radical the Mosuo family structure seems to many of us today highlights just how deeply ingrained our own patrilocal and patrilineal traditions remain.

The Political Is Always Personal

The twin traditions of patrilineality and patrilocality uphold certain customs about social relations that assume that women and children are part of a man's property. The economic considerations of the private, patriarchal family inspired even the earliest utopian thinkers to imagine different ways of organizing our domestic lives. The ancient philosopher Plato rejected the slaveholding nuclear family of ancient Greece and described the evils his elite Guardians of the Republic might avoid by having a large communal family where children were raised in common by specialized nurses. In his ideal state, the Guardians could escape "the perplexities and sufferings involved in bringing up children; the need to make the money necessary to feed the household—the borrowings, the defaults, and all the things people are compelled to do to provide an income to hand over to their wives and slaves to spend on housekeeping."[36]

Plato well understood that private family life would make the Guardians less concerned with working for the public good of Kallipolis, the beautiful city of his ideal Republic. He proposed that rethinking the structure of the Greek family would free his Guardians "from the sort of faction that the possession of property, children and families causes among people. . . ." He writes: "[I]f these people are going to be real guardians, they should not have private houses, land, or any other possession, but should receive their upkeep from the other citizens as a wage for their guardianship, and should all eat communally. . . . [This would] prevent them from tearing the city apart by applying the term 'mine.' . . ."[37]

Much closer to our own era, the physicist and mathematician Freeman Dyson—who once imagined genetically engineered trees that could grow on comets and star-encompassing biospheres able to support extraterrestrial life—struggled with the specific demands of the patriarchal family. In response to an undergraduate student who asked him in 2012 about the nonscientific issues he had grappled with during his life, Dyson replied, "[A]dapting my socialist principles to a capitalist society," after he moved from Great Britain to the United States. "In England during World War Two," Dyson explained:

> I lived in a socialist society that functioned well. . . . Money did not matter. Everyone got the same rations of food and clothes and soap and other necessities. The rationed stuff was cheap, and there was nothing else to buy. Cars were not allowed any gasoline except for official business. It was a wonderful time to be a socialist, so long as the war lasted. . . . When I started to raise a family, I discovered that my socialist principles gave way to my responsibilities as a father. As a father, I needed money to take care of my wife and kids, and the more money the better. The theoretical idea of equality faded, as the kids needed a good home in a good neighborhood with good schools.[38]

Social dreamers have long understood that building a more harmonious society depends on undermining the structures that persist in viewing the family as a private economic unit where men provide resources for their own wives and children to the exclusion of others. More important, political and economic elites can more easily divide ordinary people if key resources like housing, health care, and education are rendered scarce by a lack of public support for them. With everyone exhausted by the hustle needed to meet their basic needs, people tend to view others as potential competitors and refuse opportunities for cooperation that could make the system work better for everyone. By keeping our attentions focused on our private families, we also ignore the possibilities of public programs that would improve life for both ourselves and our children.

Although Plato's ideas about property and the family may still shock many people today, we must understand that this kind of utopian thinking provides an invaluable intellectual tool. Even if dreams don't come true, they do expand our imagination of what is possible and thereby reshape the landscape of what we can practically achieve (the so-called Overton window). The ideas of blue sky thinkers have often inspired social progress that would not have gone as far had there not been an even further point imagined. For example, Plato's works inspired later dreamers whom I will discuss in the coming chapters, people like Charles Fourier in France, John Humphrey Noyes in the United States, Clara Zetkin in Germany, and the kibbutzniks in Israel, who all advocated for some form of collective child-rearing. Although the most extreme programs for raising children in common failed, they did open minds to the idea that children could be cared for in collectively funded public kindergartens during the day. Similarly, blue sky thinkers have long imagined alternatives to traditional forms of marriage. The institution survives but it is no longer the irrevocable union that once bound husbands and wives to each other for life. The idea of no-fault divorce once seemed as utopian as the concept of asteroid mining.

Recent global realities have begun to shake people. Our innate tendency toward inertia and the lazy comforts of the status quo no longer feel viable. Younger generations have begun to challenge the way we organize our private lives, which implicitly means also challenging the long-held traditions of patrilineality and patrilocality. In addition to the growing acceptance of queer relationships, polyamory, and passionate friendships, some youth are reimagining housing, education, and kinship relations in ways that loosen the grip that patriarchy holds on our social relations.[39] Even without radical politics, coliving buildings, coworking spaces, and the rise of remote work fuel trends that undermine the old ways of marking the transition to adulthood and redefine the traditional roles of the "head of household" or the "boss." Some gravitate toward planned communal living while others avoid marriage and single-family home ownership altogether, both trends which have the effect of lessening the burdens of care work that women often bear in the private sphere.

Environmental concerns have also precipitated a BirthStrike among twenty- and thirtysomethings who feel it ecologically irresponsible to bring babies into the world.[40] And the social psychologist Eli Finkel challenges the idea of the "all-or-nothing marriage," highlighting the importance of having "other significant others" in our lives.[41] Some states now allow for three legal parents and new technologies of ectogenesis promise to revolutionize the way we bring children into this world. According to some scientists, viable artificial wombs are less than a decade away.[42] As our societies evolve and change, we must be ever mindful of the social and cultural beliefs which perpetuate patriarchal power and how they manifest themselves in our daily lives. The traditions that many of us think of as "natural" have been shaped by millennia of patrilocal and patrilineal practices which reinforce the power of a small group of (usually male) authority figures over the rest of society. It's time to change this.

In this book I will explore alternative ways of building our homes, raising our children, educating our youth, sharing our property, and defining what counts as family. Undermining the beliefs and practices that reinscribe patrilocality and patrilineality can liberate people from outdated and oppressive stereotypes about femininity and masculinity. It can also open up new possibilities for building happier and more democratic societies, ones that don't scale up to the state level the supposedly "natural" relations of authority and domination found in the traditional family. It will mean less hustle, more friends, and happier families.

I'll also discuss the persistence of dystopian fears and try to make a case for militant optimism in the face of the many challenges the future will bring. I realize that, these days, cynical apathy is more fashionable than what many might consider naive optimism. Wearing black turtlenecks and passively ruminating on the coming climate apocalypse is just hipper than trying to convince others that the world can and should be changed. But historically speaking, real social progress often begins with hopefulness, extreme dreaming, and crazy ideas. "To hope is to give yourself to the future," explains the feminist historian Rebecca Solnit, "and that commitment to the future is what makes the present inhabitable."[43] Reviewing the history of previous utopian thinkers and examining the cultures and communities experimenting with their ideas today provide a necessary first step in unshackling our collective political imaginations from the all-pervasive ideologies that try to convince us that change is dangerous. The concept of utopia helps us forge paths forward, giving us the courage, curiosity, and conviction to experiment with new and better ways of organizing our private lives.

Why Martin Luther King Jr. Loved Star Trek

I was born in 1970, a moment of sudden and unexpected challenges to the prevailing status quo. Wonder Woman's creator introduced the Princess of Paradise Island during World War II, but it's no coincidence that the image of the Amazon warrior also appeared on the very first issue of the explicitly feminist Ms. magazine in 1972 under the headline: "Wonder Woman for President." Eleven years later, I watched my other screen heroine, forced to wear a now-iconic metal bikini, free herself from the tongue-waggling and blubbery Jabba the Hutt by strangling him with the very chain he had used to bind her to him. The University of Pennsylvania only fully integrated female undergraduate students into its School of Arts and Sciences in 1974, and yet today I teach there as a full professor and serve as the chair of my department. In some ways, both Wonder Woman and Princess Leia helped me to deal with the sexism I often encountered in my own life because I could imagine worlds where sexism didn't hold women back. They were just fictional characters, but they made a difference.

Although I am too young to have seen the original series while it was airing, another science fiction show has the distinction of being the longest lasting and most influential utopian vision that ever entered popular culture. When *Star Trek* began broadcasting in 1966, its creator, Gene Roddenberry, crafted a positive view of the future where humanity had overcome all of its conflicts and lived in a sort of galactic Pax Romana within something called the United Federation of Planets, "an interstellar union of different worlds and species with shared principles of universal liberty, rights, and equality."[44] In a 2011 interview, the late actress Nichelle Nichols (who played the African communications officer, Uhura, on the original starship *Enterprise*) recounted a story of her first meeting with the Reverend Martin Luther King Jr. at a banquet. King told Nichols that he was a huge fan of the show and that it was the only thing he and his wife allowed their children to stay up late to watch. At the time, Nichols intended to leave the show to pursue a career in the theater, but King insisted she had to stay.

Nichols recalled: "He said I had the first nonstereotypical role, I had a role with honor, dignity and intelligence. He said, 'You simply cannot abdicate, this is an important role. This is why we are marching. We never thought we'd see this on TV.' "[45] For the first generation of Black Trekkies, Nichols's portrayal as an officer on the bridge of the interracial starship *Enterprise* helped them envision the possibility of equality. "When I was a little girl," explained the actress Whoopi Goldberg in 2014, "it was like, 'Oh, we [Black people] are in the future.' Uhura did that for me."[46]

"Imagination is more important than knowledge," said Albert Einstein in 1931. "For knowledge is limited, whereas imagination embraces the entire world, stimulating progress, giving birth to evolution."[47] We stand on the cusp of a new age, with many of us striving toward a more positive vision of the future like the one Roddenberry once provided, where human beings find a way to build a better world for subsequent generations of humanity. Our old ideas about patrilineality and patrilocality are no longer fit for that purpose. We need new ideas, new dreams, and the courage to imagine alternative futures. Now is the moment to "think different." If we can imagine them first in a galaxy far, far away, it's only a matter of time before we boldly go and begin figuring out how to translate these inspired visions into our own everyday utopias.

CHAPTER 2

Home Is Where the Walls Are

Thinking Outside the Single-Family Box

Imagine living in a community with hundreds of like-minded people of a similar age, all united in a common purpose. You may have one roommate, maybe two, as well as hallmates with whom you interact each day. You share common spaces and bathrooms. You eat together in large cafeterias, choosing meals from well-stocked buffets. Everywhere you need to be is within walking distance: libraries, a fitness center, a concert hall, an art museum, sports arenas, and lecture halls. Those who have lived under these conditions often consider the experience part of "the best years of their lives," filled with social occasions of all sizes—from a few friends sitting on a hard dormitory room floor to massive parties on the quad. For many students away from home for the first time, university living encourages camaraderie that often lasts a lifetime. Perhaps people idolize their university years not only because they were young, but because they enjoyed dwelling communally.

I first tasted residential campus life in 1988, but after my freshman year, I dropped out of the University of California at Santa Cruz because I thought the world was going to end in a nuclear war. I worked all summer at three jobs and bought myself a one-way ticket to Europe, where, because I needed employment to fund my travels, I worked illegally as a live-in nanny for a posh British family. Residing with the Brits exposed me to a whole new world of hereditary wealth as I shuttled between their expansive London flat and elephantine manor in Oxfordshire. Despite the luxury, living with the aristocrats felt isolating and miserable: a father, a mother, and three children locked away in their individual rooms. When the colicky baby screamed at 3:00 a.m., only I woke to comfort him, feeding him spoonfuls of alcoholic cough syrup at his parents' request. Excess speech was discouraged. When the children practiced enunciation, they clenched pencils between their back teeth to prevent their mouths from opening too widely.

Within a week of leaving England after almost four months of nannying, I found myself living in a community not too different from that of my student life: the kibbutz Hatzerim, located near the city of Be'er Sheva in the Negev Desert. But instead of attending classes, I earned my keep by rotating through a series of different jobs: picking avocados in the orchards, loading and unloading the industrial dishwasher in the dining hall, or working the night shift in the irrigation tubing factory. Compared to my lonely nannying days, my new life brimmed with human connection. Founded in 1946 and settled initially by Polish-Jewish refugees from the USSR, Kibbutz Hatzerim embodied the spirit and practice of communal living. I found myself surrounded by people who related to each other like one big extended kin network, with a nursery school and dozens of alloparents (caring adults beyond the mother and father) for every child. For the first time in my sheltered American life, I understood how profoundly the type of suburban single-family home I'd grown up in had isolated my family from others.

Put down this book for a moment and look around. If you're inside your home, ask yourself: How did so many of us find our way into spaces rented from faceless landlords or contained within privately owned but mortgaged walls that separate us from our neighbors and mire us in debt? When we search for a place to live, do we ever stop to consider what our ideal living arrangements might be, or just scan the listings for a decent place in a desirable neighborhood that we can afford? What if our individual flats and single-family homes, which feel so normal to us, also represent a particular cultural ideal perpetuated by an economic system that seduces us into the belief that square footage and privacy are both desirable goods for which we should pay a premium? As the earth's population passes eight billion, is it really sustainable for each of us to aspire to a personal abode? And what if the spaces in which we eat, sleep, and warehouse our possessions reinforce certain ideas about what constitutes a family and with whom we should share our property?

So many of us who live in modern postindustrial societies also suffer from a pandemic of loneliness exacerbated by the limited architectural options available. A 2018 report on loneliness in the United Kingdom found that nine million Britons (approximately 13 percent of the population) were "often or always" lonely, and that more than half of all parents reported feeling isolated and alone.[1] In the same year, the Cigna US Loneliness Index report found that only 53 percent of Americans had "meaningful in-person" interaction on a daily basis.[2] The youngest members of society, Gen Z, reported the highest levels of loneliness of any age cohort, and this study preceded the COVID-19 pandemic that sequestered high school and university students away from already low levels of in-person social interaction. Even though we know that loneliness undermines our mental and physical health, many of us still aspire to have our own place.

Our way of living—the very design of the dwellings we inhabit—also perpetuates the social norm that many types of care work must be provided within the individual household, usually by women. We are each tasked with cooking and cleaning up in our own kitchens, doing our own laundry in our own private washing machines that sit unused most of the week, or mowing our own little pieces of lawn—even though there are huge economies of scale to be realized in much domestic work. We know from history and from recent empirical studies conducted everywhere from Norway to Japan that more communal forms of dwelling can make everyone's lives less lonely, less harried, and less deleterious to the environment. So why do we live the way we do?

For millennia, people from different ethnic, religious, and cultural traditions have resided together in nonconsanguineous (that is, not blood-related) extended households and communities. Whether these were small groups sharing tribal longhouses; celibate, pious, and ascetic cenobites settled in monasteries, convents, or beguinages; or secularists fully engaged with the world and living in colleges, phalansteries, or planned microdistricts, many of our ancestors rejected the isolation of the individual dwelling shared only with a handful of one's blood-related or legally recognized kin. Even the history of a country as hyper-individualistic as the United States brims with attempts to find more collective ways of dwelling. Our architectural options today reflect a specific set of choices about the ideal habitat for human flourishing, choices often born of our past attachments to patrilineal and patrilocal traditions.[3] We've been convinced that single-family houses on our own private plots of land, or spacious but separate flats in urban residential towers, signal social and financial success—and yet for many of us, this habitat proves far from ideal.

Across the globe today, many communities—rural and urban, traditional and progressive—are experimenting with different forms of dwelling together, whether for cost savings, the convenience of shared responsibilities, or the furtherance of a certain set of ideals: environmental, feminist, anarchist, Christian, Buddhist, or simply to reduce the medically proven negative effects of loneliness and isolation. Instead of paying a premium for privacy, what would happen if we chose to reorganize our lives to maximize our social connectedness?

The Bones Buried in the Living Room

Utopian dreams of collective dwelling often have their roots in imaginings of how our distant predecessors might have lived. But sometimes, thanks to archaeological evidence, we don't need to imagine. In modern-day Turkey, archaeologists have excavated a large proto-city, one of the first major settlements in the world, built by humans who had only recently left their hunting-and-gathering past behind. Occupied between 7400 to 6200 BCE, Neolithic Çatalhöyük may have housed up to eight thousand people who lived in mudbrick homes clustered so close together that they essentially created one mega dwelling, as if the entire city lived together in one massive house.[4] People entered their residences through portals in the ceilings, and they socialized and worked on the interconnected rooftops of their homes. The longevity of this streetless settlement implies that the residents of Çatalhöyük enjoyed stable and prosperous lives for many generations.

In 2011, archaeologists excavating the site made a startling discovery. The people of Çatalhöyük buried their dead under their hearths and many dwellings contain the skeletal remains of long-ago residents. Researchers had assumed that the people buried under the hearths of individual dwellings at similar times would be blood relatives, but a closer examination of the dental remains of burials from a variety of different dwellings revealed that the people of Çatalhöyük may well have lived in nonconsanguineous households, suggesting they had a more expansive concept of family, including both "official" and "practical" kin.[5] "These results could be interpreted to suggest that inclusion for interment within a home was only minimally related to biological affinity. Instead, the site may have been organized by an alternate definition of kin that was not defined in terms of genetic relationships," write the anthropologists Marin A. Pilloud and Clark Spencer Larsen.[6] Nine thousand years ago, it seems our ancestors may have had little reason to establish households with only their immediate blood relatives. What's more, the thought might not have occurred to them.

Excavations also suggest that Çatalhöyük was home to a profoundly egalitarian society, with few archaeological markers signaling class distinctions and both women and men granted equivalent access to nutrition. The size and shape of the individual dwellings are remarkably uniform. In contrast to Çatalhöyük, the six-thousand-year-old Mesopotamian sites in present-day Iran, Iraq, and Syria reveal extensive evidence of hierarchy and inequality. In cities such as Uruk and Ur, agriculture allowed a class of rulers and priests to tax away the wealth of their settled populations. Differences in the size of private dwellings marked differences in social status, with palaces reflecting the wealth and power of their owners. Consanguine kinship relations then presumably facilitated the transfer of that wealth and power from one generation of rulers to the next.

By the heyday of ancient Greece in the fifth century BCE, the political and economic elites also lived in consanguineous groups in private homes. The Greek word for "family," *oikos*, is also the word for "house," emphasizing that the physical dwelling was the natural and proper container for the household. Plato suggests that the institution of the *oikos* promoted selfishness. If the Guardians "acquire private land, houses, and money themselves, they will be household managers and farmers instead of guardians—hostile masters of the other citizens, instead of their allies."[7] Instead, in Book V of the *Republic*, Plato suggests that his Guardians would live communally, like "soldiers in a camp," to ensure that their loyalty remained to the common good rather than to their own interests.

Most etymological sources claim that our English word "family" is derived from *famulus*, which is the Latin word for "servant" or "slave." The ancient Roman concept of *Familia*, therefore, referred not only to the blood-related parents and children in a given household, but also to all of the servants and enslaved people, which collectively constituted the property of the head of that household: the *paterfamilias*. There was a different word for the nuclear family—*domus*—and perhaps not surprisingly, ancient Roman elites lived in private townhouses called the *domus*, large single-family residences. The Roman lower classes lived in apartment-like buildings called *insulae* (islands), where individual families inhabited flats, but shared a common courtyard. From ancient times, therefore, the kind of communal living Plato considered ideal for his Guardians in the *Republic* reflected the living situation of people of a lesser social status in an unequal society. This ancient bias against collective housing lingers with us to this day.

Living Together to Love God

But certain minorities always maintained a commitment to the kind of possible nonconsanguineous collective living found in Çatalhöyük. For some, living in self-sufficient communities with shared moral commitments set them apart from the more material concerns of everyday human existence. The early followers of the Buddha began practicing forms of monasticism between the fifth and fourth centuries BCE. Initially, Buddhist monks and nuns practiced an eremitic (or solitary) form of monasticism, but after the death of Gautama Buddha, they settled together, first for the rainy season and later in more permanent collectives, making Buddhist monasticism one of the earliest known forms of intentional communal living practiced by a group of spiritual seekers. Living together initially allowed them to pool resources, but later helped reinforce their mutual dedication to following the Middle Way, the teachings of the Buddha.

Early adherents of Christianity desired to find communion with God by leading ascetic lifestyles. The first Christian monastics lived alone in caves or huts as hermits, but sometime between 318 and 323 CE, St. Pachomius established the first cenobitic monastery in Tabennisi, Egypt. Unlike the eremitic monastics who rarely came together to worship, the believers of the "cenobitic" tradition ("cenobite" being derived, via Latin, from the Greek words for "common" and "life"), lived together and held all of their property in common, under the rule of an abbot or abbess who directed their spiritual lives. St. Benedict of Nursia firmly established the cenobitic tradition in Europe, founding the Benedictine monastery of Monte Cassino on a hill between Rome and Naples in 530 CE. From Italy, dedicated buildings to house various monastic communities spread across medieval Europe, offering a communal life to those willing to take a vow of celibacy, give up their material possessions, and dedicate themselves to spiritual pursuits. Although celibates did not have children of their own, the Epistle of James in the New Testament made it clear that true believers had a responsibility "to look after orphans and widows in their distress."[8] For centuries, members of monastic communities have often served as surrogate parents and families for the most vulnerable members of society.

Building on the success of the Benedictines, the first Cistercian abbey was founded in 1098, and at their height in the fifteenth century, the Cistercians claimed to have 750 houses across Europe. The rise of the mendicant orders (the Dominicans and the Franciscans) who traveled across Europe and lived among the poor with little access to either individual or collectively owned property, as well as the onset of the Protestant reformation after Martin Luther's excommunication in 1521, precipitated a decline in the European cenobitic monastic tradition. In England, before Henry VIII suppressed the monasteries, historian George W. Bernard estimates the presence of about nine hundred religious houses, which provided shelter for approximately four thousand monks, three thousand canons, three thousand friars, and two thousand nuns, meaning that about 2 percent of the country's adult male population lived in a religious order.[9]

During the Middle Ages, cenobitic communities aspired to self-sufficiency, often owning their own agricultural lands, stables for livestock, workshops, and kitchens, as well as engaging in their own cottage industries, with bakeries, breweries, kilns, mills, and the like. Perhaps the most famous architectural blueprint for a utopian monastic community is the Plan of St. Gall, which dates from sometime between 820 to 830 CE and was intended to house around three hundred people.[10] One of Switzerland's most important national treasures, the calfskin blueprint depicts the Carolingian ideal of the perfect Benedictine cloister, which, in addition to its church, dormitories, and refectory, included gardens, stables, an orchard, a scriptorium, an infirmary, an on-site bakery, a brewery, and various workshops. Although scholars still debate whether the plan was meant as a blueprint for the ideal monastic community or for a specific project to be built in St. Gall, its deliberate design to promote physical closeness and self-sufficiency would echo throughout later utopian plans for collective living.

Even today, experimental archaeologists in southern Germany are building a full-scale monastery based on the Plan of St. Gall using the methods and materials from the Middle Ages: the Campus Galli in Baden-Württemberg. When I visited in July 2022, one young carpenter told me that he had given up a lucrative career in Germany to work at Campus Galli because he longed to learn preindustrial building techniques, such as working with painstakingly dried wooden dowels instead of metal nails or installing windows of translucent white leather instead of clear glass. He and his fellow workers didn't live on site, but they did strive to recreate the social ecosystem that would have allowed a Carolingian monastery to thrive in the Middle Ages. In the mornings, they often met to discuss and debate the *Regula Santi Benedicti* (Rule of St. Benedict), a 516 CE text with advice on how to live harmoniously with others in a communal setting.[11]

Since most European institutions of higher learning grew out of the Catholic Church, the architecture of medieval colleges and universities mirrored the communal living arrangements of the abbeys. When teaching at Oxford University began sometime in the late eleventh century, the first academic houses were actually monastic halls run by various religious orders that accommodated lay students.[12] The first three residential colleges—University, Balliol, and Merton—weren't built until between 1249 and 1264 CE. Like the monasteries that inspired them, the great medieval universities established their own kinds of utopian communities. One famous alumnus of Oxford University is none other than the father of *Utopia* itself, Thomas More, who began his studies at Canterbury College in 1492. On his ideal island, all families ate their meals in common in great halls and lived in identical houses with no locks on the doors so that "every man may

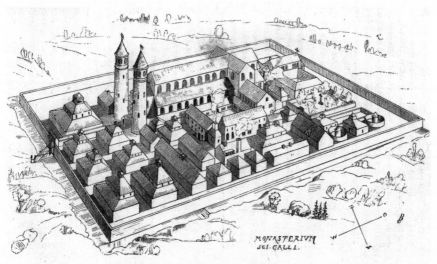

* Kloster Sanct Gallen nach dem Grundrisse vom Jahre 830. (Lasius).

Figure 2.1. "*Reconstruction of the buildings of the abbey of Saint Gall according to the historical plan from the early 9th century.*"

freely enter into any house whatsoever"—details perhaps reminiscent of his university days.[13] Although students did not give up their worldly possessions, they worshipped, studied, ate, and slept in vast common spaces. These scholarly enclaves united students in a shared quest for knowledge as they fully immersed themselves in the life of the mind, debating lectures together over common meals or exploring theological quandaries while strolling the grounds.

Of course, the most famous monasteries and universities were overwhelmingly male spaces. Women who chose to become nuns often found themselves locked away in convents living under the strict authority of the Mother Superior and a male hierarchy that controlled their access to resources. Many convents were much poorer than monasteries, and some orders demanded dowries or other maintenance fees from the aspiring nun's family. Nuns enjoyed fewer freedoms than monks, particularly their ability to leave their cloisters. But beginning in 1190 CE, some women found a way to live communally with other women without taking vows. They became the first Beguines (sometimes referred to as Beguine nuns), a special lay order of women who lived together in urban areas in what is now modern-day Belgium, the Netherlands, and northern Germany. In contrast to cloistered nuns who took religious vows and lived apart from the world, lay nuns lived their faith within their communities. A 2001 book, *Cities of Ladies* (a title that plays off of Christine de Pizan's 1405 utopian feminist text, *The Book of the City of Ladies*), surveyed more than two hundred beguinages over almost four centuries to reveal that the Beguines enjoyed an autonomy and independence rare for other women of their era.[14] Beguine nuns walked the city streets unchaperoned, and they visited the sick in their own homes, flouting the strict rules of propriety that governed women's mobility in the Middle Ages.

North European societies revered the Beguines for their piety, industry, and generous care for the poor, the elderly, and the infirm.[15] Some beguinages ran schools for children, while others made lace, wove textiles, or brewed beer. Like the original cenobitic monastics, the beguinages strove to be economically self-sufficient. But unlike ordinary nuns, the Beguines could leave their communities at any time—even to marry. And whereas the church obliged cenobitic nuns to donate all personal property to the convent, the Beguines retained rights to their property if they chose to leave.

Two of the most famous thirteenth-century Beguines were Hadewijch of Antwerp and Mechthild of Magdeburg, who both left a wide variety of mystical writings about their unique spiritual communities and the difficulties they faced living as lay nuns within a profoundly patriarchal religious hierarchy that mistrusted them. In a letter to her young Beguine sisters, Hadewijch encourages them to do God's work despite the resistance of medieval society: "Whether you make a good impression or a bad impression, do not renounce truth in your good works," she writes. "We can willingly put up with derision when it is aimed at good works in which we recognize God's will. . . . The affliction of our sweet God which he suffered when he lived as Man, merits our gladly bearing for his sake all afflictions and every sort of derision. . . ."[16]

Eventually, the male hierarchy felt threatened by the defiant independence of the beguinages, which attracted greater and greater numbers of single women and widows into their all-female fellowship. Partially for their lack of formal religious vows, the Catholic Church castigated the Beguines as heretics and ordered that the beguinages be disbanded at the Council of Vienne in 1311. Despite this, the Beguine way of life continued for centuries beyond the official auspices of the Catholic hierarchy because they never lacked customers for their beer, cloth, and lace, and they remained in high demand as nurses and teachers. Today, a collection of thirteen beguinages are protected as UNESCO World Heritage Sites.[17] The last known Beguine nun died as recently as 2013 at the age of ninety-two.[18]

Get Thee to a Phalanstery!

Unlike the cenobitic monastic communities that provided homes for those who wanted to set themselves apart from the world and lead singular lives of spiritual or intellectual contemplation, the utopian socialists who emerged after the French Revolution wanted to change the world for everyone: "Newton was their favorite hero and they imagined themselves achieving for the social universe what he had for the physical," write Frank and Fritzie Manuel in *Utopian Thought in the Western World*.[19] Of the three men most identified with utopian socialism—Robert Owen, Henri de Saint-Simon, and Charles Fourier—the latter provided the wildest visions of alternative ways of living and is often credited with coining the word "feminism."[20] Writing in 1808, Fourier asserted that "the extension of the privileges of women is the basic principle of all social progress,"[21] "the happiness of men is proportionate to the freedom enjoyed by women,"[22] and that "women, in a state of liberty will outdo men in all mental and physical functions which are not dependent on bodily strength."[23] Born in 1772, Fourier was the son of a cloth merchant who propounded theories on how to achieve a global "transition away from social chaos to universal harmony."[24] Although some of his ideas raised eyebrows, such that the melting of the polar ice cap might one day "give the sea a flavour of the kind of lemonade known as *aigresel*,"[25] his thoughts about women's rights and the advantages of communal living would leave their definitive mark on the history of the nineteenth and twentieth centuries, not least because of his acknowledged influence on the works of the Germans Friedrich Engels and Karl Marx.

Fourier's vision of the secular phalanstery (sometimes called "phalanx") drew direct inspiration from the abbeys of the Roman Catholic Church. The portmanteau *phalanstère* comes from blending the French words *phalange* (an ancient Greek military formation, perhaps in a nod to Plato's wish that his Guardians live as "soldiers in a camp") and *monastère* (monastery) in recognition of the utopian impulses of the cenobitic tradition. The phalanstery was a massive complex designed for 1,620 men, women, and children together in a self-sustaining community where people theoretically only labored at tasks that they enjoyed based on their particular passions. (Children supposedly did all of the dirty work because they could make a fun game out of anything.) Fourier believed that individual homes created unnecessary barriers between neighbors, exacerbating alienation and loneliness—emotions that made people selfish for the attention of others and stood in the way of social harmony. Individual households also failed to take advantage of the economies of scale possible for domestic work. Rather than one woman cooking and cleaning and looking after her own children, an entire community would share the necessary labor and avoid duplication of the appliances of the day (such as winepresses and stoves).

Fourier imagined that the architecture of his phalanstery would reinforce his utopian socialist ideals. "The lodgings, gardens and stables of a society . . . must be vastly different from those of our villages and towns, which are perversely organised and meant for families having no societary relations," he wrote. "Instead of the chaos of little houses which rival each other in filth and ugliness in our towns, a Phalanx constructs for itself a building as perfect as the terrain permits."[26] Built in rural areas and divided into three sections, the phalanstery included a central residential structure flanked by two wings with covered galleries. Noisy workshops as well as the children's living quarters and schools would take up one wing, while a traveler's inn and various meeting rooms would be clustered in the other. The phalanstery strove for balance between agriculture and industry, as well as the private and the communal. And unlike the poverty and chastity demanded of

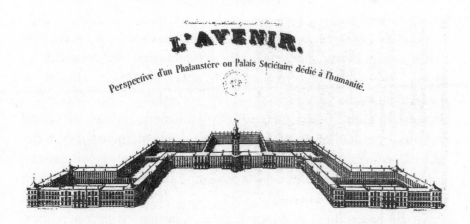

Figure 2.2. Perspective view of Charles Fourier's phalanstère.

monastics, Fourier imagined collective abundance, free love, and communally raised children, although he allowed for private property and some social stratification. Residents who had joined the community with preexisting wealth enjoyed more luxurious rooms, but they took their common meals in a dining hall with anyone in the community who had a taste for more exclusive foods and wines. Fourier believed that some level of inequality was unavoidable, and as long as all residents lived in conditions of relative abundance, differences in dispositions (or what Fourier called "passions") would not fuel envy or discord.

Many progressive Americans enamored with imported European ideas for building self-sustaining communities outside of the existing hierarchies of wealth and power tried to establish phalansteries over the nineteenth century. In places like the North American Phalanx in Monmouth County, New Jersey, the South Bay Phalanx in western New York, and Ceresco (or the Wisconsin Phalanx) in Fond du Lac County, the followers of Fourier joined a much larger communitarian movement that endeavored to settle the West and avoid wages and chattel slavery. During this time, utopian religious and socialist communities sometimes cooperated to build an earthly paradise, promoting abolition, pacifism, and temperance.

A Utopia Realized

Inspired by Fourier's work, another Frenchman named Jean-Baptiste André Godin built his first *Familistère* (Familistery or Social Palace) in 1859 in a small village in northern France called Guise. This experiment in collective living lasted for 109 years. Like Robert Owen had done in Scotland, Godin married utopian socialist visions with local industrial production to build a successful (if paternalistic) community of workers, giving proof that Fourier's sometimes fanciful ideals could be adapted to practical purposes and promote greater concord between capital and labor.

Godin had trained as a locksmith and, during his time as a journeyman, he witnessed the poverty and suffering of ordinary French workers as they grappled with the onset of what was later called the Industrial Revolution. After he invented a patented, cleaner-burning, double-combustion cast-iron (and sometimes enameled) stove, Godin designed the plans for, and plowed his profits into, the Familistery, arguing that it must be "a space of freedom, calm, peace, tranquility; it must be surrounded by everything that is convenient and agreeable, in particular, it must bring men closer together and unite them in the idea of the common good."[27] Although individual families resided in their own private apartments, the Social Palace resembled a large hotel with a beautiful vaulted glass ceiling where residents shared a vast array of communal spaces designed for their enjoyment, including assembly halls, dining rooms, a theater, gardens, courtyards, a laundry, a swimming pool, a bar, and an observatory. All children accessed childcare and education according to their ages: a nursery for infants; a *pouponnat* for toddlers who could walk, up to four years old; and a *bambinat* for children from four to six, after which they began their education. Godin boasted of the health of the children living in the Familistery:

> In the Familistere neither abandonment, want of cleanliness, inanition [exhaustion from malnourishment], poverty, nor indigestion are any longer the causes of that mortality among young children to which society closes its eyes. In the palace the child receives all the attention demanded by its age. The halls of the nursery and the *pouponnat* are in the building itself, near to the home of each one, always open to the child and the mother, while night and day good nurses watch with a tender care over all the children in the cradles, as soon as their affairs call the mothers away.[28]

At its height, about two thousand workers and their families chose to live together at Guise, including Godin and his wife and children. He shared in daily life and managed to run a profitable enterprise, reinvesting those profits to ensure that the Social Palace's residents had access to services and opportunities rare for other members of the working classes in France at the time: theater performances, lectures, education for their children, and leisure associations. Daily life presented many challenges, particularly since workers sometimes lacked the inclination to send their kids to school and rejected the high standards of education and cleanliness demanded by Godin because of their unfamiliarity. Posted notices reminded residents not to throw rubbish out of their windows into the common courtyard and that all children should wear clothes and shoes.

Godin also created rules against drunkenness, vandalism, and unruliness, and enforced behavioral standards on and off the factory floor. He encouraged industriousness and education by awarding bonuses, diplomas, and various public honors. An elected council of men and women workers could also impose fines and other sanctions on those who continued to flout the rules. An American who visited the Social Palace in 1870 reported that many French industrialists despised Godin's successful social experiment with communal living and spread negative rumors about his life and work: "The word went out that Godin was a rich manufacturer who employed a large number of hands, and he had devised this hotel merely to board and accommodate them; that he had no other wish in his mind than to get the largest amount of profit out of his men; and consequently, like any other slave-master, it behooved him to keep them well in order to get this quantity of labor from them."[29]

Over time, the workers, who compared their conditions within the Familistery with that of their peers outside of it, accepted Godin's paternalism as a necessary price for their improved standards of living. Godin provided them with inexpensive but high-quality housing near their workplaces, medical care, and even parties and celebrations on major holidays. At a time in France when women needed their husbands' permission to work outside the home, Godin encouraged wives and older daughters to find work within the Familistery, providing rather exceptional opportunities to working-class girls and women.

In 1872, a journalist for *Harper's Magazine* waxed lyrical about the success of the Social Palace, writing, "M. Godin, though obliged legally to remain the owner of the capital represented in the Familistere, has placed the control of the affairs in the population, who elect those who carry on its operations, and the result has shown how quickly men demonstrate, where the only law is liberty, that human nature is inherently good, and learn to seek their own happiness in that of others."[30] Four years later, the *American Socialist* celebrated that, in Guise, "a new human habitation has been invented against which even our prejudice in favor of individualism or isolation can make no attack,"[31] and in 1875, the weekly journal *American Artisan* reported that the experiment sparked international conversations about how industrial life could be better organized to maximize the happiness of workers "all over the civilized globe."[32]

The Familistery model never caught on in the way these American periodicals predicted. In an 1872 series of articles on "The Housing Crisis," Friedrich Engels criticized the Familistery as an unworkable "bourgeois" solution: "No capitalist has any interest in establishing such colonies, and in fact none such exists anywhere in the world, except in Guise in France and that was built by a follower of Fourier, not as profitable speculation but as a socialist experiment."[33] Eight

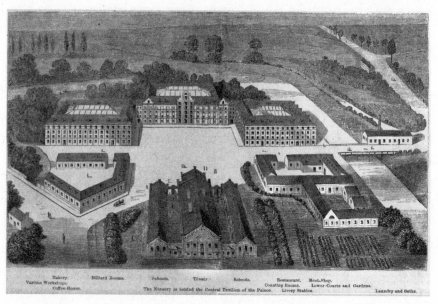

Figure 2.3. Sketch of the Familistère at Guise.

years before his death, Godin converted the ownership structure of the Familistery into a cooperative enterprise owned in common by its employees.[34] Although he died in 1888, the community of workers Godin left behind in Guise continued to flourish as a cooperative for another eighty years, until the enterprise became less financially viable as the market for iron stoves dried up and French ironworkers faced growing international competition. In 1968, the factory was privatized and for a brief period made enameled cast-iron Le Creuset cookware. Although the factory still works today, private owners inhabit the apartments, and the Social Palace is a museum. In the gift shop you can buy a mug that celebrates Godin's creation as *une utopie réalisée*, a utopia realized.

Dreaming in Concrete and Steel

Charles Fourier's visions of collectivity, abundance, and gender equality also had a strong influence on Russian nihilists, communists, socialists, and anarchists, many who lived in exile in France in the late nineteenth century and who brought those ideas back to Russia after the 1917 Revolution, and eventually established the Union of Soviet Socialist Republics.[35] In the early years of the new Bolshevik regime, acute housing shortages forced government officials to subdivide the aristocratic apartments they had expropriated to house multiple families. In an era of massive rural to urban migration, the new city dwellers of Petrograd shared kitchens, stairways, corridors, and bathrooms in apartments that became known as *kommunalki*.

These communal dwellings (which persist to this day) placed severe limitations on privacy. People from many different professions and regional backgrounds found themselves sharing a *kommunalka*. One of the opening musical numbers of the charming 2008 Russian film *Stilyagi* (*Hipsters*) beautifully parodies the unique camaraderie of the residents of the *kommunalka*, including happy dancing babushkas cooking together in their shared kitchen.[36] The film's representation of communal living is an affectionate exaggeration of the specific kind of sociality experienced by those who once shared these spaces. According to a Colgate University project dedicated to preserving the history and unique culture of the *kommunalka*: "Tenants in a communal apartment are like family in some respects and like strangers in others. The transparency of the space they occupy means that they are privy to things about each other that otherwise would be known only by close relatives."[37] Writing in 1994, the Russian cultural theorist Svetlana Boym also opined that "the communal apartment was the cornerstone of the now disappearing Soviet civilization" with its blurred boundaries between "intimate and public, with a mixture of ease and fear in the presence of foreigners and neighbors."[38]

Later, when the Soviet Union industrialized, the idea of self-sufficient rural communities like the phalanstery and the Familistery, as well as the work of the Swiss-French urban planner Le Corbusier, inspired architects to design new integrated city neighborhoods where workers would reside near their workplaces and enjoy easy access to services. Massive new planned cities like Magnitogorsk sprang up, filled with microdistricts, known as *mikrorayoni*: large housing complexes within walking distance to parks, health clinics, schools, and groceries, and connected by free or subsidized public transportation to universities, factories, and offices. Planners also designed these microdistricts to help promote women's emancipation: if women had easy access to stores, cafeterias, playgrounds, and mass transit networks, many of their domestic burdens could be reduced.

Soviet architectural ideals slowly spread across the globe. On the left bank of the Sava River, just before its confluence with the Danube, a collection of stunning microdistricts cluster in the area still known today as New Belgrade in Serbia. After the defeat of the Nazis and the liberation of Yugoslavia in 1945, socialist planners poured their dreams of a brighter future into concrete and steel. Looming modernist tower blocks housed a diverse range of Yugoslavs from different social classes, many of whom were moving to the city for the first time. "I loved being young there," explained Radina Vučetić, a professor at the University of Belgrade who grew up in Block 45. "For a kid it was great."

The ground floors of almost every residential tower included cinemas, culture centers, libraries, kindergartens, pediatricians, supermarkets, hairdressers, cafés, and a wide variety of services that existed primarily to lessen the burdens associated with daily life in the private sphere. Wide pedestrian-only promenades linked parks and children's playgrounds, where kids could roam freely with their friends around the residential towers.[39] A construction worker or miner might live next door to a physicist, a neurosurgeon next to a seamstress, and, "On the top floor of many of the taller blocks," Vučetić explained to me, "the planners had built ateliers for creative workers. Each building had a working writer, a painter, a designer, and a composer in apartments with terraces as big as the apartment they lived in." Even when I visited in 2021, the ground floors of these microdistricts still contained various businesses to service people's daily needs: appliance repair shops, dentists, butchers, green grocers, and stationers.

Figure 2.4. Block 23 in New Belgrade in 2021.

Neighborhoods like New Belgrade, and their brutalist counterparts around the world (including places like the Park Hill housing estate in England) functioned as "15-minute-cities" even before the term came into fashion among urban planners in the West.[40]

Soviet-style microdistricts also inspired the *xiaoqu* in China and neighborhoods like Nowa Huta in Krakow, Poland. And architects from Eastern Europe helped to build similar housing complexes across the Global South in countries such as Afghanistan, Algeria, Angola, Chile, Cuba, Egypt, Ethiopia, India, Iran, Iraq, Libya, Mongolia, Nigeria, Sudan, Syria, Tanzania, Vietnam, and Zambia. In his discussion of two microdistricts in Accra, Ghana, the historian of architecture Łukasz Stanek explains: "The program of the housing neighborhoods conveyed a vision of a socialist everyday life. Facilities such as People's Art Club were to provide a venue for collective education and leisure, while nurseries, kindergartens, laundries, and canteens were to alleviate domestic work of women, thus advancing their professional prospects."[41]

Downtown Dormitory Living

This history of utopian architecture inspired many contemporary Western experiments in collective living, which spring up to address the particular needs that societies fail to meet in a given era. While twentysomethings have long shared flats or houses with roommates to mitigate the high cost of urban rents, recent start-ups in New York, San Francisco, and Los Angeles offer fully furnished rooms, flexible leases, and ample amenities in buildings with curated common spaces designed to promote community. Some of these spaces operate as a kind of high-end hotel, but residents increasingly stay for longer periods because of the convenience. Through innovative design choices, co-living keeps rents low by increasing shared livable space. Bedrooms and sometimes small bathrooms remain private, but living rooms and dining rooms are communal. Building one large kitchen costs less than building dozens of individual kitchens and these savings get (at least theoretically) passed on to residents.

Commercial co-living companies highlight both collectivity and convenience in their marketing materials. Starcity claimed that its mission was "redefining the meaning of home,"[42] while the Collective wants to "build and activate spaces that foster human connection and enable people to lead more fulfilling lives."[43] *Business Insider*'s Zoë Bernard referred to Common as offering "a sleek reconfiguring of communal life"[44] and Common suggests that its co-living projects allow for "urban living's closest thing to utopia."[45] Among the "testimonials" on Common's website, James from Brooklyn, New York, explains: "Since becoming a part of Common, I, along with others, have thought more about how physical space affects the ways we interact with each other."[46] The cofounder of Starcity, Jon Dishotsky, also emphasized that certain forms of privacy are a waste of money. "What are the things you can do with other people? Eat food, drink wine, watch TV," he explained in a *New York Times* profile. "You don't need to do that in your own unit alone, so why pay for it?"[47]

In the absence of state commitments to public housing, these forms of commercial collective living might provide one practical solution to urban housing shortages. Although rents for one room are more in line with what one might pay for a studio in the United States, they include utilities and amenities like weekly cleaning, Wi-Fi, and the provision of basic goods like toilet paper and coffee.[48] Co-living might also help reduce individual carbon footprints because of the economies of scale gained by the heating and cooling of communal kitchens, living rooms, and dining rooms, the sharing of large appliances designed to become obsolete within a decade, and the general reduction of excess consumption possible when a large group of people share a variety of ordinary household goods: pots, pans, plates, blenders, espresso machines, tools, vacuum cleaners, Wi-Fi routers, printers, furniture, etc. And yet these for-profit co-living facilities also care about the bottom line. In a 2019 article, journalist Will Coldwell suggested that with its focus on marketing to millennials, co-living may be seen "as a cynical ploy by property developers to cash in on a generation living in the 'age of loneliness,' locked in a perpetual struggle to find a place they can call home."[49] According to the co-living company Outsite, the average age of their residents was thirty-five, and 70 percent of them declared themselves "single."[50]

The 2008 financial crisis certainly left many US millennials less enamored with the idea of owning a traditional single-family home after home values plummeted beneath the amount of the loans people had taken out to buy them. According to a February 2021 survey on the website Apartment List, millennials lag far behind previous generations in terms of homeownership. By the age of thirty, only 42 percent of millennials owned homes, compared to 48 percent of members of Generation X and 51 percent of the Boomers.[51] But these numbers hide egregious racial disparities since the rate of homeownership for white millennials is two and a half times greater than that of Black millennials. After the shocks of the COVID-19 pandemic, almost one in five millennials claimed that they planned to rent forever, and of those who still wished to buy their own home, 63 percent reported not having enough money saved for a down payment. But for many, that style of residence remains the ideal.

The co-living model rarely provides opportunities to buy rooms or shares in the property, and the proliferation of co-living spaces is at best a temporary solution to what is ultimately a systemic crisis in affordable housing, one exacerbated by rampant real estate speculation and discriminatory zoning laws (which restrict the construction of multifamily units in wealthier neighborhoods) and premised on a specific ideal of how "grown-ups" should or should not live. Co-living spaces allow young singles to thrive in cities in their twenties and thirties, but the ideal remains a coupled-up existence in a single-family residence. The turnover of tenants also prevents the formation of the close community bonds promised on aspirational websites. Rather than working together to share chores and maintain their collective spaces, co-living residents benefit from the labor of others hired to work for the community. And since most residents are young and single, co-living is not set up to meet the specific needs of parents. (Although one certain way to undermine the lingering cultural influences of patrilineality and patrilocality is to never marry or have children.)

Despite these shortcomings, co-living developments continue to expand in major cities around the world. Investors predict further growth as younger generations embrace the sharing economy. Between 2016 and 2021, Starcity grew to include twelve locations in the Bay Area, seven in Los Angeles, and three in Barcelona.[52] As of 2021, the co-living provider Habyt owned more than four thousand micro apartments across thirteen metropolises in five countries.[53] And the growing popularity of co-living has already sparked a backlash against it. In April 2022, the Shawnee City Council in the Kansas City area unanimously banned the possibility of more than three unrelated adults living together in a house.[54] The city explicitly defined a "co-living group" as a group of four or more adults who share a dwelling as long as any two members of the group are unrelated by blood or marriage.[55] This means that it is legal for three brothers to reside together with one of their wives, but illegal for two unrelated married couples to share a household. In the future, more city councils and property owners may resist creative attempts to deal with rising rents and housing shortages. And while co-living may only provide a temporary solution to much bigger structural problems, it could also serve as a gateway to the creation of more permanent forms of collective housing.

"Danish Blueprint for Utopian Existence"

Just outside of the town of Brunswick, Maine, off a rural road that leads away from the Atlantic Ocean, there's a small wooden sign for the Two Echo Cohousing community. Conceived of and constructed in the 1990s, Two Echo consists of twenty-seven homes clustered around a common house. Built on an old dairy farm, residents share ninety-seven acres, which include wilderness trails, a soccer field, spacious garden plots, and a wood-fired sauna. "It's great if you have kids," explained one older resident when I visited in August 2021. "You can just let them go outside and play freely anywhere they want. Everyone looks out for them and it's completely safe." The children could roam down by the pond or make their way to the

Common House, where a playroom includes a wide variety of games, toys, a ping-pong table, a foosball table, a synthesizer, and a small library. The playroom connects to a quiet sitting room, a communal kitchen, a guest bedroom, and a large dining room with a piano. In the foyer of the Common House are storage cubbies marked with the names of each of the households, maps of the garden plots, and information about permaculture (sustainable native agriculture) and neighborliness. Community residents come together for regular potlucks and concerts. "The best thing was the multigenerational aspect," explained another woman, who lived in Two Echo for two years before a new job forced her family's relocation to Florida. "They [older residents] have to be patient with us, and we have to be patient with them, but in the end, it benefits everyone. I wish we'd never left."

The recent upsurge in interest in co-living builds upon a much longer tradition of cohousing often associated with early develop-

Figure 2.5. Houses at Two Echo Cohousing in Brunswick, Maine, in 2021.

ments in Denmark in the 1960s. These communal housing projects (*bofællesskab*), which sparked an international movement against the single-family home, have been called a "Danish blueprint for utopian existence."[56] Unlike co-living, cohousing tends to be intergenerational and attempts to find an ideal balance between privacy and community. Cohousing also allows for private or collective homeownership, as opposed to the rental options primarily available through co-living, making cohousing a more permanent arrangement.

Scandinavian feminists played a critical role in promoting early private cohousing developments as a way for groups of families to share common chores more equitably between the genders. As the state-owned model of the microdistrict proliferated throughout the socialist world, the Danes tried to create a housing alternative that combined this communitarian spirit with private property. In 1964, a Danish architect named Jan Gudmand-Høyer conceived of the idea of building a community of twelve row houses that would surround a shared common house and swimming pool. Gudmand-Høyer and some of his associates actually bought land and gained municipal approval for their development, but the neighbors objected to having a multifamily complex built near their homes (assuming it might diminish their property values), and so the project failed.

Around the same time, in 1967, a Danish feminist named Bodil Graae wrote a groundbreaking article called "Children Should Have One Hundred Parents," where she argued that communal living would lead to a safer, more supportive, and happier environment for children.[57] Graae's essay explicitly challenged the nuclear family and single-family dwellings, advocating for a profound transformation of the prevailing concept of "home." The following year, when Gudmand-Høyer published an article defending the communitarian goals of collective living in a Danish national newspaper, over a hundred families wrote in to express their interest in living in such a development.[58]

In 1972, Bodil Graae and a group of Danish families started an intergenerational cohousing project now known as Sættedammen—often credited as the world's first modern cohousing community. Britta Bjerre and her husband were among the first residents to move into

Sættedammen. "We didn't want our family to spend our lives in an insular way in a house on a suburban street somewhere," she explained. "And one day we saw a newspaper ad saying that some people had their eyes on a plot of land, and they were looking for twenty-five to thirty families to buy it and build houses as well as a communal house."[59] Gudmand-Høyer founded a community called Skraplanet the following year,[60] and like Britta Bjerre, many other Danes saw ads in the newspaper and found their way into living arrangements with strangers who valued the idea of living cooperatively.

Over the next decade, cohousing communities spread across Denmark, usually in suburban or semirural areas with an architectural style known as "dense-low," dense because people lived close together and low so that the developments would maintain a greater harmony with nature. Much like the initial plans devised by Gudmand-Høyer, the physical layout of cohousing usually included a cluster of independent homes—much smaller than single-family homes, but still with private bedrooms, bathrooms, and a kitchen—together with shared walkways, gardens, parking, laundry facilities, workshops, tools, recreational equipment, and play spaces. The collective facilities encourage sociality, and many cohousing communities include labor requirements that compel residents to work together toward common goals. The architecture of cohousing communities varies, with some building fairly similar single-family homes for traditional nuclear families, while others offer a variety of accommodations for older residents, singles, multigenerational families, or childless couples.

One example of a Danish cohousing community is Ibsgården in suburban Roskilde about twenty miles west of Copenhagen.[61] Established in 1983, and functioning continuously since then, the community contains twenty single-family homes and a large common house, where residents share meals four to five times a week. Members must provide four hours per week of labor for the community, but otherwise the obligations are relatively light. Community labor includes normal things like landscape maintenance, cleaning common spaces, and cooking common meals, but it also often includes tasks like organizing and leading activities for children as well as driving elderly residents to doctor's appointments or doing the kinds of care work that would otherwise fall disproportionately on the shoulders of women. By recognizing many traditional care activities as labor contributions to the wider community, cohousing collectives help alleviate some of the stresses involved in daily life. And to the extent that women often provide a disproportionate amount of emotional support within families (particularly in heterosexual relationships where male partners rely primarily on their wives or girlfriends for their emotional needs), the close proximity between cohousing residents creates a wider network of people with whom to share thoughts and feelings.

By 2017, about 1 percent of the Danish population lived in official cohousing communities.[62] Cohousing residents are often a bit wealthier than their average compatriots, perhaps because while owner-occupied homes in cohousing communities cost about the same as regular single-family homes in similar neighborhoods, there are monthly association fees to pay for occasional expenses like a new roof for the common house. Cohousing residents also have, on average, higher levels of education.[63] One 2016 report found that rather than being the continuation of the anti-establishment experiments of the 1960s and '70s, cohousing in Demark had become "a sort of practical 'lifebelt' for the modern human and an attempt to recreate the meaningful social relations that are no longer automatically provided by the nuclear family. . . ."[64] Today, rural Danish municipalities hope to encourage regional development initiatives and to fight depopulation by increasing the construction of cohousing communities to attract disenchanted city dwellers to their environs.[65]

Since the 1970s, cohousing has spread from Scandinavia through Europe and the world. Across the Netherlands, there are over a hundred cohousing projects, and the city of Berlin boasts one of the highest densities of cohousing projects in the world: over 150 different communities as of 2017.[66] Unlike in traditional cohousing developments, Berliners often join together in *Baugruppen* (building groups) to pool their money and build their own multistory, multi-family urban dwellings without using a developer as an intermediary.[67] Because German

banks approve mortgages to *Baugruppen*, groups of families can design and oversee the construction of their own buildings at considerable cost savings since they cut out the middleman. One of the most
famous *Baugruppen* projects is R50 in Kreuzberg, named after its location on Ritterstrasse 50. R50 is a seven-story complex built by nineteen households who self-financed the project with the cooperation of
the Berlin Senate Department for Urban Development, a public body
interested in protecting city residents from the predatory machinations of real estate corporations.[68]

Néo-Béguinages and Matriarchal Villages

With so many cohousing projects springing up around the world, it's
no surprise that some communities have begun to tailor their offer-
ings to specific demographics. Nor should it astonish that the fastest
growth area for cohousing is among seniors, where the isolation and
loneliness of the traditional single-family home get exacerbated when
adult children move out. Because women's life expectancy exceeds
that of men, many older single women in particular seek to reimagine their lives through cohousing. Women's pensions are also typically
smaller than men's, so older women have a harder time remaining
independent after they are widowed or divorced. And so a modern
Beguine movement has emerged in Western Europe, beginning with
the founding of Midgaarden in Denmark in 1987.[69] While some of
these all-female communities are explicitly religious, many have been
established by secular feminists. In London, New Ground Cohousing,
developed by the Older Women's Co-Housing group, finally became a
reality in 2016,[70] and in Paris, a group of twenty older women created
a *néo-béguinage* called the Maison des Babayagas, after a long battle
with municipal officials, who objected to the single-sex and communal
nature of the proposed dwelling because it purportedly violated zoning and antidiscrimination laws.[71]

It's not only senior women who move into all-female collective complexes. The intergenerational and "matriarchal" ecovillage Nashira in

Colombia, which was a finalist in the 2015 World Habitat Awards, contains over eighty homes built by women and children who have been victims of domestic violence or found themselves displaced by Colombia's decades-long civil war.[72] The residents constructed their own houses on free land using recycled materials.[73] Once women contribute a fixed amount of "sweat equity," they become full co-owners in the cooperative community, sharing in its collective revenues and partaking of its many facilities, including a computer lab, a community center, and a shallow pool for children to play in.[74] Although some men live in the community, all authority rests with the female residents who grow their own food, have their own source of clean drinking water, and operate a restaurant run on solar power and a Saturday market.[75]

American cohousing communities have also taken on their own particular character. The concept of cohousing came to the United States by way of two architects who met while studying at the Royal Academy of Art and Architecture at the University of Copenhagen in 1980. But Kathryn McCamant and Charles Durrett detached the idea of cohousing from its communitarian and feminist roots.[76] While cohousing experiments in Europe often attempted to challenge the nuclear family (as in Denmark) or undermine commercial property relations (as in Germany), the more than fifty communities McCamant and Durrett's architectural firm has developed have been adapted for North American sensibilities, focusing instead on giving their residents a chance to lead more meaningful and connected lives with nicer neighbors. In general, American cohousing often retains a more explicit commitment to autonomous, owner-occupied households, with fewer obligations for collective labor, distinguishing itself from the much derided idea of "communes" or "cults" that populate the American imagination of cooperative living.[77] As of 2017, more than a hundred and fifty cohousing communities flourished across the United States, many of them like the community at Two Echo in Maine, where people built their own homes on a property that they purchased in common with their neighbors.

Happy Kids and Collective Chores

Although the empirical research is relatively sparse, the studies that have been conducted reveal that cohousing usually delivers on its many promises—even when its more traditionally feminist and communitarian histories are de-emphasized. One 2010 study comparing women's time use among residents of cohousing and more conventional neighborhoods in the southeastern United States found that women living in cohousing spent less time on domestic chores and lived in households where their partners contributed more time to housework. The author highlights the differences in the spatial dynamics of these two ways of living, contrasting "cohousing developments, which contained collectively owned spaces for socializing housework through neighborhood networks" with "new urbanist developments, which contained isolated, individualized suburban houses where a woman's highest priority is to serve and care for her own family."[78] Perhaps because the cohousing development attracted residents with more unconventional household structures, women in cohousing arrangements spent 24 percent of their time at home on housework compared to women in urban developments, who spent 31 percent. Among cohousing residents living with a partner, 40 percent claimed that their partners "were involved in housework activities at least once in a typical day" compared to only 27 percent of residents with a partner in the urban development.[79] Since organizing collective chores and responsibilities creates economies of scale (that is, watching children with other residents, cooking and cleaning up together after communal meals, and gardening on collective plots), the cohousing women not only saved time (perhaps as much as a half hour per day), but their otherwise unseen private labors at home become valued as contributions to the community.

More important, 30 percent of cohousing residents reported sharing or trading off a chore with members of other households in the community, whereas none of the residents of the urban development reported sharing or trading off household activities with their neighbors. This was at least partially a function of cohousing's unique architecture and design. While the new single-family homes in the urbanist development clustered around planned commercial centers that contained movie theaters, grocery stores, child care, and recreational facilities such as pools and gyms, the study found that the "communal facilities, communal management, and a consequent tight-knit community" of the cohousing developments "accommodated more egalitarian ideas of gender" and "patterns of sharing housework within and among households."[80]

Another study, which interviewed Danish and Swedish cohousing residents in six different communities between 2015 and 2018, suggested that children raised in cohousing move more fluidly across the boundaries of private and communal spaces than their parents. Based on her findings, sociologist Cathrin Wassede proposed that children growing up in cohousing communities enjoyed the benefits of a close-knit group of other adults and children that acted as an extended family. Although some parents remained invested in maintaining time for their own children in their private spaces, children seemed happier and more comfortable with the constant collectivity. They developed a more capacious concept of home that included the kitchens and living spaces of their neighbors in a way that transcended the tight linkage between home and the nuclear family.[81]

In her interviews with children who grew up in cohousing in the United States, the journalist Courtney E. Martin also found that "coming of age in a cohousing community has wide-ranging and long-term impacts."[82] One college student raised on Sandhill Farm in Missouri reported that growing up with many adults in a wide community enhanced her interpersonal skills: "Our weekly check-in meetings, garden work parties, and shared meals developed in everyone the skill of open, honest conversation, which I have relied on my entire life and believe is really valuable in any situation."[83] Another young woman raised in a cohousing community in Durango, Colorado, recalled the relative freedom she enjoyed. "We all grew up with a sense of adventure," Helen Thompson explains. "We would run around the neighborhood and take care of ourselves, with an adult there only if we needed them."[84] Not everything was rosy; other kids who grew up in American cohousing communities complained about the lack of privacy, the constant gossip, as well as of the racial and economic homogeneity. But at the end of the day, Martin found that "for all its potential flaws, almost all of the young adults I interviewed said that, given the chance, they would raise their own kids in cohousing."[85]

Researchers show particular interest in the success of the cohousing model among the elderly, since most populations in postindustrial economies are graying. In March 2020, the Pew Research Center found that 27 percent of American adults aged sixty and above lived alone, compared with only 16 percent of over-sixties in the other 130 countries and territories surveyed.[86] The spousal age gap around the world also means that women are twice as likely to age alone.[87] Promisingly, one 2020 study of eighty-six (mostly female) inhabitants of five senior cohousing complexes in the United States found that self-reported levels of loneliness were below the national average. The study also found that self-identified introverts especially enjoyed the cohousing environment because they'd feared becoming recluses in their previous housing arrangements. This is consistent with other studies that show that older introverts understand the importance of regular social interaction for healthy aging.[88] "Respondents reported it was less effortful to get together socially in this setting," the study found. "They appreciated being part of a community where neighbors were looking out for each other."[89] Another 2020 study of the quality of life in a senior cohousing complex in Canada found that residents specifically appreciated the possibility of aging in place, making cohousing a far more desirable option than a commercial assisted living facility.[90]

A 2020 literature review of available research on cohousing and life satisfaction suggested that in addition to the quality-of-life benefits typically touted (benefits borne out by their review of the extant studies, mostly in Western Europe and North America), cohousing residents enjoyed more protection from price volatility. "[C]ohousing has been considered a housing model that could help to decrease the commoditisation of housing . . ." the authors write, as "housing construction costs are often less subject to the capital gains of promoters" and "there is greater long-term stability of housing prices and mutual economic support that results in stable economic and social security for residents, who are less exposed to the precarious conditions of the neo-liberal housing market."[91] In other words, cohousing arrangements can challenge real estate speculators and house flippers who exploit the volatility of housing markets to buy low and sell high, or property management companies that buy up hundreds of thousands of homes and convert them into rental properties.

Unlike condominiums or single-family homes, individual units often cannot be sold without the approval of the whole community. In Two Echo, owners can sell their properties to any potential buyer, but the buyer has to be willing to abide by all of the rules and responsibilities of the community. Property values do not fluctuate as much because speculators and house flippers find cohousing community covenants anathema to their desire for quick profits. Also, since aspiring cohousing groups like the *Baugruppen* in Germany build their communities without the middleman of a commercial developer, these savings are passed on to owners in the form of lower initial housing prices.

Studies have also shown that cohousing arrangements make it easier to maintain commitments to environmentalist goals and that cohousing reduces domestic energy consumption.[92] Common facilities obviate the need for twenty different dwellings with twenty different dishwashers and washers and dryers, which will break and end up in landfills every decade or so.[93] Shared libraries full of books, shared magazine and newspaper subscriptions, shared Wi-Fi connections, and shared cable or streaming subscriptions mean both cost savings and less waste. A 2019 study found evidence that buying less stuff makes people happier than buying "green" stuff, and it's easier to buy less stuff when you're sharing things with a wider group of people.[94] "After we left Two Echo and moved to Florida, one of my new neighbors went out and bought a wheelbarrow when we already had a wheelbarrow. I couldn't understand why he didn't just ask to borrow ours," explained the woman who lived with her family at Two

Echo for two years. "It just makes so much more sense for everyone to share."

Cohousing arrangements also mitigate the isolation that results from more remote working and the migration of our public spaces from the material to the digital world. As brick and mortar stores give way to Amazon fulfillment centers, we have fewer reasons to leave our homes to interact with others. With new technology, you almost never have to wait in a line anymore, and while I realize that in most cases this is a good thing, some of my fondest memories are of the shared excitement and effusive conversations I had with other fans while queuing for hours to get tickets for live concerts or midnight premieres of highly anticipated films. In our time-pressed, hyperactive societies, we consistently give up community for convenience without really thinking about it.

"I Don't Want to Sugarcoat It"

And yes, there will inevitably be conflicts and tensions associated with communal living, especially for those of us used to dwelling in single-family homes. "I don't want to sugarcoat it," explained the older woman resident I spoke to at Two Echo in August 2021. "You have conflicts with neighbors here like you would have conflicts with neighbors anywhere. And oh, the number of emails can be overwhelming!" Unlike co-living spaces, most cohousing communities perform their own maintenance, and Two Echo is no exception—they only hire outside help for snow removal, felling large trees, and inspecting their septic tank. Conflicts arise when some residents prefer to use their pooled association fees (each household paid about $180 per month in 2021) to hire out more of the collective labor when others insist that it should be done by the community. Another common conflict is the use and abuse of the pedestrian road. Like most cohousing communities, Two Echo is meant to be car-free. Residents park their cars on the periphery and agree to shuttle their groceries and children to and from their cars using carts or wheelbarrows. The rules allow for exceptions in specific circumstances, such as packing up a car for a vacation or delivering large items. This can lead to tensions when some residents take what their neighbors consider too many liberties.

But unlike other neighborhoods, cohousing communities have regular meetings of all residents and have agreed to a certain set of protocols regarding conflict resolution and collective decision-making. Two Echo works on a consensus-based model that requires the consent of all residents, a process that can be lengthy and tedious, but that demands good-faith cooperation when tensions do arise. Sometimes the issue is small, such as allowing a resident to build a new porch on their house or put up a larger-than-usual antenna or satellite dish. Other times the issue can be more fundamental, such as allowing gun ownership on the property. If residents fail to reach consensus after repeated attempts, they can put the issue to a vote if 75 percent of people agree to suspend the consensus process. Once a vote is called, a motion will pass only if three-fourths of all residents vote in favor. Having a clear process helps bind the community together.

We've all had bad roommates and nasty neighbors, and for those of us accustomed to living in our own isolated homes, it might be hard to deal regularly with other people's habits, quirks, or demands: the playing of noisy instruments, the cooking of smelly food, or the whining of a local hypochondriac. But unless you are wealthy enough to live on a large private estate, most of us will have to deal with the people who share our neighborhoods. Imagine the advantage if those we lived near agreed beforehand on a set of protocols to handle any future conflicts. In a cohousing community, residents move in knowing the rules and come with a commitment to a more collective ideal of living together. Dealing with interpersonal issues and facing shared challenges can bind people together the same way we learn to live with the idiosyncrasies and annoying habits of our romantic partners. In Eastern Europe, people used to complain bitterly about the crowded living conditions due to housing shortages, but after the collapse of state socialism in 1989, ethnographic research suggests that many citizens missed the sociality of their former lives and reported that the arrival of free markets increased personal isolation.[95]

Our bathrooms, bedrooms, kitchens, and dining rooms are places of great physical intimacy, and we often measure our closeness with others by the rooms we are willing to share with them. Close proximity also means vulnerability, and trust is an essential component of inhabiting common spaces and microbial environments. But our preferences are malleable. Both individualism and cooperation are learned traits; like muscles, the more we use them the stronger they become. Some of us just uncritically accept the private apartment or single-family home for ourselves because it is what our societies consider "normal." We might be more flexible than we imagine. We also know that children who grow up within large extended networks are more likely to feel comfortable in those types of communities as adults, the same way that women who attended day care as children are more likely to send their own children to nurseries and preschools.

Still, critics point out that cohousing, especially in North America, has devolved into gated communities for leftists.[96] Perhaps one of the biggest problems in the United States today is the sequestering of citizens in their own private echo chambers. People of different political orientations watch different cable channels, read different news sources, and scroll through hyper-curated social media feeds that reinforce their own preexisting beliefs. In some ways, the current trend in American cohousing might exacerbate this extreme polarization, and it could be that only public commitments to affordable cohousing developments would allow for different demographics to live together and find ways to overcome their political divisions, in the same way that some sports fans can put aside politics when it comes to rooting for their home team. Of course, like co-ops in New York City, cohousing could also exacerbate discrimination if approval is needed from existing members. But in the United States, the Fair Housing Act applies to cohousing communities and, at least in theory, provides some protection for certain categories of potential residents.

Cohousing arrangements could encourage more multigenerational living and promote the mixing of childless singles, couples, triads, traditional families, and extended families all in one community. The benefits of cohousing might also support greater racial, religious, and socioeconomic integration as people spend more time socializing at meetings, potlucks, soccer games, concerts, and craft nights with a greater diversity of neighbors. If we look at the different kinds of friendships formed among first year students when they move onto university campuses, there exists the possibility that cohousing could provide a part of the solution to growing political divisions.

But in the short term, the more likely scenario is the proliferation of small, privately funded cohousing communities of people with shared beliefs, whether these be spiritual or secular. A common commitment to a goal, such as living sustainably or bringing up children in a community of faith, helps us live together. Although I am an introvert and would definitely need my own private space to retreat to occasionally, I could more easily imagine myself living with a gaggle of Trekkies than with a clutch of sports fans (and we would definitely have a full replica of Ten Forward as our common room). When I'm feeling playful, I can imagine cohousing for horticulturalists, cohousing for motorcycle enthusiasts or opera aficionados, and maybe even multigenerational cohousing for feminist Wonder Woman fans.

Today, the Cohousing Association of America (or CohoUS), the Foundation for Intentional Community, the Canadian Cohousing Network, the UK Cohousing Network, the National Union for Cohousing (or Landelijke Vereniging Centraal Wonen) in the Netherlands, the association Kollektivhus NU in Sweden, and many other organizations around the world are helping to connect interested individuals and families with old and new cohousing developments. But you can also reap the benefits of cohousing without living in a designated cohousing community. Some might find it easier to buy a shared house or property and live together with a group of close friends, *Golden Girls* style. In a January 2022 essay, a single mother named Holly Harper described her existence at Siren House, a four-unit home she bought together with three other single mothers, and how their sharing of emergency expenses saved her $30,000 in one year (although her arrangement would now be illegal in Shawnee City, Kansas).[97] Existing neighbors might find new and innovative ways to coordinate neighborhood potlucks or the sharing of snowblowers, lawn mowers, hedge trimmers, and wheelbarrows. Residents might also put pressure on local government officials to promote public cohousing developments or at the very least to challenge zoning laws that prevent the construction of more dense and multifamily forms of housing.

No More Empty Penthouses

In the end, cohousing models can decrease isolation, increase housing stock as existing buildings are retrofitted to house more people, and reduce overall consumption, putting a dent into the materialism that fuels the climate crisis. But scholars of feminist political economy don't think this goes far enough. Given that cohousing in the West started as a uniquely feminist project to disrupt the nuclear family, Lidewij Tummers and Sherilyn MacGregor argue that too many cohousing developments today have been watered down or stripped of their radical histories and so "fall short of the transformation needed to build a post-capitalist and post-patriarchal society."[98]

In 1892, the Russian anarchist, polymath, and prince Peter Kropotkin proposed that housing should be completely decommodified in order to ensure the true liberation of the working classes. "If the people of the Revolution expropriate the houses and proclaim free lodgings—the communalizing of houses and the right of each family to a decent dwelling . . . [i]t will have struck a fatal blow at individual property," he wrote.[99] Cohousing communities can challenge the idea that housing should be a commodity rather than a social good by allowing citizens to pool resources and cut out commercial property developers. In precarious societies where the wealthy and the upper middle classes store value in tangible assets, real estate was (and is) too often conceived of as an investment rather than a basic need of all citizens. Hundreds of penthouses in places like New York and London sit empty today, while tens of thousands of people in those cities go homeless. Even before the pandemic swelled his billions, Amazon CEO Jeff Bezos bought a 13,600-square-foot Los Angeles mansion for $165 million in February 2020, the same year that the Los Angeles

Homeless Services Authority reported that more than sixty-six thousand residents of the city lived on the streets.[100]

From this perspective, modern co-living and cohousing arrangements may be a tepid reform rather than a world-shaking revolution, although there are certainly some communities that go beyond the sharing of dwellings, as I will discuss in my later chapter on productive property. For now, most of us, but particularly women, would benefit from taking any steps, however small, away from the rigid walls of the single-family home. By thinking more deliberately about how, where, and with whom we live, we can all recover some of the spirit of cooperation and sharing that modern life has robbed from us.

CHAPTER 3

Kids as Public Goods

Why the Privatization of Childhood Is Bad for Families

When I got pregnant at thirty-one, one of my graduate school professors at Berkeley, a then childless woman in middle age, warned me that I would jeopardize my chances for a career if I became a mother before earning my PhD. For two agonizing months during my first trimester, as I struggled with horrible fatigue, I feared she was right. The hustle required to land a tenure-track position felt incompatible with my growing stomach and fogging brain. Marshaling all of my resolve, I plowed ahead with my thesis and threw myself out onto the job market just before my due date.

I landed my first phone interview with a small liberal arts college in Maine. I did the entire thing from the car so they wouldn't hear the baby crying in the background. When they invited me to fly from the West to the East Coast only two weeks after my caesarean, I considered withdrawing my application. But my dissertation chair convinced me to go. "It will give you a valuable opportunity to practice your interview skills," he said. But he also advised that my choice to have a baby could bias the search committee. They might assume that caregiving responsibilities would hamper my ability to produce the quality and quantity of research and teaching necessary to succeed. Fearing my new mother status would harm my candidacy, I never mentioned my daughter's existence.

I thought I had everything planned. Because I was nursing, I carried a handheld breast pump in my messenger bag, hoping to use the breaks between my campus interviews to express my milk. But every moment of my day was scheduled as I walked from faculty office to faculty office, guided by a program coordinator who waited outside of the bathroom for me when I went in. By my four o'clock interview, my breasts had swelled up like basketballs. No doubt encouraged in their dairy production by the furious pumping I'd done before leaving California to ensure that my husband had enough milk for the baby while I traveled, they sprang a leak. As I sat with the dean and associate dean around a small circular conference table in an austere New England office, I felt fluid trickling out of the special nursing pads I'd put into the cups of my bra. My body betrayed me. I could do nothing to stop it. As I listened to the two deans discuss health and dental insurance plans, my stomach clenched in horror as I felt the force of the squirting and saw the milk soaking through the fabric of my suit under my arms. I hugged my elbows into my sides, praying it looked like perspiration.

I marvel to this day that I got that job: my first in academia. I know many other women who weren't so lucky. It comes as no surprise, then, that when I look around at my female peers, I estimate that about half are childless. For some of my colleagues, they made a deliberate choice: a successful career in a world where professional timetables revolve around male biology precluded having babies. For others, their childlessness stemmed from what the economist Sylvia Ann Hewlett calls "creeping non-choice."[1] Women delayed childbearing until they felt professionally accomplished enough to settle down (they'd finished their residencies, earned tenure, became a partner, etc.). Already in their mid- to late thirties, they now either couldn't find partners, couldn't get pregnant, or just decided that they were too old or too financially precarious to start families.

Having kids requires a major commitment of time and resources for anyone, particularly when the entire responsibility for their upbringing devolves onto just one or two parents. But what if it didn't have to be that way? For millennia, utopian thinkers have proposed that children should be raised by a wider collective of adults. Usually accompanying the development of more collective forms of housing, social experiments with alternative forms of child-rearing demonstrate that ideas once considered fanciful or extreme can pave the way for practices most people accept as normal today. For as long as we have had children, people have found ways to raise them together, pooling the energies and resources of the wider community for the benefit of all families. But the opposite practice has coexisted, particularly among the wealthy and powerful who often raise their own children apart from the children of others, historically with the help of wetnurses, nannies, cooks, governesses, and other staff. In recent times, the ideal of an early childhood spent within the confines of the nuclear family usually means that one parent must fulfill all of these roles, an exhausting and often impossible task. For those considering parenthood, some kind of collective support for child-rearing remains an essential pillar of building an everyday utopia.

Calculating the Cost of Kids

According to the United States Department of Agriculture, a child born in 2015 would cost a middle-income married couple $233,610 to raise from birth to age seventeen, not including the price of any higher education.[2] And this fails to account for the opportunity costs of mother's time: what she might have been doing for the period that she withdraws from the labor force for family reasons. For college-educated women this can exceed a million dollars of lost earnings over a career.[3] Almost all of this cost is borne by the family, which means that in societies where children no longer work on the family farm and are not expected to care for their parents in old age, childbearing and rearing are simply bad financial investments.

On top of the rational economic considerations, some research also contradicts the idea that children bring happiness. One 2006 study of German life satisfaction over time showed that while happiness initially increased after the birth of a first child, happiness levels for both men and women fell significantly below their baseline by the time their child reached the age of three or four.[4] A 2003 meta-analysis found that parents also report much lower levels of marital satisfaction than nonparents.[5] And another study of twenty-two Organisation for Economic Co-operation and Development (OECD) nations found an overall happiness gap between parents and nonparents in most advanced economies, with parents reporting lower levels of happiness. The largest happiness gap was found in the United States.[6]

And yet, people continue to procreate despite the difficulties. For some, marriage and kids are just an expected part of adulthood, the completion of a life stage. Others long for the opportunity to give and receive the unconditional love and care often inherent in parent-child relations, or to project something of themselves into the future through the lifelong project of supporting the next generation. Still others strive for the full human experience, which for them must include the bringing of new life into the world and raising that life to maturity so that the cycle can begin again (interestingly, grandparents have historically reported higher life satisfaction and quality of life than non-grandparents, but this requires that their children must live long enough and be willing to have children of their own).[7] Given that having children satisfies a basic biological instinct, surely it should be increasing rather than decreasing the happiness of parents. What accounts for it having the opposite effect? According to the authors of the study comparing twenty-two OECD nations, the reason for the greater happiness of nonparents compared to parents in the United States is quite clear: "Less generous family policies, especially subsidized child care and paid leave," explain this gap.[8]

Even in countries that have made commitments to provide subsidized national childcare, it can be difficult to find a place, the quality of care isn't always very good, and there may be a large delay between when women wish to return to work and when the subsidized childcare begins. Progressive Americans often look overseas to find models for their own dreams of universal childcare, but the reality in many countries means they may have to dream bigger. In Germany, for instance, all children enjoy a legal right to a place in preschool. In 2019 the federal government approved $6.5 billion in subsidies to expand childcare facilities. But less than two years later, Germany still had a shortage of 342,000 childcare places for children under the age of three, accounting for about 14 percent of the nation's younger children.[9] Because of the ongoing shortage, it was German mothers, many of them educated professionals who desperately wanted to return to work, who stayed home with their kids. And even for parents who could find a place, a separate 2020 study revealed that the child-to-caregiver ratio was higher than optimal and that many day care centers lack qualified personnel (the German Bertelsmann Foundation recommended one caregiver per three infants under the age of three and one caregiver per 7.5 children over that age).[10] Despite Germany's public commitments to expand childcare options, the supply simply could not keep up with the demand.

Similarly, in New Zealand, the government fully subsidizes twenty hours per week of early childhood education for all children between the ages of three and five.[11] But when I spoke to women in Wellington in March 2020, I learned that many new mothers wished to return to work before their children turned three. The cost of care during these years must be borne by individual families—either by paying a caregiver or by staying at home. In a competitive market where labor is a commodity, three years out of that market can put a worker at a significant disadvantage with regard to their professional ambitions. At the same time, the system penalizes those women who do choose to stay home for the full three years because it treats those years as value-less. The policy also reinforces a gendered division of labor in the heterosexual family, as most couples rationally choose to have the parent with the lower wage stay home. Since women generally earn less than men, New Zealand's policy perpetuates a vicious cycle wherein heterosexual mothers (rather than fathers) must sacrifice their aspirations for the sake of their children. As a result, New Zealand recorded its lowest-ever fertility rate in 2021, and all indications suggest a continued decline. This is probably good for the planet, but not so great for New Zealand's future tax revenues and ability to pay its pension obligations.[12]

For many families, both available options—paying for childcare or losing one parent's income for three years—exceed their financial means. In the past, grandparents and other relatives provided more alloparental care. But economic changes due to outsourcing and globalization mean that more people move away from home to find work. Even if grandparents live nearby, they often spend more years in the formal labor force because of rising retirement ages and fears of economic precarity in old age. The erosion of multigenerational support networks particularly hurts racial and ethnic minorities, working-class communities, and single mothers. Post-pandemic labor shortages in the United States partially resulted from the lack of childcare. Even if American women wanted to get back to work, they either couldn't find or couldn't afford to have someone else help look after their kids.

Raising children in isolated nuclear families not only places a disproportionate burden on mothers but may also undermine the social and emotional needs and psychological development of the next generation. Research has consistently shown that the early years of life prove the most important for cognitive development and emotional attachment. What is needed is consistent loving care by a number of adults. A 2004 working paper from the Harvard University Center of the Developing Child and the National Scientific Council on the Developing Child, "Young Children Develop in an Environment of Relationships," emphasized that "healthy development depends on the quality and reliability of a young child's relationships with the important people in his or her life, both within and outside the family. Even the development of a child's brain architecture depends on the establishment of these relationships."[13] These relationships often include nonparental caregivers in high-quality childcare settings where close connections can be forged over time between attentive professionals and young children.

Devolving care for babies onto their mothers also ignores the reality of postpartum (or postnatal) depression. According to the Centers for Disease Control, about 13 percent of American mothers suffer from emotions that may make it difficult to adequately care for their babies, although this percentage varied across states and reached as high as one in every four new mothers in Mississippi.[14] Having other nonparental caregivers around to support both the mother and the infant can mitigate the deleterious effects of this condition. But societies continue to idealize the mother-child bond. We ignore the stress that this places on mothers and the benefits that can be gained by having several loving carers.

And even without depression, anyone who has ever spent days, weeks, or months on end looking after infants knows that it is tedious, exhausting, and repetitive work punctuated by sleep deprivation and ceaseless demands, which is why the wealthy often hire live-in nannies and au pairs. A growing number of women now (anonymously) admit that they regret having kids, despite the social outrage they face for challenging pervasive stereotypes about motherhood.[15] Others struggle with their emotions in private, fearing that they are "bad mothers" and that they alone feel disappointment and resentment at the level of self-sacrifice now demanded of them. Our competitive economies lionize individualism and enlightened self-interest until someone starts calling you "Mom."[16]

Not surprisingly, birth rates across the Global North have plummeted in the last four decades, now falling well below what demographers call replacement levels. Many individuals make the economically rational decision to forgo family formation in cultures where the choice to have babies is framed as an individual privilege rather than a social endeavor. In countries such as Japan or Italy where government media campaigns try to shame young people into procreating for the sake of ethno-national preservation, women respond with anger and frustration at the persistence of outdated cultural ideals of selfless motherhood. Around the world today, debates over universal childcare still often get framed as a trade-off between what's best for women and what's best for children, but utopian visions of universal and collective childcare have been tried in many countries. The evidence shows that everyone benefits.

Economists define a "public good" as a service or commodity in which the consumption by one person does not use up the good. Since all members of society benefit from their availability, public goods should be funded collectively through general taxation. National defense, roads, a legal system, or clean air are classic public goods. In the sense that children represent future workers, taxpayers, and consumers, the American economist Nancy Folbre argues that they, too, are public goods because all current citizens will (if they live long enough) one day depend on their contributions to society.[17] Every person drawing pension payments today relies on the labors of children that other people helped to raise. Every employer hiring new workers reaps the rewards of someone else's kids. During times of war, other people's sons and daughters fight to protect their compatriots. In 2022, the US Department of Defense "death gratuity" (that is, the compensation parents will receive in case of the death of their unmarried enlisted child) was $100,000, less than the direct costs that most parents incurred in raising that child to adulthood.[18] And yet in most countries, this valuable public good (the next generation) gets paid for privately, which means that parents are subsidizing our futures with their time, energy, money, and love. Eschewing parenthood provides one way to avoid this situation, but those who do commit themselves to an eighteen-or-more-year project of raising children provide a public service for all of us. They both need and deserve our help. Even beyond the practical necessity of childcare, raising our kids together builds the emotional connections and community supports necessary to realize other efforts to transform our everyday lives. Anyone who has spent years raising children knows that our closest comrades-in-arms are other mothers and fathers jousting on the chaotic tiltyards of parenthood.

The Kids of Kallipolis

As early as 375 BCE, Plato took issue with the lack of civic-mindedness perpetuated by private family relationships. Remember that he wrote the *Republic* in the aftermath of the Peloponnesian War when Athens got its butt kicked by Sparta. The Spartans embraced a more collectivist spirit than the individualistic Athenians, and Plato's ideal form of an enlightened society may have drawn from his understanding of

Spartan social customs regarding women and children. In Book V, he argues that all children of the Guardians (and possibly all children in the Republic) should be raised collectively, "with no parent knowing its own offspring, and no child its parent."[19]

Plato divided his society into three groups: the philosopher-kings, the auxiliaries, and the producers. When Plato first speaks of "the Guardians," he means both the philosopher-kings and the auxiliaries, but then makes a distinction between the two: the auxiliaries are warriors who protect and ensure order in the Republic, while the philosopher-kings (and queens) are those deemed wise enough to rule it. The producers grow the food and practice the trades to support everyday life in Kallipolis. Scholars still debate whether Plato meant *all* children in his ideal society should be raised collectively or whether he meant this only for the offspring of the Guardians, but it is clear that any child could end up in any one of the three groups depending on their innate abilities. "I think it makes more sense for all kids to be raised communally given his goals, which include discovering true talent," a professor emerita of philosophy, Sarah Conly, explained to me in an email in March 2022. "[But] it is more important for the Guardians because they have power and must be prevented from trying to amass more to pass onto their families."

Plato (through a dialogue featuring his mentor, Socrates) suggests that after birth children should be "taken by the officials appointed for this purpose, whether these are men or women or both—for surely our offices are also open to both women and men."[20] The children would be cared for by a designated group of professional infant caregivers, trained women as well as men, who cooperatively endeavor to raise up the next generation. Plato understood the necessities of biology and he explained that "these nurses also take care of the children's feeding by bringing the mothers to the rearing pen when their breasts are full, while devising every device to ensure that no mother will recognize her offspring. . . ."[21] Plato's scheme also ensured that if a mother had insufficient milk, her child would be fed by wet nurses and that the "sleepless nights and similar burdens" would be assigned to professionals rather than to the birth mothers. This is not so different from the way British aristocrats raised their own progeny for centuries. As almost any lactating person can attest, your milk can let down at the cry of any baby, not just that of your own biological offspring. Plato's heavy-handed paternalism and his specific prescriptions may seem harsh to us today, but the goal of this separation of a mother from her own child may have been, in part, to ensure that all children had the best possible care and nutrition, because some mothers have more milk than others. Nursing babies collectively ensures that each receives adequate sustenance, which also supports the argument that Plato meant all children in Kallipolis to be raised in common.

Collective child-rearing provided another benefit, one even more important to Plato: that no Guardian became too attached to his or her own offspring to the exclusion of others. Plato makes it clear that the raising of children in common allowed the women more freedom, but his primary objective was to lessen the competition and rivalry between the auxiliaries and the philosopher-kings of his Republic. If the Guardians treated all children as if they were their own, the theory went, they would place the collective interests of the Republic above the selfish interests of their own families, and everyone would be better off, especially in a time of war. They would also avoid the presumed guilt and disappointment if their own biological progeny lacked the innate abilities necessary to become an auxiliary or a philosopher-king.

Too Radical for The Communist Manifesto

Over a thousand years later, Plato's ideal of publicly funded collective child-rearing found renewed relevance as the Industrial Revolution drew increasing numbers of working-class women and children out of unpaid labor in the rural home and fields and into wage labor in the factories. By the mid-nineteenth century, proletarian mothers worked twelve-to-fourteen-hour days and had precious little time to look after their sons and daughters, as Friedrich Engels knew so well from his time spent living among the workers in Manchester for his 1844 book,

The Condition of the Working Class in England. Proponents argued that collective child-rearing would protect kids from the care deficit that resulted. Outraged at the high rate of child mortality, Engels understood that "in many families the wife, like the husband, has to work away from home, and the consequence is the total neglect of the children, who are either locked up or given out to be taken care of."[22] Engels discovered that women who took in children usually did piecework at home (that is, work paid by the unit of the product produced), and often gave infants drops of something called Godfrey's Cordial, an opiate derivative, to keep them in a quiet stupor. Babies died of overdoses while their parents toiled. Children old enough to go to school usually labored in factories instead, exposed to all sorts of danger.

Engels demanded some form of universal childcare beginning as early as possible and including a strong educational component to ensure that all children had a fair start in life. He believed that encouraging the literacy and numeracy of working-class children could liberate them from the lifetime of difficult manual labor awaiting the uneducated in an industrializing society. In 1847, Engels wrote two early drafts of what would eventually become *The Communist Manifesto.* In the first draft, a "Communist Confession of Faith," dated June 19, Engels asserts that "all children will be educated in state establishments from the time when they can do without the first maternal care."[23] In his later "Principles of Communism," written sometime between October and November of that year, Engels reasserts that an essential component of the revolution to come will be the "education of all children, from the moment they can leave their mother's care, in national establishments at national cost."[24]

But in *The Communist Manifesto,* cowritten the following year with Karl Marx, Marx and Engels walk back this plan, proposing only "Free education for all children in public schools."[25] The specification that a child's education begin "the moment they can leave their mother's care" had been taken out, a change probably necessary to protect the coauthors from hysterical accusations that communists wanted to "abolish the family," accusations that both authors specifically addressed and refuted within the text of the *Manifesto*. In their rhetorical struggles with the proponents of socialist ideals in the nineteenth century, bourgeois polemicists often appealed to traditional family and religious values to convince workers to maintain the status quo. Reducing the burdens of childbearing and child-rearing for women or "abolishing the family" could all too easily be framed as an affront against God, since women's pain and suffering was a specific punishment for Eve's sin of eating of the Tree of Knowledge. It's amazing to think that the idea of publicly funded nurseries and kindergartens, something that many parents take for granted today, proved too radical for *The Communist Manifesto*!

American Spiritual Perfectionism

While Marx and Engels embraced atheism and believed that religion was the "opiate of the masses," other proponents of collective childcare took their inspiration from scripture. John Humphrey Noyes founded the Oneida Community in upstate New York in 1848, the same year that Marx and Engels published *The Communist Manifesto*. Noyes was born into a relatively wealthy family in Vermont in 1811. In the early 1830s, after a brief attempt to become a lawyer, he abandoned his studies to attend the Andover Theological Seminary and the Yale Divinity School. He hoped to become a Christian preacher and helped to organize against the institution of slavery. Noyes came to believe in a Christian doctrine called "Perfectionism," in which humans could find a way to live free from sin by emulating the lives of the Apostles, the earliest disciples of Christ, who dwelled together and owned all of their property in common.

Like Plato, Noyes believed that individualism bred selfishness. This undermined the Christian values necessary for salvation. Because of his unorthodox views, Noyes was forced to leave his studies and refused the necessary credentials he needed to preach. Instead, he eventually founded a spiritual collective to reflect the values of communalism in all things, including love. Like Godin before him, Noyes had the wealth and privilege necessary to invest in his utopian visions. At its height, the Oneida Community consisted of about three hundred men, women, and children all living together in one massive ninety-three-thousand-square-foot mansion house for over thirty years, making it one of the longest-lasting utopian communities in the United States.

The Oneidans practiced a form of "complex marriage," whereby every man was married to every woman in the community. Because they believed in the equality of the sexes, women worked alongside men, had their own rooms, and could choose to engage in sexual relations with any husband they desired at any time; they also had the right to refuse. Because the Oneidans believed that sexuality was sacred, men in the community practiced a form of "male continence" (penetration without ejaculation), which, in Noyes's view, allowed women to enjoy sensual pleasure without fear of pregnancy. According to one source, "women had between two and four sexual encounters a week, with several men."[26] Despite the frequency of encounters, very few babies were born into the community in its early years, until Noyes decided that the Oneidans needed to create a new generation to carry on their unique way of life.

Babies born into the Oneida Community remained with their birth mothers for the first twelve to fourteen months of their lives, much like they would have in a traditional family of the time. But soon after weaning, the children were moved into a separate part of the mansion called the "Children's Department." Up to the age of three, children spent their days in the nursery playing with other kids their age and forming attachments to other adults in the community. At the end of the day, their mothers would collect them, and they slept together in their mother's room until morning. At the age of three, the toddlers moved into the East Room, a wing of the mansion where all of the three- to six-year-olds lived and often slept together.

Although their mothers could visit, sustained contact was discouraged to allow the child to form stronger attachments with their peers and the designated caregivers. The East Room was not so different from a modern-day care center filled with toys, but even the youngest children had fairly regimented schedules of exercise, meals, work, play, and Bible study. At the age of six, the children graduated to the South Room, where their formal education began. These older children studied a wide variety of subjects in small classrooms in the mansion, including reading, writing, arithmetic, and Latin.[27] The children in the South Room also helped in the community's various enterprises, for instance, making chains for the animal traps that the Oneidans sold across the country. Between the ages of ten and twelve the children usually moved into their own rooms in the main part of the mansion.

In the East Room, the younger children were cared for by special nurses and teachers who volunteered for the job, including at least one, but sometimes two or three, men. A rotating group of mothers also volunteered to work with the children, but there was a good continuity of care for the toddlers, so that they saw the same groups of adults almost every day, although caregivers did work in shifts to ensure each some time off. Sometimes younger children from the East Room shared rooms with other members of the community at night, but never for more than a week at a time. Children also never slept with their biological parents to ensure they formed strong attachments to other adults. In general, the children accommodated themselves to life in the East Room rather quickly, and according to the memoirs of some of these children, it was much harder on their mothers, who ached to share time with their kids. Noyes's vision of collective child-rearing prioritized the needs of the community over the desires of the mother. What Plato had imagined in theory, the Oneidans instituted in practice.

When learning about the Oneidans, the parent in me initially rebelled against Noyes and his disrespect for the bond between a mother and child. While pregnant, I had harbored an intense feeling of connection between myself and my daughter. I believed that after birth I would easily be able to identify her as *my* particular baby in a room full of other babies. We were naturally linked by some unique metaphysical bond, right? But even though the nurses had brought her in to suckle every few hours, I could not pick out my own daughter when faced with five neat rows of babies in their individual cribs, swaddled in identical blankets, and wearing little blue and pink stocking caps.

I remember closing my eyes and waiting for my instincts to take over, but unlike my smartphone pairing wirelessly to a Bluetooth speaker, no magical connection helped me identify her. Over the years, I've heard many mothers admit the same secret fear that I had then—that our babies might have been switched at birth, because we couldn't tell them apart from others.

Rather than fighting this realization, many Oneidan women embraced the idea that they could harbor maternal feelings toward all children in their community. Although the initial separation was difficult, one Oneidan mother reported that, "The benefit to me is very great; it relieves me of a care that was too great for my strength; it gives me time and opportunity for other occupation, it chastens my affections and frees me from absorbing distractions."[28] Another Oneida woman, Harriet Worden, recalled in her 1871 memoirs that, "At first the real mothers experienced considerable distress in giving up their little ones to the care of others, but a new sphere of existence opened

THE INFANT SCHOOL. ONEIDA COMMUNITY.

Figure 3.1. The Infant School at the Oneida Community.

to them and they now found time for educational pursuits. Besides, the improvement in the behavior and general condition of their children was of greater value than the luxury of a sickly maternal tenderness."[29] Finally, John Humphrey Noyes's granddaughter, Imogen Stone, also extolled the benefits of collective child-rearing as someone who grew up in the system, noting, "If a child is subjected to the hangups and neuroses of just two people, it has a hard time. There is something spacious and good about having many caretakers."[30]

But children rebel against their elders. As the younger generation came of age, they began to question the stricter doctrines of Noyes and rejected some of the more problematic aspects of complex marriage. Men in the Oneida Community were encouraged to approach all women through a third party so that the latter could more easily decline proposals "without embarrassment or restraint," and the *Hand-Book of the Oneida Community* made it absolutely clear that women had the right to reject any and all unwanted offers: "Every woman is free to refuse every man's attentions."[31] But some women may have felt pressured to accept the attentions of certain senior men in the

Oneida Community, Home Building, Kenwood, N. Y.

June 26 1907

McGuinness, Oneida, N. Y.

Figure 3.2. A postcard from the Oneida mansion in 1907.

community, while others longed to form more exclusive attachments. The Oneidans maintained an explicit prohibition on stable couples, noting: "[I]t is not desirable for two persons, whatever may be their standing, to become exclusively attached to each other—to worship and idolize each other—however popular this experience may be with sentimental people generally. They regard exclusive, idolatrous attachment as unhealthy and pernicious wherever it may exist. The Communities insist that the heart should be kept free to love all the true and worthy, and should never be contracted with exclusiveness or idolatry, or purely selfish love in any form."[32]

When younger Oneidans attended university outside of the community—with the thought that it would behoove the community to have a few resident doctors, for instance—they returned with new ideas and desires that conflicted with "Perfectionism." Teenagers and young adults who felt ridiculed by mainstream American culture demanded more autonomy and wanted the choice to form stable couples with romantic partners. This internal dissatisfaction coincided with increasing scrutiny from the outside world, which considered the kind of complex marriage practiced at Oneida as criminal adultery. Facing the threat of persecution, Noyes fled to Canada. Fearing that they would all be arrested and have their children taken away from them, the remaining Oneidans hastily married. The community was abandoned in 1880. But unlike so many other utopian communities that could not survive an onslaught of negative attention and criticisms of mainstream society, the enterprising Oneidans evolved into a successful capitalist enterprise making tableware that continues to be sold to this day.[33] Although the unique Oneidan way of life died out, their beautiful mansion in upstate New York still stands as a testament to their utopian social dreams.

Dreamers Near the Sea of Galilee

If Marx and Engels believed that the collective education of children proved essential to building a socialist society and John Humphrey

Noyes saw raising children in common as a stepping-stone to spiritual Perfectionism, the kibbutzniks (people who live in a kibbutz) took inspiration from European socialist movements and mixed them with the Zionist goal of returning to their ancestral homeland. The kibbutz (plural: kibbutzim) is a cooperative multigenerational community founded in the territories that eventually became the state of Israel.[34] Early kibbutzim were primarily agricultural communes where members owned their modest amounts of property in common. Later, they developed to include successful collectively owned and operated industrial enterprises. The first kibbutz was Degania, established near the Sea of Galilee in 1909, when the Ottoman Empire controlled the territory. Fleeing pogroms in Europe, many early kibbutzniks settled on poor-quality land where the local insects and waters carried diseases such as malaria, typhus, and cholera. They lived in tents, striving to build their own utopian communities under difficult conditions.

After World War I, when the British took over this territory from the Ottomans, they initially encouraged Jewish migration from Eastern Europe and Russia, much to the consternation of the local Arab and Bedouin populations. Many of the Ashkenazi youth who traveled to Palestine were enthusiastic pioneers filled with ideals of egalitarianism. The socialist principle of "self-labor," of not having one's work exploited by owners of the means of production, meant that all members labored together, including the women. Living on desolate land with few resources, these early kibbutzniks did everything themselves, including growing their own food and sourcing their own water. By 1928, there were forty-one kibbutzim in British Palestine, with a population of roughly 2,400 adults and 300 children.[35] The kibbutz movement continued to expand rapidly until the Holocaust drastically reduced the population of potential new immigrants from Europe. By 1948, the kibbutzniks represented about 8 percent of the Jewish population in the area, which was their peak, coinciding with a generally positive attitude toward socialist ideals before Winston Churchill gave his Iron Curtain speech in 1946 and launched the Cold War.[36]

The organization of child-rearing differed somewhat from one kibbutz to the next, so I'll describe here the basic structures that they shared. In many of the earliest kibbutzim, the only brick building was the children's house, built even before the adults had permanent dwellings. All of the other tents and structures surrounded the children's house and, later, when the kibbutzniks grew in wealth and resources, they built campus-like communities with communal kitchens, large collective dining rooms, and dormitories. The design of the kibbutz allowed for most things to be within walking distance, although outlying fields could be reached by bicycle. All property was shared, and all members lived, worked, and ate communally. Unlike the Oneidans, the kibbutzniks hewed much closer to traditional gender roles, lived in monogamous pairs, and made no prohibitions against procreative sex. Women and men would have different roles in the community, but none was supposed to be superior to the other.

Also unlike the American Perfectionists, many kibbutz mothers took their infants to live in the children's house only days after their birth. Because the agricultural success of the community also depended on women's labor, it made practical sense to designate a handful of women to look after all of the children in common. Kib-

Figure 3.3. The Kibbutz Degania with the Sea of Galilee.

butzniks theoretically committed themselves to gender equality and believed that communal childcare would promote women's emancipation from the conservative values typical of East European and Russian Jewish communities in the early twentieth century. Although mothers of infants often went to the children's house to nurse—and by the 1960s, parents of older children visited daily for what became known as the "love hour"—the kibbutz kids spent most of their time together in the children's house. On some kibbutzim, in addition to the love hour, families shared time together in the afternoon and early evening when sons and daughters visited in their parents' dwelling, but they always returned to the children's house each night to sleep. Kibbutzniks believed that this arrangement fostered social solidarity and cooperativeness among the families, and that the relative expertise of the designated caregivers compensated for the shortcomings of new parents.

The children's house was the heart of the kibbutz, designed to maximize the health and welfare of its youngest members. Each children's house usually contained a large playroom and dining area. Groups of three or four children shared bedrooms, where they each had a private corner to keep their favorite things and decorate their walls. Women—and it was almost always women—volunteered to serve as a *metapelet* (Hebrew for "caretaker"; plural: *metaplot*). In the earliest days of the kibbutzim, only a few *metaplot* would look after twelve to eighteen children during the day. As the kibbutzim became more established, the ratio of children to *metaplot* steadily decreased, as did the size of the children's groups, until there was one *metapelet* for every two or three infants. These *metaplot* stayed with the children as they grew up; the relationship between the children and their caretaker was stable and warm. Mothers tended to their children's emotional needs, while the *metaplot* took care of child development and early education: weaning, potty training, and teaching toddlers how to dress, feed, wash, and generally look after themselves.

As the children grew, the *metaplot* also began educating them in the basics of reading, writing, and arithmetic until they were old enough to attend the kibbutz school. At night, two different women looked after all of the children under twelve, usually from a station in the infant room. They circled through the older children's rooms, but couldn't give too much individual attention to children having nightmares or otherwise unable to sleep. This all-night job rotated among the women in the kibbutz every week. Compared to the constant and reliable presence of the daytime *metaplot*, the night watchwomen didn't provide the same feelings of security.

As time passed, traditional gender roles remained rather fixed even in these supposedly egalitarian communities. Women continued to be judged as "good" or "bad" partners based on criteria such as selflessness and a willingness to sacrifice their personal desires for the sake of others. Girls found themselves groomed for caregiving jobs on the kibbutz. As the decades wore on, many women gave up the fight against these stereotypes, and mothers demanded to bring their children home at night so they could forge closer attachments with their own sons and daughters. Children also stayed longer with their mothers after birth, although they still moved to the children's house at the age of three months, when almost all mothers returned to work. Nevertheless, there emerged a growing sense that kibbutz infants lacked the amount of emotional love and attention they needed to thrive. Eventually, when the kibbutzim began expanding into industrial enterprises and generating profits, residents could increase the size of their individual dwellings, which allowed children to have bedrooms at home. Almost all kibbutzim abandoned collective sleeping arrangements by the early 1990s.

This long history of almost-universal nonparental care in kibbutzim inspired hundreds of research projects in the field of child psychology. Most experts agree that the experiment with communal sleeping was a failure; it was too extreme an arrangement for infants and toddlers, who require more constant and intense forms of attention. Some adults raised as children in kibbutzim later complained of feeling abandoned when they slept away from their parents, resulting in lasting trauma.[37] And yet, apart from the acknowledged problems with communal sleeping arrangements, kibbutz childcare is still widely considered to be the gold standard for day care. One 1991 study compared the quality of kibbutz childcare with that of urban day care and family care in Israel. It found that the unique physical and social setting of the campus-like kibbutz, the higher educational levels of the *metaplot*, and the relatively greater number of *metaplot* assigned to look after smaller groups of children, contributed to a better-quality experience for the kids.[38] For this reason, many Israeli parents living nearby pay to have their children looked after on kibbutzim.

A typical fear that parents (especially mothers) express when considering putting their infants in day care is that the presence of regular nonparental caregivers might interfere with the formation of secure attachments between biological parents and their children. But a retrospective study of the first seventy years of collective child-rearing on Israeli kibbutzim found that children's ability to connect emotionally with multiple caregivers contributed positively to children's overall well-being by "adding to a network of secure attachments, or possibly, compensating for their absence," all without compromising the parent-child relationship. The security of an extended network of attachments to multiple adults was also "related to higher IQ and more independent behaviour in kindergarten, as well as to higher ego resilience, ego control, field independence, dominance, goal-directed behaviour, and empathy."[39] It seems that growing up in a collective environment provides children with an earlier and stronger form of personality development that builds on secure attachments with their parents and immediate caregivers, but expands as children learn to negotiate a more complicated social environment at an earlier age.

In short, the long kibbutz experiment with collective child-rearing shows that having multiple nonparental caregivers may be more beneficial to children's long-term development than being cared for exclusively within a nuclear family. According to one 1997 study in the journal *Early Child Development and Care*, the success of the kibbutz experience complicates "the predominant Western view of family and childcare settings as separate systems," demonstrating that familial and institutional childcare systems can work together for the benefit of parents, children, and society as a whole.[40] And from the evolutionary anthropological perspective, researchers also conclude that,

"Human children are well adapted to having nonparental helpers, so much so that they have positive effects on children's development. Exposure to multiple caretakers expands a child's social sphere and is associated with cognitive and psychological benefits."[41]

"Why Do People Form a State, If Not for This Purpose?"

While the kibbutzniks built their children's houses in Israel, social democrats, socialists, and communists back in Europe also understood that some form of communal childcare was not only necessary to nurture and protect the children of the working class, but that nurseries and kindergartens proved essential to ensure women's full incorporation into the labor force. Building on the works of Marx and Engels, but also that of utopian theorists like Flora Tristan in France and August Bebel, a cofounder of the Social Democratic Party in Germany, a new generation of activists proposed that women's work outside the home was a necessary condition of their future emancipation, ushering in the concept of paid parental leave. A German social democrat named Lily Braun proposed a public "maternity insurance" in 1897. Some form of universal tax would create a special fund to replace women's lost wages immediately before, during, and after childbirth.[42] Once women returned to their jobs, Braun proposed that infants and toddlers should be looked after in community-based childcare collectives. Braun appealed to the German bourgeoisie, arguing that their own long-term economic interests depended on lowering infant mortality rates and ensuring the health of future German workers and soldiers.

Braun's willingness to work with industrialists to protect proletarian mothers led her to clash with Clara Zetkin, the leader of the socialist women's movement in Germany, who rejected the idea that childcare should be funded through philanthropy or self-organized on a voluntary basis. Lily Braun was an aristocrat involved with the women's movement; Clara Zetkin was a middle-class schoolmaster's daughter who grew up in a peasant village in Saxony and came into her socialist commitments before she embraced the question of women's emancipation. Although members of the same party, Braun and Zetkin often disagreed over issues of policy and represented different visions of social democracy, with the former more enamored of philanthropy and the latter demanding state intervention. Zetkin's vision prevailed at the Second International Congress of Socialist Women, held in Copenhagen in August 1910. The platform of the social democratic women of Germany specifically demanded the "establishment of lay nursery-schools and 'kindergarten' (play schools)" as well as special homes where the state would provide for orphaned or abandoned children.[43] In the following years, these new institutions began to pop up across northern Europe.

But it was the Russian Alexandra Kollontai, the first Soviet commissar of Social Welfare, who took the platform and, seven years later, used the public resources of the world's first workers' state to expand collective childcare for all working women. Born to an aristocratic family in Saint Petersburg in 1872, Alexandra Mikhailovna Domontovich grew up in relative luxury, but chose to marry a poor cousin, Vladimir Kollontai, when she was twenty-one. She had one son, but soon found herself disenchanted with married life and the limited educational opportunities available to women in the Russian Empire at the time. A trip to a textile factory radicalized her after Kollontai witnessed the horrific conditions suffered by the women and children who lived and worked there. She left her husband and young son to pursue university studies in Switzerland and she never returned to any form of conventional domestic life.

In 1916, the year before the Russian Revolution, Kollontai outlined a utopian vision for a form of collective child-rearing similar to those of centuries past: that society would support families by helping mothers raise happy and healthy children "in the kindergarten, the children's colony, the crèche and the school under the care of experienced nurses."[44] But there was one crucial difference: general state funds would pay for everything. "When the mother wants to be with her children, she only has to say the word; and when she has no time, she knows they are in good hands," Kollontai wrote in her pamphlet "Working Woman and Mother."[45] "Every member of society—and that means every working woman and every citizen, male and female—has the right to demand that the state and community concern itself with the welfare of all. . . . Why do people form a state, if not for this purpose? At the moment there is no government anywhere in the world that cares for its children. Working men and women in all countries are fighting for a society and government that will really become a big happy family, where all children will be equal and the family will care equally for all."[46]

The early years following the Russian Revolution were times of great upheaval as the Bolsheviks tried to remake their world through a series of sweeping administrative decrees. Of the many programs

Figure 3.4. Portrait of Alexandra Kollontai.

Kollontai implemented, a massive expansion of state-run kindergartens, crèches, and children's homes, as well as maternity clinics,
were among her first priorities. She pushed an ambitious package
of social reforms that would increase the health and well-being of
working-class children, while also promoting the full emancipation of
women through the liberalization of divorce and the decriminaliza-
tion of abortion in 1920.

Despite her best efforts, World War I, the Russian civil war, and a
horrendous famine crushed the Soviet economy and undermined the
viability of her social dreams. Worse still, her decision to liberalize
divorce resulted in a social crisis as men forsook their pregnant lovers.
The new Bolshevik state found its major cities flooded with abandoned children who formed large gangs and survived through petty
crime. By 1926, the Soviet Children's Commission estimated that
there were about 250,000 children living in state-funded orphanages
and another 300,000 living on the streets.[47] Conditions in the children's homes proved rather miserable, especially for infants and toddlers who needed the most attention. The general economic chaos also
limited the resources available for the kindergartens. Quality suffered.

Given the costs of feeding, clothing, and providing shelter to more
than half a million parentless kids, let alone paying the nurses and
educators necessary to look after them, Soviet leaders preferred a retreat to the traditional family, where women would provide this labor
without cost to the state budget. To fund women's return to the home,
Kollontai's Bolshevik colleagues proposed to strengthen laws around
alimony collection so that fathers would bear the responsibility for
their offspring. Kollontai objected to the reversion to the traditional
family and considered alimony both demeaning to women and impossible to enforce. Instead, she proposed a universal tax of two rubles
per person so that the state could properly fund nurseries, kindergartens, and children's homes and also support single mothers. Her male
comrades considered her proposal untenable given the stark realities
of the Soviet economy. Then, in 1936, fearing demographic decline,
Joseph Stalin forced the passage of a new Family Code. This reversed
many of the early gains of the Bolshevik revolution with regards to

women and the family, making it more difficult to obtain a divorce and illegal to get an abortion.

Kollontai's dreams for a state-funded system of universal early childcare combined with job-protected, fully paid maternity leaves resurfaced in Eastern Europe after World War II, particularly in East Germany. Although job-protected maternity leaves for industrial workers began in Finland as early as 1901, postwar centrally planned economies of Eastern Europe expanded provisions to all workers. One year after the Soviet zone of Germany became the German Democratic Republic (GDR), the new nation introduced a maternity grant for all mothers and a special child allowance for working women with more than two children. The state also paid for almost three months of maternity leave. Eight years later, the country increased the value of the maternity grants and expanded the generous monthly child allowance to all families, in an attempt to defray the indirect costs of motherhood and increase the number of families with more than one child.

By 1976, the state guaranteed job-protected paid maternity leave for six months, followed by an additional six months at a lower standard rate of pay for second and subsequent children, the so-called *Babyjahr* (baby year).[48] In 1984, this maternity leave was extended to a year and a half for second and subsequent children, and by 1986 even first-time mothers got the full *Babyjahr*. After twelve months, most children went into formal childcare, first to a nursery (*Krippenplatz*), up to the age of three, and then to a kindergarten between the ages of three and six. This pattern of childcare echoed the experiments of the Oneida Community, where children under three were cared for more intensively in small groups and children over the age of three played together in larger groups with fewer caregivers.

Unlike their Soviet predecessors, the East German government committed the resources necessary to make the system work. In 1949, only 17 percent of East German children had access to childcare centers, but by 1989 the government claimed to guarantee a place for 100 percent of parents who wanted a space.[49] On the eve of the fall of the Berlin Wall, 80 percent of all infants and toddlers under three were in nurseries and 95 percent of children between three and six attended preschools.

In contrast to the miserable conditions of the Soviet children's homes in the 1920s, the East German kindergartens had professional staff and decent facilities.[50] Similar combinations of paid parental leave and subsidized or free universal childcare spread throughout the Eastern Bloc countries and eventually to socialist-leaning countries in the Global South such as Cuba, Vietnam, Afghanistan, Namibia, and Nicaragua. Even in nonaligned Zambia, experts from the Bulgarian Women's Committee helped set up a network of urban kindergartens in the 1980s.[51]

The Benefits of Getting It Right

Today, the idea of raising children collectively has migrated from the realm of the utopian visions of spiritual Perfectionists and revolutionary Bolsheviks into an everyday reality for women in many high-income countries, although its availability within those countries remains uneven. According to a 2020 World Bank report investigating the global availability of early childhood education, "40 percent of all children (nearly 350 million) who are below primary-school-entry age worldwide need childcare, but do not have access to it" across all countries.[52] This lack of childcare access largely affects the poor, whose children grow up in "suboptimal conditions," with parents whose struggles to survive necessarily limit the time they can invest in the care for their kids.[53]

Sweden is a fascinating case study of a country that made a massive public commitment to supporting both parents and children. Swedish feminists demanded that the government create a National Commission on Childcare in 1968 to deal with the increasing number of mothers entering the labor force. In 1975, the National Preschool Act forced Swedish municipalities to expand the availability of publicly funded childcare, and by 1991 all children between the ages of eighteen months and six years had a guaranteed place in a day care facility as long as both parents studied or worked. Demand for childcare places continued to grow and municipalities could not keep pace—even though the facilities largely paid for themselves through the economic boost resulting from women's greater labor force participation and increases in local tax revenues. A new law in 1995 obliged all municipalities to ensure that places be made available, "without reasonable delay," for all Swedish children between one and six in day care centers and for kids between seven and twelve in after-school recreation centers.

This rapid expansion of childcare caused some issues with quality. As demand for places surged, the government allowed the participation of for-profit childcare centers and an increase in home-based care, which did not follow the strict curricular guidelines of the public centers and lacked the same qualified staff. Despite this, by 1998, more than 95 percent of Sweden's municipalities could offer children a place within three to four months of their parents' application.[54] All Swedish mothers take at least a year of parental leave before returning to the labor force, and now that the system has been in place for more than a generation, mothers who once attended public day care do not hesitate to send their own children to the same institutions when they're ready to return to work. In 2005, 88 percent of all children between the ages of one and five were enrolled in preschools. In the same year, 93 percent of Swedish parents reported being happy with their childcare situation. Less than 2 percent said they would rather stay home with their child.[55]

Multicultural France also has a high-quality publicly funded childcare program. Approximately 52 percent of children under the age of three are in crèches, and 97 percent of all French children begin preschool at age three. These services are available to all parents regardless of their circumstances. Empirical research on the effects of early childcare and preschool is fraught with politics, especially in the United States, where conservatives insist on the superiority of exclusive at-home maternal care. But findings from France confirm that most children benefit from earlier exposure to peers and nonparental caregivers. Scholars concur that children who attend preschool are better prepared for formal education and have better academic outcomes than children raised at home.[56] More surprising is that attending preschool also appears to have benefits for children's health. Children who start school earlier do get more infections than those who stay home with their parents, but they get fewer infections in elementary school. In other words, the number of infections remains the same, but the timing of their occurrence differs. Earlier exposure to infection builds earlier immunity, which means that children miss school in the years before they begin their academic work.[57]

Where the research is contradictory is in the realm of children's behavior in the United States, with a significant number of studies showing that American kids who spent long hours in institutional childcare may be more aggressive and disobedient later in childhood, although this may reflect the mediocre quality of much American childcare with high turnover rates among badly paid caregivers. One 2013 Norwegian study of seventy-two thousand mothers with children between the ages of eighteen and thirty-six months found no relationship between hours in childcare and aggression or disobedience.[58] The Norwegians compared children from different families as well as siblings who spent different amounts of time in good-quality center-based childcare. "These are exciting findings because they contradict research from the USA," explained Henrik Zachrisson, the lead author and researcher at the Norwegian Institute of Public Health and the Norwegian Center for Child Behavioral Development.[59]

Another study from France published in 2018 used a sample that followed the same subject population over time. The researchers tracked the lives of children under the age of three who attended two different forms of childcare in the cities of Nancy and Poitiers, and found that "access to high-quality childcare in the first years of life may improve children's emotional and cognitive development, prevent later emotional difficulties and promote prosocial behaviors."[60] The French experience, which dovetails with the Israeli findings about kibbutz-style childcare, suggests that when done well, public childcare can benefit both parents and children if societies are willing to commit themselves to the shared costs of raising and educating the next generation. "I have seen hundreds of studies showing no ill effects and yet we can't seem to be done with this research question," the American feminist economist Rachel Connelly, who regularly teaches a class on the economics of the family, explained to me by email in 2022. "In truth, the effect of childcare on children depends on the quality of the care, which varies substantially from excellent to mediocre with far too much of it falling on the mediocre side because we don't subsidize the price and parents are stuck between a rock and a hard place."[61] This question of costs often stands in the way of efforts to ensure that all children benefit from high-quality childcare. Why, many politicians still ask, should taxpayers foot the bill for a service to society that parents, but usually mothers, can provide for free?

Parents Are All Nepotists

While most extant research shows that high-quality childcare benefits both parents and children, there exists a persistent resistance to investing the resources necessary to provide the level of quality demanded, because, let's face it, it costs a lot of upfront money to get it right. Rather than relying on individual parents in their individual homes, the universal public provision of childcare requires safe buildings in multiple neighborhoods with paid professional staff. Based on the history of experiments with collective child-rearing and the study of their outcomes, it seems the ideal combination of policies would be a job-protected, paid parental leave for the first six months to a year of an infant's life, followed by universally available and publicly funded high-quality care during the workday with educational requirements for preschool teachers and pay commensurate with their education.

Caregivers for toddlers would ideally have professional training as nurses, child psychologists, or teachers specializing in early childhood education. Good salaries and working conditions for caregivers would reduce turnover and ensure a continuity of care for the infants and toddlers, encouraging the formation of secure attachments. At all ages, appropriate child development curricula would equip kids with the skills necessary to succeed intellectually and emotionally through their formal schooling. If the relatively poor East Germans could do it, and the Swedes and French continue to do it, why isn't childcare a basic right of citizenship everywhere?

One part of the problem is the calcification of beliefs about the benefits of exclusive parental care. But another part stems from the idea that raising children in common is too utopian, because it challenges our ideas of the traditional family. As Plato recognized in the *Republic* so long ago, the prioritizing of consanguineous family ties over all other relationships can undermine the cooperation necessary for a healthy society. Many people harbor a natural aversion to what we call nepotism (the favoritism specifically shown to our own family members), but when it comes to their own children, most parents openly behave as nepotists. Many good-hearted, charity-giving, community-minded folks let their ideals fly out the window if there exists a scarce resource or opportunity for which their own child competes.

Many of us have been raised to think of "good" parenting as doing everything to secure a safe, healthy, and prosperous future for our children. We rarely stop to think about how the economic systems within which we live shape the efforts required to be a "good" parent. Because parents remain primarily responsible for their children's current and future welfare, our competitive economic system pits us against each other and undermines solidarity and community. Where childcare is a commodity rather than a public good or basic right of citizenship, households that start out higher on the socioeconomic ladder can reproduce their status by using their wealth and influence to confer privileges on their offspring, not because their children are particularly worthy for any meritocratic reason, but simply by their accident of birth, exactly as Plato predicted so long ago.

In contemporary economies where a large part of the gross domestic product is generated through consumer spending, and where we require future consumers, workers, and taxpayers, economic elites reap the rewards of the parental sacrifices needed to produce and rear future generations of children, including the humiliation of spontaneous lactation during a job interview. In the long run, everyone benefits from a better-educated, emotionally stable, and healthy populace.

By making early childcare a *socially* provided good, we can ensure that children born into all families—no matter what their economic situation—enjoy the education and the emotional attention necessary to build a more harmonious society. Collective childcare allows us to acknowledge our connection to, and responsibility for, our fellow citizens of the next generation, even while we might feel especially emotionally attached to the specific children we have helped to raise.

CHAPTER 4

The Good School

Educating the Next Generation of Social Dreamers

Middle school sucks. For most American kids, these weird limbo grades that coincide with the onset of puberty provide ample opportunities for petty or great personal traumas that scar for life: unrequited love, friendship dramas, vicious bullying. Just as little bodies begin to surge with hormones, schools ratchet up their academic demands and begin to sort nascent adults into different kinds of students, putting them on predetermined tracks that shape their future positions in society. Given this universal truth of middle school suckage, how much worse could it be to do a full year of it in a language you don't speak?

That's a question I found myself asking when I won a fellowship in Germany for the 2014–15 academic year. We planned to move to a town in the Black Forest, and I had to figure out what to do with my nerdy thirteen-year-old daughter. The nearest international school was too far, and a year of homeschooling: impossible. It is a serious crime in Germany for parents to prevent their kids from attending a formal school, and snooping neighbors would report offenders, even naive foreigners, to the police. So, my daughter did a one-month summer crash course in German, and we registered her as an official guest student at the local academic secondary school: the Geschwister-Scholl-Gymnasium.

As we sat down to pick out her classes with the kindly principal and her homeroom teacher, I noticed a spot in her schedule reserved for "religion." I asked with incredulity, "Is this a required class?"

The Germans seemed confused. "Of course, it is required of all students."

We had to choose one: Catholicism, Protestantism, or a catch-all multidenominational class called "Ethics." At first, I balked. Couldn't she just take an extra study hall? No, religious education is mandated by the German constitution, they told me.[1] I remember shaking my head. Not only were the Germans forcing my poor daughter to attend school in a language she couldn't understand, but they insisted on religious indoctrination as well!

Noting my resistance, her teacher suggested that we go ahead and register for all her other classes and take a few days to decide on a religion class. He sent us home with information about the "Ethics" course. It included visits to a local church, a synagogue in the nearby town of Emmendingen, and the Islamic Center in Freiburg with the idea of exposing children to the beliefs and practices of multiple faiths. It didn't seem too bad. Maybe my daughter would actually enjoy having teacher-led discussions "about the meaning of life" and the "acquisition of competence for moral action."[2]

In the end, my daughter's "*reli*" classes, as she affectionately called them, gave her a safe space to ask questions about who she was, what the world expected of her, and how to figure out who she wanted to become. It turned out to be less about religion and more about values. The kids learned a motto from the German children's author Erich Kästner, "*Es gibt nichts Gutes, ausser man tut es*" (roughly: There is nothing good, other than what one does), meaning that goodness requires us all to choose good actions. The Germans used this course called "Religion" to teach kids the intellectual skills and self-confidence required to grapple with difficult moral quandaries. They read philosophical texts and studied the lives of historical figures, such as Hans and Sophie Scholl, after whom her Gymnasium was named. The *Geschwister Scholl* (Scholl siblings) were members of a nonviolent German student group, White Rose, that opposed World War II and the dictatorship of Adolf Hitler. In February 1943, the brother and sister were arrested for handing out anti-Nazi flyers at the university in Munich and guillotined. The siblings became powerful symbols of German anti-Nazi resistance and of maintaining the courage to stand by one's convictions in the face of social pressures. After learning about their lives, my daughter reasoned that doing seventh grade in German was a lot simpler than standing up to Hitler. She struggled at times, but she managed it. And we avoided any unpleasant encounters with the local police.

Schooling in Capitalist America

Children are the most creative, open-minded, and flexible members of our societies. The ability to shape the worldview of the next generation infuses the visions of pedagogues on all points of the political spectrum and inspires many questions. Should education promote individual autonomy and self-sufficiency or teach cooperation and interdependence? Is education an end in itself or merely the means to a specific, socially determined goal, such as producing productive workers? Is education a public good for the creation of an enlightened citizenry or an individual investment to pursue meritocratic opportunities for social mobility? The possibility of shaping the minds and hearts of children, once they are old enough to leave their parents' care, has motivated social dreamers to reimagine traditional forms of schooling.

Back in 1976, the economists Samuel Bowles and Herbert Gintis published a scathing indictment of the sorting role that education played in the United States, *Schooling in Capitalist America*, a book that fundamentally changed my way of thinking about why and what kids are taught. According to the authors' "correspondence principle," governments often organize public schooling to reflect the prevalent attitudes, norms, and values required by future employers—what kids get to learn in their classroom corresponds to what employers think they need to know. Even outside of the formal curriculum, the types of skills and behaviors encouraged—such as sitting still, paying attention, being punctual, meeting stated deadlines, and following instructions—might take precedence over critical thinking, problem-solving, or English composition if resources are scarce and teachers are overworked.

I was still in elementary school in 1978 when the successful passage of Proposition 13 capped California property taxes under then governor Ronald Reagan and devastated funding for our local public school district. When he became president of the United States in 1981, Reagan and his advisors promoted an economic vision that saw government spending as a problem, encouraging localities to slash taxes and further undermining revenues for schools. Knowledge and education became scarce commodities that parents coveted for their own offspring at the expense of others. To this day, children from immigrant, minority, and working-class families still too often get tracked into "regular" classes, while the kids of the wealthy take "honors" or "advanced placement" classes or abandon the public education system altogether to attend expensive private schools.

In the more than twenty years that I've been teaching at the university level, I've witnessed attitudes about education shift dramatically. Rather than students seeking knowledge and learning critical-thinking skills to better understand the world around them, young people often now consider themselves customers paying for a product that will enhance their individual value on a mercurial job market. In 2019, according to the US Bureau of Labor Statistics (BLS), the median weekly earnings of workers twenty-five and older with only a high school diploma was $746, compared to $1,248 for those with a bachelor's degree, a difference of about $26,000 per year.[3] Unemployment rates for those with lower levels of education are also higher, which incentivizes aspiring matriculants to take out loans, contributing to Himalayan levels of student debt.[4]

The commodification of education has become so extreme that the American millennial scholar Malcolm Harris suggested a dystopian future where individual children might be listed on some form of schooling stock exchange, where the rich could buy, sell, and trade shares.[5] One of Ronald Reagan's favorite economists, Milton Friedman, explicitly suggested this model in 1980, when he proposed that individual private investors could " 'buy' a share in an individual's earning prospects, to advance him the funds needed to finance his training on condition that he agree to pay the investor a specified fraction of his future earnings. In this way an investor could recoup more than his initial investment from relatively successful individuals, which would compensate for the failure to do so from the unsuccessful."[6] Friedman's view of the instrumentalization of education has seeped its way into our culture.

The irony of all of this is that rather than a mechanism for the reproduction of privileges from one generation to the next or another investment vehicle for the rich, education was once imagined as a social project for liberation, particularly for women and other disadvantaged populations. "Free education for all children in public schools" was the tenth point in *The Communist Manifesto*, and nation-states around the world once embraced this utopian vision. So how did we stray so far from this idealistic view of education to a place where parents in the United States bribe their children's way into elite universities and American student debt has surpassed $1.7 trillion in 2021?[7] If our schools now uphold one particular way of organizing our society, can they become new sites for social dreaming?

So far in these pages, I've explored utopian ideas for reimagining where we dwell and how we care for our infants and toddlers. I've focused on how each of us can make positive changes in our personal lives by expanding our definitions of what counts as a desirable home or what it means to be a "good" parent with the goal of lessening the burdens of unpaid care work in our families. This chapter takes a slight detour to examine the role that formal education can play in either nurturing our imaginative capacities to buck the status quo or socializing us into accepting that things cannot change. When five- and six-year-olds head off to primary school, they face a whole new world of assessment, sorting, and judgment about their particular skills and abilities, as well as social pressures to fit in and be liked by their teachers and peers. As children move through the formal education system, they internalize a specific set of norms and expectations about how to be a "good boy" or a "good girl" and what it means to lead a "good life." As someone who has spent my entire adult life in classrooms, either as a student or a teacher (three years teaching in middle school and high school in Japan, and twenty-three years as a professor in the United States), I have witnessed firsthand the many struggles of young people trying desperately to live up to external standards of success.

Utopians have long understood that lasting social change requires an investment in the education of the next generation, and that this endeavor should not fall exclusively on parents. In this chapter, I want to reflect on the challenges of educating for self-reliance, creativity, and personal contentment in a world where schools often emphasize conformity, standardization, and professional accomplishment. Although my focus here is on the unique needs of older children, teenagers, and young adults, I promise that even readers without kids will find some thoughts and suggestions for how to make their own lives more utopian as well. But in order to understand why it often feels so difficult to engage in blue-sky thinking, we must turn our attention to the primary institution that first encouraged most of us to give up daydreaming for studying and to trade in our own imaginations for other people's knowledge.

How Many Einsteins Did We Miss?

By now, you may have predicted that, as with so many other visions deemed utopian, most ideal imaginings of education trace their roots back to our ancient Greek radical in robes, Plato. Although many aspects of his plans for social engineering are problematic, his influence on subsequent generations of political philosophers in the Western world is undeniable. The *Republic* is often considered the first work of educational theory. The French Enlightenment philosopher Jean-Jacques Rousseau drew inspiration from the *Republic* for *Emile*, his own book about the ideal education system for boys, calling Plato's work "the finest treatise on education ever written."[8] Rousseau believed that the public provision of schooling for all, as opposed to private and domestic schooling for a select few, played an essential role in the creation of an enlightened citizenry. He recognized that schools could forge the characters of men who subsumed their own interests to the needs of the common good. "The smaller social group, firmly united in itself and dwelling apart from others, tends to withdraw itself from the larger society," Rousseau wrote in 1763. Plato's utopian vision of public education could mold a new kind of citizen "so that he no longer regards himself as one, but as a part of the whole. . . ."[9]

In his quest to create the perfect city of Kallipolis, Plato spent much of his book outlining in specific detail how to educate the Guardians: both the auxiliaries (the warriors) and the philosopher-kings. Gymnastics (sports and physical training) and music (which included literature and speechmaking) provided the foundational subjects of Plato's system of education, but the overall goal was to teach the virtues of wisdom, courage, moderation, and justice. The philosopher-kings required wisdom and the auxiliaries courage, whereas moderation would be encouraged in all members of society. Every pupil followed the same basic and strictly regimented curriculum, which involved the heavy censorship of stories and tales deemed unsuitable for young minds: a classical analog of extreme "parental controls." Although some of Plato's specific ideas about the education of his Guardians were rather severe (he wanted to prohibit laughter and sentimentality), his system endeavored to excavate as much latent talent from as many children as possible.

Rather than only looking to the offspring of the extant aristocracy for the leadership positions in his Republic, Plato understood that raw intelligence, the love of knowledge, and the capacity for wisdom were distributed randomly throughout the population. Once, when asked to account for Albert Einstein's exceptional intelligence, the evolutionary biologist Stephen Jay Gould replied: "I am, somehow, less interested in the weight and convolutions of Einstein's brain than in the near certainty that people of equal talent have lived and died in cotton fields and sweatshops."[10] And in kitchens and nurseries, I would add, since for thousands of years the talents and intelligence of girls have been systematically overlooked. But Plato may have been a feminist before anyone had a word for it.

Given the prevailing gender norms in ancient Greece when the *Republic* was written, and although Plato still held some sexist views, I marvel that Plato recognized the inherent potential of girls, unlike his protégé Rousseau centuries later. He asserts that while the ability to be a good Guardian or a "lover of wisdom" may be distributed unequally among the population as a whole, it is equally distributed among men and women, and therefore women must have access to the same sort of education as men and be equitably trained in the arts of war, music, and literature.[11] When challenged that women cannot be effective Guardians because of their reproductive roles in society, Plato defends his position through an analogy to domesticated dogs. "Do we think that the females of our guard-dogs should join in guarding precisely what the males guard, hunt with them, and share everything with them? Or do we think that they should stay indoors and look after the house, on the grounds that they are incapable of doing this because they must bear and rear the puppies, while the males should work and have the entire care of the flock?"[12]

When his interlocutors accept that the ability to hunt or guard a flock is unaffected by the sex of the dog, Plato explains that the sex of the person does not affect the skills necessary to be a Guardian. In a key passage on the traits necessary for leadership in Kallipolis, Plato asks whether bald or hairy men are more suitable for positions of authority. Baffled, his interlocutors point out that relative hairiness has no bearing on the skills necessary for leadership. "There is no pursuit relevant to the management of the city that belongs to a woman because she is a woman, or to a man because he is a man," Plato wrote. "But the various natural capacities are distributed in a similar way between both creatures, and women can share by nature in every pursuit, and men in every one, though for the purposes of all of them women are weaker than men."[13] Considering that our modern schools and universities segregated students on the basis of their sex well into the late twentieth century, Plato's arguments in favor of co-education were quite literally millennia ahead of their time.

An Imagined Medieval Wikipedia

Like Plato who was his inspiration, Thomas More also understood that a good educational system could form the bedrock of an ideal society. More believed that men and women should be educated equally, and that educational opportunities should be extended to all citizens, not just those destined to lead or protect. Utopians cultivated a collective love of learning so that "children and a great part of the nation, both men and women, are taught to spend those hours in which they are not obliged to work in reading; and this they do through the whole progress of life."[14] On the island of Utopia, citizens of all ages could attend special lectures offered in the morning before the workday started. But these lectures were not mandatory. As More explained, "[I]f others that are not made for contemplation, choose rather to employ themselves at that time in their trades, as many of them do, they are not hindered, but are rather commended, as men that take care to serve their country."[15] In More's egalitarian society, those who preferred to work with their hands rather than their minds would not be deemed less-worthy citizens.

More's vision of educational access for all probably appeared preposterous to his early sixteenth-century readers. The idea that every person would be fully literate, willing to read for leisure, and desirous of continuing education throughout their lives may still push the boundaries of credulity today. Let's face it: some people just hate formal learning. But even if we are inclined toward bookishness, the chaos of our daily lives robs us of hours we might spend on hobbies that have little productive purpose. I have often flaked on my book club because I never found the time to read the month's novel. For my daughter and her American high school friends, sports and extracurricular activities—meant to be opportunities for fun outside of the formal school day—felt like extra burdens. I have watched many college-bound kids cram as many things into their schedules because they think it might look good to an admissions committee. Instead of the constant hustle of a society where competition requires repeated investments in our so-called human capital, More's vision of utopia was one where collective ownership and cooperation would give people both the opportunities and the free time to treat education as a pleasure rather than a means to an end.

In his 1602 *The City of the Sun*, the Italian Tommaso Campanella built on the utopian visions of his predecessors, but kicked it up a notch. Rather than having his citizens educated in designated classrooms or lecture halls, he conjured a world where knowledge would be woven into the fabric of everyday life. The unique architecture of Campanella's ideal city consisted of a series of concentric walls painted with a kind of illustrated encyclopedia of human knowledge. Children learned about their world by living, playing, and being led around the walls of their city by designated guides, who'd help them grasp the more difficult concepts. At a time of widespread illiteracy, Campanella imagined a society where knowledge would not be hidden away in books or cloistered behind monastery walls, but available to all. Campanella's walls enclose and protect his city, but they also stand as a testament to his egalitarian views on education:

> On the interior wall of the first circuit all the mathematical figures are conspicuously painted—figures more in number than Archimedes or Euclid discovered, marked symmetrically, and with the explanation of them neatly written and contained each in a little verse. There are definitions and propositions, etc. On the exterior convex wall is first an immense drawing of the whole earth, given at one view. Following upon this, there are tablets setting forth for every separate country the customs both public and private, the laws, the origins and the power of the inhabitants; and the alphabets the different people use can be seen above that of the City of the Sun.[16]

On the outer rings of the walls, citizens learned about the mineral, vegetable, and animal world in great detail, as well as astronomy, geography, and a comprehensive history of humanity. They even practiced a kind of early ethnography in taking the time to learn about the languages and cultures of others. In his imagined "Poetical Dialogue between a Grandmaster of the Knights Hospitallers and a Genoese Sea-Captain," Campanella, taking the role of the visiting seaman, reports: "And when I asked with astonishment whence they had obtained our history, they told me that among them there was a knowledge of all languages, and that by perseverance they continually send explorers and ambassadors over the whole earth, who learn thoroughly the customs, forces, rule and histories of the nations, bad and good alike."[17] The residents of the City of the Sun displayed all of this accumulated knowledge freely for daily perusal and pleasure, no matter what a citizen's station in life. Campanella used the walls of the city as one big open book—a kind of medieval Wikipedia.

A Unique Ukrainian Vision

For centuries after the works of Plato, More, and Campanella, other utopian thinkers embraced the call for universal public education because they understood that society could only progress if children were given opportunities to think beyond the traditions and dogmas that governed their daily lives. After the consolidation of the nation-state and the onset of the Industrial Revolution, less utopian reformers accepted demands for various forms of universal public education because they recognized the role that formal schooling could play in creating a literate, numerate, productive, and patriotic citizenry. As a social institution that exists at the intersection between the public and the private sphere, schools often provide the first contact that many children have with other children and adults who are not already members of their families or familial networks.

A good and well-funded public education can equalize disparities in children's home life and help teachers to recognize exceptional talent that might have otherwise been ignored. Formal schooling also supports parents by alleviating some of the burdens associated with educating their children in a wider variety of subjects than they can manage on their own. (I can't even begin to describe my panic when my daughter needed help with her calculus homework.) In progressive educational settings with high-quality health education, children can learn about their bodies, their emotions, and their relationships from qualified adults who are properly trained to address awkward or embarrassing questions, sparing many squeamish parents from having to explain the birds and bees by themselves. (My daughter had a better Sex Ed class in German seventh grade than I ever attended in all four years of my American high school.) Many utopian educational reformers believe the same burden sharing can be true for ethical education; rather than just teaching physics and history, schools have a role to play in teaching what Plato called virtue. Why place the entire project of raising the next generation of well-adjusted and decent human beings on the shoulders of already exhausted parents?

One reformer who advocated for a more wholistic view of education was the Ukrainian Anton Makarenko, who developed a unique approach to formal schooling. Makarenko, who would be chosen by UNESCO as one of the four most influential pedagogues of the twentieth century, was a railway worker's son who in 1914 entered the Poltava Teacher's Institute, a university for training future educators.[18] Upon his graduation, he became the headmaster of a higher primary school and forged close bonds with the working-class parents of his pupils. From his experiences in the classroom, Makarenko believed that the education of children must extend beyond the school, and that children would only embrace learning if they felt that their lessons related to their experience of the world. Pupils wanted teachers to act as guides rather than arbitrary authority figures. And so, Makarenko created a new pedagogy that fully integrated manual and mental labor and taught youth the values of cooperation, community, and self-reliance.

In 1920, the education department in Poltava, Ukraine, put Anton Makarenko in charge of creating a colony for "juvenile delinquents," which is to say orphaned or abandoned children who had lived on the streets (called the *besprizornye* or *bezprizorniki*—the "unattended" ones).[19] Makarenko understood that these children had survived on their own, sometimes for years, through creative forms of self-reliance born out of desperate necessity. So rather than treating them as mere pupils, Makarenko gave them control of what eventually became known as the Gorky Colony, collaborating with the young people to create a self-sustaining community where pupils took charge of their own working, learning, and well-being. "Children are living their lives, splendid lives," Makarenko wrote, "that's why you have to treat them as comrades and citizens, have to respect and keep in view their right to enjoy life and their duty to bear responsibility."[20]

Makarenko organized the children into autonomous and co-educational groups he called "detachments" of no less than seven and no more than fifteen members. Each detachment had an elected "commander," chosen by the children, and these commanders had to attend spontaneous "Commander's Councils" to discuss the business of the colony. When the famous Russian writer Maxim Gorky visited the colony that bore his name (because the colonists so admired his nov-

Figure 4.1. Portrait of Anton Makarenko.

els) in 1928, he marveled at the initiative of the four hundred children he met there. "All of the Colony's business and life routine is virtually run by the twenty-four elected chiefs of the workers' detachments," Gorky wrote. "They have the keys to all the stores, they draw up all the work places, manage the work and take part in themselves on an equal footing with the rest of the detachment. The Commanders' Council decides questions such as the admission or rejection of voluntary newcomers, and sits in judgement on fellow-colonists guilty of slipshod work or of a breach of discipline and 'traditions.' "[21]

Over time, the detachments grew less hierarchical as Makarenko ensured that each member—particularly the girls—had leadership opportunities by creating temporary detachments for specific tasks, such as organizing a special Guest Committee to host international visitors or preparing for holiday events. The "Commander's Councils" soon transformed into "Detachment Councils" after the children decided that anyone could attend a council meeting as long as each detachment was represented. Later, the children began self-organizing into their de-

Figure 4.2. Students at the Gorky Colony with Anton Makarenko in 1928.

tachments, which they treated as their families; they remained within the same group of age-mixed and gender-mixed kids throughout their stay in the colony. The children worked for four hours a day and spent the rest of their time studying for a traditional secondary education.

Makarenko further developed his unique pedagogy in the Dzer-zhinsky Commune, which opened in 1927 to house and educate not only orphaned juvenile delinquents, but also runaways. The commune began its life with one hundred boys and fifty girls from between the ages of thirteen and seventeen, and among them Makarenko refined his pedagogy and methods of working with teenagers, eventually writing: "I am convinced that the object we pursue in education is not only to bring up a creator and a citizen capable of effectual participation in the development of the state. We should rear a person who is [destined] to be a happy man."[22] Like the Gorky Colony, all of the Dzer-zhinsky communards combined their education with work, but unlike the Gorky Colony, which started out with far fewer resources, the Dzerzhinsky Commune had an initial state subsidy. Makarenko used the funds to build various workshops (for joiners, turners, tailors, locksmiths, etc.) and eventually a full-fledged facility for the manufacture of electric drills and Leica-type cameras.

All of the communards worked in the various enterprises, and Makarenko became famous for integrating labor into a holistic education system. "When I watched that factory at work—and that work meant an exact, detailed plan, standards of tolerance, standards of quality, servicing by dozens of engineers, a design office, etc. etc.—only then did I realize what such production meant . . ." Makarenko wrote. "I discovered that the teaching process at school and the production process were strong personality builders, because they tended to eliminate the distinction between manual and mental labour and turned out highly skilled people."[23] Like Thomas More, Makarenko and his contemporaries attempted to ensure that all citizens knew their work was valued so that even the most basic of manual laborers could take pride in their roles in society.

Makarenko's unique vision of education, with its emphasis on teaching children self-reliance as well as a respect for the value of manual labor, influenced the organization of schooling in countries across the globe, particularly those that fell into the Soviet sphere of influence after World War II. One example comes from socialist Bulgaria. By the late 1970s, the government grew concerned about the role education played in dividing society into manual and mental laborers, which increased the class divisions in a supposedly classless socialist state.[24] Bulgaria's rigid track system funneled some students into academic high schools, where they prepared for university entrance exams, while others attended technical high schools, where they trained for specific careers in the planned economy. Bulgarian leaders noticed that the children of high party members and intellectuals gravitated toward the former, while the children of ordinary laborers found themselves in the latter, contrary to the state's official goals of egalitarianism. Part of this resulted from different parental expectations, but it also reflected a growing devaluation of manual labor in a supposedly worker's state.

To address this, the Bulgarian government introduced a novel program between 1983 and 1989 that forced all academic high school students to pick a trade, earn a formal qualification in addition to their academic diploma, and work full-time in that trade before going to university. Until the very end of the communist era, no university-bound student graduated from an academic high school without working as a manual laborer, whether it be typing, plumbing, or driving. This program, referred to as the *Uchebno-Profesionalni Kompleksi* (Educational-Professional Complexes), meant that in the 1990s I had a friend who got her hair cut by a high court judge because the judge had taken a high school trade certificate in hairdressing. My ex-husband, who eventually became a lawyer, earned his qualification in construction and carpentry. This made him very handy around the house.

My colleague, the anthropologist Maria Stoilkova, was among the last class of students in Bulgaria who participated in this program. She spent the final year of secondary school learning to be a seamstress. Stoilkova chose sewing because she thought it would be a practical skill that would allow her to make her own clothes, but the work turned out to be much harder than she expected. Although she earned her lowest grade in sewing (which prevented her from earning an academic gold medal at school), she ultimately found the experience a valuable one. "You know, at the time I hated going [to the garment factory] because it was difficult work and I wasn't any good at it," she told me over coffee one day in Sofia in 2021. "But now that I have my own son, I wish he could have a similar experience. It is important to know how difficult factory work is, so you can appreciate the hard work that other people do."

As they try to figure out who they want to be and what they want to do in the world, children understand their society's definitions of what it means to be a "winner" or a "loser," and how those categories differ for boys and girls. Parents and popular culture instill these definitions, but schools also play a significant role in imparting ideas about which goals in life are deemed worthy of pursuing. In American high schools, graduating seniors sometimes take a vote to determine who among them is "most likely to succeed," which means becoming either rich, powerful, famous, or all of the above.[25] Raising a family or living a happy life surrounded by friends gets excluded from many Western definitions of success. Universities often celebrate the achievements of wealthy or celebrity alumni. CEOs, professional athletes, and entrepreneurs are held up as role models for current students who feel pressured to "make something" of themselves, implicitly relegating the valuable work of caring and nurturing to the category of "nothing."

The values taught in our schools can uphold a particular vision of the world, one that generally tends to reinforce the way things are, including the systemic injustices of the past. These social expectations and biases can be hard to challenge if they become entrenched in a society over time. Which is exactly the problem Julius Nyerere, another utopian educational reformer, faced as he tried to lead a newly liberated Tanzania out of its British colonial past.

"Every School Should Also Be a Farm"

When the British territory of Tanganyika achieved its independence in December 1961, about 80 percent of the population was illiterate, and only 50 percent of children attended primary school.[26] Of those who completed their primary education, only 5 percent entered secondary school. Nyerere was elected president of Tanganyika in 1962, and following a coup in neighboring Zanzibar two years later, Nyerere negotiated for the unity of the two countries into the new Republic of Tanzania, of which he was elected president in 1965. Nyerere grappled with a wide variety of challenges, including how to transform the elitist colonial legacy of formal schooling into a mass education system capable of supporting his plans for a unique form of African socialism.[27]

Born in 1922 into the family of a tribal chief, Nyerere excelled at school and won successive scholarships to further his education within the colonial system, including grants to Makerere College in Uganda to train as a secondary school teacher. He taught biology and English in Tanganyika for three years before he left for a master's degree at the University of Edinburgh. Upon his return, he worked again

Figure 4.3. Portrait of Julius Nyerere.

as a teacher—this time of history, English, and Kiswahili—at St. Francis' College near Dar es Salaam, until he founded a pro-independence party, the Tanganyika African National Union (TANU), and began his political career.[28] In March 1967, Nyerere published his groundbreaking pamphlet, *Education for Self-Reliance*, a stinging critique of the way the British had used formal schooling as a tool in their imperial strategy for the subjugation of Africa.

Nyerere argued that the colonial education system taught African boys and girls to embrace Western values and attitudes, such as prioritizing competition over cooperation, urban over rural living, and mental over manual labor. The system also reinforced racial and class inequalities and disdain for traditional African cultures. For too long, secondary and tertiary students had also prioritized academic knowledge over practical skills and work experience because they hoped to win coveted administrative posts. Nyerere's curricular reforms centered the history of Tanzania and of Africa rather than prioritizing European history, philosophy, and culture. Schools moved away from the formal examination system that encouraged students to cram facts through rote memorization. An "Education for Self-Reliance" had to "foster the social goals of living together and working together, for common good. It has to prepare our young people to play a dynamic role and constructive part in the development of a society in which all members share fairly in the good or bad fortune of the group, and in which progress is measured in terms of human well-being, not prestige buildings, cars, or other such things whether privately or publicly owned," Nyerere wrote. "Our education must therefore indicate a sense of commitment to the total community and help the pupils to accept the values appropriate to our kind of future, not those appropriate to our colonial past."[29]

Nyerere wanted pupils to combine labor and studies in financially self-sufficient communities, similar to Makarenko's communes. "Each school should have, as an integral part of it, a farm or workshop which provides the food eaten by the community . . ." Nyerere explained. "This is not a suggestion that a school farm or workshop should be attached to every school for training purposes. It is a suggestion that every school should also be a farm; that the school community should consist of people who are both teachers and farmers, and pupils and farmers."[30] Nyerere hoped his compatriots would embrace the ethos of cooperative self-sufficiency, while also ensuring that young Tanzanians learned skills useful to the future development of their now independent country. Rather than treating education as a privilege for academically exceptional individuals, Nyerere imagined schools that cultivated and valued all talents: "[T]he education system of Tanzania must emphasize . . . the responsibility to give service which goes with any special ability, whether it be in carpentry, in animal husbandry, or in academic pursuits."[31] Although Nyerere met resistance from students and teachers who looked down on agricultural labor, his example in Tanzania became a model for other postcolonial African countries throughout the 1970s and '80s, which instituted similar Education with Production (EWP) programs.[32] His social dream of schooling for cooperation and self-reliance continues to inspire progressive pedagogues around the world today.

The Handicapper General

The common element behind these utopian visions of education, and many others that I have not discussed here, is that schools must teach children values. This might sound odd in the United States for it is usually conservatives who speak of teaching children "the proper values," such as unquestioning patriotism, American exceptionalism, or some version of the Protestant work ethic. But by teaching girls as well as boys, Plato reinforced the idea that girls were equally capable and worthy of education. When Makarenko let young students collectively make their own decisions about their education, he was teaching them to think about democratic consensus and the need to cooperate with others, rather than encouraging obedience to what a headmaster or boss decrees. When Nyerere included agricultural labor as an integral part of education, he wanted students to appreciate the importance of such work within Tanzania and to reject the

British colonial notion that work on the land was only something to the "losers" of society.

A typical reaction to utopian visions for reimagining what and how we teach our children in school is that instilling youth with a particular set of ideals, no matter how well-intentioned, is some kind of social engineering or brainwashing, and it's probably true that Makarenko enjoyed so much success with the Gorky Colony and the Dzerzhinsky Commune because the children he taught were orphans and runaways and he never had to deal with their mothers and fathers. Spend just fifteen minutes on the websites of groups like Parents Against Critical Theory (PACT) and you will see the word "indoctrination" used multiple times. In 2019, conservative American legal groups sued public schools that taught children mindfulness meditation techniques and yoga because they supposedly endorsed Buddhism and Hinduism.[33] And all sorts of books exploring teen sexuality are being challenged or banned.[34] Many people feel that ethical education is the sole purview of parents and religious institutions, while others believe that children should find their way into their own "authentic" set of personal values independent of outside influence.

But I think it naive to pretend that our modern schools don't already teach particular values and worldviews. I grew up in a country that lauds its commitment to the separation of church and state, but I spent my entire youth attending public institutions where every morning I stood, with my right hand over my heart, and recited in unison with my classmates the same words from memory as we faced the Stars and Stripes: "I pledge allegiance to the Flag of the United States of America, and to the Republic for which it stands, one Nation, under God, indivisible, with liberty and justice for all." Congress adopted the Pledge in nearly this form in 1942, but they added "under God" during the Cold War in 1954 to distinguish Americans from the atheists in the Soviet Union. When I consider the history of my country and look around at the political polarization today, it's laughable to suggest that the United States is "indivisible" and provides "liberty and justice for all." But I always stood and repeated the words. I never learned to question them until much later.

ıy German colleagues about the Pledge of Allegiance,
ror that children would be taught to accept such bla-
ɯı. As the philosopher Susan Neiman observed, postwar
ɯɯans are uniquely progressive about teaching kids to think for themselves and to recognize the difference between right and wrong.[35] I'll never forget the day when my daughter came home from her German ethics class excited to share details of the discussion they'd had about the Scholl siblings, who resisted the Nazis in 1943. They were good students from a good family. Did they throw their lives away resisting Hitler when their protest ultimately made no difference? Would it have been better for them to have kept their mouths shut? How many of their classmates also hated the Nazis, but chose life instead of almost certain death? These were not easy questions, and my daughter and I talked about them long into the night. When I finally got her to bed, I was deeply impressed that her teachers expected thirteen-year-olds to engage in such profound moral searching. I thought back to my own middle school years to see if I could excavate any similarly explicit ethical questioning.

I could only remember a discussion about Kurt Vonnegut's short story "Harrison Bergeron" in 1982. In this dystopian tale, a married couple sit together on a couch watching a ballet performance after government officials have arrested their fourteen-year-old son. "The year was 2081, and everybody was finally equal. They weren't only equal before God and the law. They were equal every which way . . ." Vonnegut writes. "All this equality was due to the 211th, 212th, and 213th Amendments to the Constitution, and to the unceasing vigilance of agents of the United States Handicapper General."[36]

This Handicapper General, Diana Moon Glampers, ensured absolute equality by forcing exceptionally graceful, strong, intelligent, or otherwise talented people to counterbalance their gifts. The ballerinas are masked and weighed down by bags of birdshot; the above-average-intelligence father has a radio device in his ear that emits unpleasant sounds to scatter his thoughts. Hazel and George Bergeron, the story's protagonists, refer to the era before the coming of equality as the "dark ages," a time with "everybody competing against everybody else." In his short story, Vonnegut captures a moment of resistance to this enforced equality, which ends in sudden tragedy.

We read the story aloud in our class, and as part of the lesson, my teacher brought out thick Halloween masks and a heavy weighted vest for us to try on. She had a ball horn that she squeezed near each of our ears. As we discussed how natural it was for different people to have different abilities, my teacher impressed upon our young minds how horrible it would be to live in a society where everyone was equal. I remember her telling us that even striving toward a state of more equality was perilous because we would have to give up the things that "made us each special." Our individualism was sacred, and we should appreciate living in a society that allowed us to celebrate our differences.

It never occurred to me to ask her if differences in how much money our parents made counted as a difference that made us more or less special. Or if it was okay that some of us were more "special" because we had lighter skin, or a Y chromosome, or worshipped in a church rather than a mosque or synagogue. And how does advocating for equality in opportunities necessarily lead to a demand for the equality of abilities? It didn't really make much sense, but I was twelve. Like my thoughtless recitation of the Pledge of Allegiance, I accepted my teacher's words as gospel: individualism was good; equality was dangerous.

I learned a powerful lesson at an impressionable age, and it is a lesson that millions of American children still learn each year. When the Libertarian Futurist Society inducted "Harrison Bergeron" into its Prometheus Hall of Fame in 2019, the educational director of the Kurt Vonnegut Museum and Library confirmed that the story was "one of the most widely taught texts in schools around the country."[37] Although we don't call it ethical education, the curricula we teach in our schools already impart specific values and beliefs to the next generation, and this includes what our societies believe to be the "normal" way to live our private lives.

Learning for the Good Life

Teaching students values can prepare them for life in the "real world" just as much as teaching them to fix cars, sew clothes, or program computers. By not allowing kids to cheat on their exams and papers, we reward honesty. When we punish bullying, we encourage kindness and camaraderie. When we prevent disruptive behavior, we teach children to respect the ability of others to learn. When we ask young children to share and play nicely, we emphasize the importance of cooperation. We tend to think of values as something inherently controversial, but most people across the political spectrum dislike cheaters, bullies, loudmouths, and selfish jerks.

Once we recognize that our schools inevitably teach values, the question is *what* values to teach and *how*. If we want to move toward different ways of organizing our domestic lives, we need to start by rethinking the basic institutional structures that promote competition over cooperation or that value paid work in the formal labor force over unpaid labor done in the home. Or those that promote material success as more worthy than healthy and happy relationships. But we can also think about teaching the next generation to better protect the environment or to appreciate the labor that goes into producing the food and other resources necessary to sustain ourselves. In Ohio, the Quaker Olney Friends School is the first USDA-certified organic campus that requires students to learn farming-related subjects as a graduation requirement, similar to the vision once promoted by Nyerere.[38] At Olney, the practical aspects of farming blend fully into the educational experience. Lessons in academic classes such as biology, chemistry, and even art and literature are integrated with applied tasks so that students learn about abstract concepts through hands-on experiments on the farm campus: a chemistry lesson that focuses on fertilizers, a biology lesson about photosynthesis that takes place in a greenhouse, a literature class that includes stories about the lives of farmers. While caring for a wide variety of chickens, goats, and cattle, students also learn beekeeping, greenhouse gardening, and sustainable farming methods.

Running the farm forces students to work together in a common endeavor outside of the formal classroom, teaching them the values of both cooperation and self-reliance, as well as a profound appreciation for the hard work involved in agriculture and animal husbandry. Knowing where the food they eat comes from, how it was planted, grown, harvested, and prepared exposes students to the most fundamental processes required to sustain life on our planet. The integration of these lessons into the basic academic curriculum at Olney provides opportunities to teach about the climate crisis and its projected effects on our environment. A 2019 National Public Radio survey found that 80 percent of American parents and 86 percent of educators supported the teaching of climate change in schools.[39] By linking academic subject material to the real world, teachers will have more opportunities to explore issues that impact students' everyday lives, not only the climate crisis but also the evolving nature of our economies and societies in the face of outsourcing and automation.

Rather than aiming for simple allegiance arising from mindless recitation, we could also teach students to *think* about moral questions using the tools of disciplines as diverse as philosophy, history, theology, psychology, anthropology, sociology, or neuroscience. One of the most highly attended courses in Harvard College's history is the philosopher Michael Sandel's course on "justice," taken by more than fifteen thousand students, and offered online for free.[40] And among the most popular courses in the history of Yale University is "Psychology and the Good Life," taught by Professor Laurie Santos.[41] The class reviews the psychological literature to examine the science of well-being, to equip students with tools that will help them make better choices and live a more fulfilled life. When Santos first offered the course in 2018, 1,200 students enrolled. When she taught it again in 2022, the five-hundred-person class had another six hundred students on the waiting list. Obviously, massive demand exists for educational exploration about how we can determine what we want out of life, not just what our societies want us to want. Figuring out answers to these questions inevitably leads us back to questions about the private sphere and how we arrange our personal lives. If youth learn that the best available empirical research suggests that healthy relationships are better predictors of life satisfaction than professional accomplishment or material success, they may make different choices in life: about where to live, who to love, and when or whether to form families.

The hysteria and hypocrisy surrounding the politics of school curricula reflect a clear reality: the fight for our collective future will inevitably be fought in our classrooms. Although many parents are exhausted by the culture wars being fought at the level of individual school districts, it's a mistake to think that we can return to some nonideological place of just teaching basic subject matter and nothing else: there is no value-neutral way of educating citizens. As Plato understood so well over two millennia ago, a society's virtues are taught through public education, and all of us have a stake in determining which virtues we wish to prioritize. Such an important task cannot be left to parents alone.

Contemporary schools also fall short when it comes to teaching kids the resilience necessary to deal with stress, particularly after the upheavals of the pandemic and in the face of the climate crisis and growing economic precarity. In nuclear families, it is often mothers who tend to the emotional needs of their growing children while also teaching the interpersonal skills, appropriate manners, and acceptable behaviors necessary to thrive in different social contexts. This is difficult work, and not all parents have the bandwidth necessary to assuage their kids' anxieties, especially those of teens and young adults. As mentioned earlier, when schools do try to introduce mindfulness techniques or yoga sessions, they are sometimes sued for promoting Eastern religious doctrines, even if these techniques are widely used by secular practitioners for stress reduction. Makarenko understood the importance of teaching young people self-confidence, self-reliance, and how to settle interpersonal conflicts within a group. Nyerere wanted to teach young Tanzanians to be proud of their African heritage and to find ways to work together for a better postcolonial future. Public schools can support parents by equipping young people with healthy coping mechanisms and strategies for dealing with the unpredictability of real life. These skills should be as important as learning history or algebra.

Festivals of Philosophy and Campanella Walls

But beyond the walls of the schoolhouse, we should also think about other ways of bringing ongoing education to the public, particularly for adults. Learning new things together with others is a wonderful way to forge bonds with strangers, widening or strengthening our social networks and modeling curiosity for the next generation. More's idea of free and lifelong education has found various outlets online, particularly in projects like Wikipedia, TED Talks, Duolingo, the original edX courses offered by Harvard and MIT, and other attempts to democratize knowledge. Although many people would still rather binge a streaming series than take an online course after a long day at work, a potential future of shorter hours, or, with the rise in remote work, fewer hours lost in commutes, might free up time to engage in more self-directed learning.

By liberating education from its credentialing functions, knowledge can become a public good and a shared pleasure, rather than an investment that reinforces the divide between blue-collar and white-collar laborers and forces young people into debt. In the United States, some of today's pervasive distrust of experts results from a deep and growing strain of anti-intellectualism.[42] The democratization of knowledge might help people understand the evidentiary bases upon which expert opinions are formed, making it easier for them to access and understand the basic facts about things that directly affect their health and well-being—and that of their children.

One wonderful contemporary example of More's vision for lifelong education is the Festival Filosofia (Festival of Philosophy) held annually in the Italian city of Modena. When I attended this event in September 2021, the packed piazzas astounded me. Over the course of three days, the city hosted forty-five free talks, concerts, and other events in the streets and squares around its old center. Fabio Brancolini, a fifty-one-year-old banker who grew up in Modena, adores the festival, explaining to me that: "Instead of people talking about football, you hear ordinary people walking on the street discussing the ideas of Aristotle and Gramsci." In Modena, construction workers and university professors mingled happily in the crowds, listening to the latest ruminations about what it means to be human in the twenty-first century.

Another way to democratize education includes modern attempts to implement Tommaso Campanella's education walls. While for Thomas More lectures and festivals would be fully voluntary pursuits that people could choose to attend or not, Campanella endeavored to weave education inescapably into everyday life. One excellent contemporary example of this can be found in various initiatives to plaster poetry across shared public spaces. Private citizens in the city of Leiden in the Netherlands launched the *muurgedichten* (wall poems) project in 1992. Over the course of thirteen years, 101 international poems graced the city's walls.[43] The Dutch embassy in Bulgaria later sponsored a similar project in Sofia under the slogan "Unity in Diversity," suggesting that since so many cultures revere poetry, humanity

Figure 4.4. Setting up for the 2021 Festival of Philosophy in Modena.

can connect through verse.[44] Also in 1992, the New York City Metro-politan Transit Authority and the Poetry Society of America launched the "Poetry in Motion" project, which initially placed poems in the subway in New York, before spreading to Los Angeles, Nashville, Providence, and San Francisco.[45] The Poetry in Motion project reaches millions of commuters each year, and is itself indebted to the Poems on the Underground initiative launched in London in 1986, which proved a huge success.[46] Shanghai's own "Poetry on the Metro" initiative was spearheaded by the British Council after the Poetry in Motion selection committee decided to feature four Chinese poets.[47]

While it is wonderful that major cities around the world have de-cided to forgo thousands of dollars of potential advertising revenue to provide an intercultural exchange of beautiful words, we could take things even further. Imagine if instead of being flooded with images of photoshopped people trying to sell us things we don't need, our pub-lic spaces featured useful and interesting tidbits of fun information. Etymology: have you ever thought about how the word "disease" is literally a compound word made up of "dis" (not) and "ease?" As-tronomy: wouldn't it be nice to know which constellations or planets would be visible in the sky on each cloudless night? Psychology: might we not all benefit from knowing the results of the latest studies on happiness and well-being? Even though we have access to so much of the world's knowledge on our electronic devices, we still have to actively seek out that knowledge. But if this kind of non-commercial content was readily available *and* integrated into our everyday sur-roundings, education would become less of a means to an end, and more of a shared, lifelong pursuit.

According to the official Times Square website, an average of 380,000 visitors enter New York's Times Square on foot per day with about 115,000 driving or being driven through. About 1.5 million people will see a Times Square ad, but almost all of the billboards serve commercial purposes. One notable exception is when John Lennon and Yoko Ono purchased a Times Square billboard in 1969 during the Vietnam War to say "WAR IS OVER! IF YOU WANT IT."[48] In 2012, Yoko Ono once again invaded Times Square with her "Imagine Peace" art installation in twenty-four languages.[49] Campanella walls put public space back into the commons, share knowledge, and challenge the idea that education and culture are only things to be acquired in schools or hoarded by the rich. In our everyday utopias, everyone can be lovers of knowledge.

At the end of the day, our education systems operate as institutions that must prepare the next generation for life in an increasingly precarious economy. For parents struggling to meet the emotional needs of their growing children, a strong public education system with well-trained and well-compensated teachers can provide much needed support. And yet, instead of working together, parents compete to get their kids into the best schools possible in the hopes of procuring for them a more secure future in an increasingly unstable world.

We rarely stop to ask: What if we were all less worried about the future because we lived in societies where one's ability to have a decent life had little relationship to one's profession? If we valued

Figure 4.5. A wall poem in Oostende, Belgium, in 2021.

all workers who contributed to the functioning of our societies—including those who provide care for our children, elderly, and other vulnerable members of society—would our formal education systems be liberated from their role in sorting us into "winners" and "losers" based on the schools we attend and the jobs we end up doing? And to the extent that schools inculcate the values that perpetuate the need to sort children into people whose future labors will be worth more or less, can't we use our schools to teach a different set of values: those of cooperation and collaboration instead of self-interest and competition? And shouldn't we continue reinforcing these values throughout our lifetimes? As so many social dreamers in the past have realized, any utopian reimagining of the private sphere needs to challenge basic ideas about how societal resources are distributed and how our formal education system legitimates that distribution. This requires a discussion of private property.

CHAPTER 5

Imagine No Possessions, I Wonder Why We Can't

How Sharing Our Things Can Open Our Hearts

My daughter and I are wardrobe communists. Except for my extra three inches of height and my slightly bigger shoe size, we share identical proportions. This means that my closets—carefully curated over the last three decades—occasionally fall victim to the pillage of a quirky Gen Z-er in search of what she considers cool vintage finds. At first, I designated certain items off-limits: concert T-shirts with particular sentimental value or designer items once patiently saved up for, cleverly thrifted from consignment stores in San Francisco, or purchased when I taught English in Japan and earned my first real salaries in yen. But once the coronavirus hit and she spent her first year of university remote-learning from her bedroom upstairs, I released all embargoes. Now clothes and accessories flow freely between us. I actually feel a deep joy when I see my grown-up baby wearing a French silk scarf or Vivienne Westwood corset that I splurged on in 1995. Since I only have one child, I suppose she will inevitably inherit all of these things anyway.

But then I catch myself and consider that word: "inherit." As someone who has inherited nothing material from my own parents, I recoil from the thought that somehow my daughter is more worthy of my clothes than other children. But I have to be honest. If any one of her peers came to my house and started rummaging through my dresses and sweaters, I would be profoundly uncomfortable. Why? Although

I have made many sartorial gifts to former students in need of professional clothes after they graduated, I've never once let any of them have at my stuff with the same abandon that I allow my daughter.

When I think back on my life, the only time I ever participated in a similar form of mutual exchange was with my college roommate during the 1988–89 academic year. I'm not sure why. Was it because we shared a domicile? Was cohabiting the necessary inducement to extreme sharing? Or were we able to share because neither of us had particularly nice things? We both came from households headed by working-class Hispanic single moms with limited resources. I wonder how our situation might have been different if we hadn't been socioeconomic equals. In the grander scheme of things, when I see my daughter wearing my favorite fleece pajamas (turquoise with little pink tea roses), I wonder if there could be a world where I felt as generous with other children as naturally as I felt with my own. What would it take, to quote John Lennon, to "imagine no possessions"?

What's Property Got to Do with It?

In my earlier chapter on housing, I looked specifically at various utopian visions for cohabitation with nonconsanguineous others and how living together with larger groups of people can bind us in quasi-familial types of relationships, or what some people call "chosen families." Chosen in the sense of forging and maintaining nontraditional kinship relations with people who are not your biological or legal relatives, but for whom you maintain an affective bond that involves a reciprocal expectation of care. In this chapter, I want to explore the history of the ideas and the communities that take things one step further: in addition to living together, they have practiced some kind of income sharing and own large parts of their property in common. While many of us freely join our finances and intermingle our possessions upon marriage or in order to demonstrate our status as domestic partners, this practice only rarely occurs with our friends, neighbors, classmates, or colleagues with whom we maintain clear boundaries.

Flatmates designate private shelves in the shared refrigerator and collective expenses such as utilities get divided equally and paid out of individual bank accounts. Yet I blithely transfer funds to my daughter in a way that would probably arouse suspicion if I did so to a former student or some other young person in need of financial support. No one ever thinks to ask what I "get out of" my relationship with my own daughter.

But where did this criterion come from? Evolutionary biologists and psychologists might claim that giving my daughter money is "natural" because my selfish genes want to maximize my chances of having grandchildren. Raising a biological child successfully to adulthood increases the likelihood that some genetic traces of me will continue on in the world after I am gone. But before we understood about DNA, aristocrats and priests claimed that inequalities in access to property, or even worse, the reduction of some subset of our population to the status of property was divinely ordained: slaves, serfs, women, and children. God, or the gods, just created the world that way. We had to accept it. Contemporary evolutionary arguments replace dogma with rational and scientific legitimation for the idea that private property, and heritable property in particular, is "natural."

The odd thing about thinking of private property as a natural proclivity is that our evolutionary ancestors spent the vast majority of our history as hunters and gatherers moving from place to place. Other than a few basic tools or weapons, some rudimentary jewelry, and maybe a spare loincloth, they owned little beyond what they could carry on their backs, ranging freely across terrain undivided by artificial boundaries, fences, or "Keep Out" signs. Although our ancestors may have competed with other groups for access to natural resources (a particularly nice cave or a choice watering hole), these resources were generally shared in common with all members of the group and abandoned when they were no longer needed.

Of course, recent investigations using technological innovations in archaeogenetic testing, such as the study of ancient DNA, have revealed that not all hunting-and-gathering societies were the "noble savages" or egalitarian communalists we have long been taught they were. And while the hunting-and-gathering societies that survived into the twentieth century did practice a form of egalitarianism, other preagricultural societies enforced strict hierarchies. Far from being a "natural" state of innocence, archaeologist and anthropologist David Wengrow and David Graeber suggest that egalitarianism was a chosen way of life, one fiercely defended by ensuring that no one person or group of people could establish arbitrary authority over others.[1] In either case, our forebears coveted far fewer material possessions than most of us today. The key point is that different belief systems about the owning or sharing of property emerged from specific historical and cultural circumstances, but property regimes, once in place, always seek to justify themselves by claiming their own naturalness and inevitability. As the French economist Thomas Piketty explains, "Every human society must justify its inequalities: unless reasons for them are found, the whole political and social edifice stands in danger of collapse."[2]

If cultural practices such as patrilocality and patrilineality exist in part to justify the intergenerational transfer of property from fathers to legitimate sons, then we must step back and understand the origins of the property that is to be passed down. The French anarchist Pierre-Joseph Proudhon proposed in his 1840 book, *Qu'est-ce que la propriété?* (*What Is Property?*), that: "*La propriété, c'est le vol!*" (Property is theft!).[3] He meant that there was some point in our distant past when we went from living in a world where everyone owned all productive resources (land, trees, streams, bushes, and other aspects of the natural world that could provision the population) in common (to the extent that we can even use the word "ownership" at all) to a world in which some individual or group cordoned off a parcel of land or guarded an alcove around a waterfall and claimed it for their exclusive use in perpetuity. Even the English philosopher John Locke, a fervent advocate for the necessity of private property in order to encourage industriousness, believed that the appropriation of land or other natural resources for private use was only justified if "there is enough, and as good, left in common for others."[4]

But the word "property" is misleading because Proudhon makes an important distinction between what he calls "property" and "possession." A significant difference exists between the personal property needed to meet one's individual needs and the private (or productive) property owned for the purpose of seeking rents or extracting labor from others. Almost all communist and anarchist thinkers following Proudhon recognize that people can maintain personal possessions, such as tools, jewelry, and loincloths, even in a society based on the common ownership of land and other productive resources. Unlike in religious traditions that eschew material possessions on moral grounds, in Proudhon's view, people should be allowed to own their homes and the various implements necessary to provide for their own health, safety, and sustenance. The problem of private property lies with those who own such property for the sake of extracting payments or labor from those without it.

In the case of my wardrobe, my vintage Vivienne Westwood corset is a piece of personal property that I choose to share with my daughter. Other than the value of looking pretty cool when she wears it, she can't generate additional wealth from the mere ownership of it. Now let's assume that 1990s corsets start enjoying another fashion moment. My daughter asks to borrow the piece and finds a way to rent it out to different Instagram influencers for $300 a day. Then she turns up one weekend and asks if she can take nine or ten other vintage pieces back to campus with her. Let's say she sets up a little business renting out my old clothes to influencers on a regular basis (don't get any ideas, honey!). Suddenly the personal property that I shared with her becomes productive property in the sense that she now uses this property to generate income. When utopians talk about "private property," they generally mean property that people own for the sake of making money, not the property we own for our own personal use.

And yet, much of our economic system today is premised on the inviolability of productive property rights. Many of our government structures and institutions exist to protect and facilitate the accumulation and intergenerational transfer of this property and the various privileges arising from it. One only has to recall that in most ostensibly democratic states, property ownership earned men the right to vote. In ancient Athens, democratic reforms devolved power from the aristocrats to four specific classes of property owners. These classes were named on the basis of how much dry grain each man's estate produced in a given year; and it was only propertied native men born of two Athenian parents who enjoyed the franchise.[5] Women, even the daughters of Athenian parents; foreigners; and enslaved people were excluded from political participation. Perhaps not surprisingly, landed Athenians governed their state with an eye to protecting their own economic interests.

Half a century before Plato, Pythagoras advocated for his followers to live communally and take their meals in common at his school in Kroton.[6] One saying attributed to the Pythagoreans was "*koinà tà philōn*," which means that all things should be shared among friends.[7] Plato, therefore, imagined a class of rulers in his ideal Republic who would not own property at all: "In the first place, none of them [the Guardians] should have any property of his own beyond what is absolutely necessary; neither should they have a private house or store closed against any one who has a mind to enter. . . ."[8] Plato proposed that no system of government could be just if the leaders were primarily concerned with their own personal wealth and the future wealth of their children. How can any leader successfully work for the health and prosperity of their society if they are simultaneously trying to preserve or grow the contents of their own purse? Property, by its unequal distribution in society, made people selfish. Plato believed that this selfishness weakened the state. Citizens would be divided in the face of external enemies because they would care more about the well-being of their own families than about the collective defense of the city. And to the extent that Plato also expected his auxiliaries and philosopher-kings and queens to be the most courageous and the wisest citizens of Kallipolis, he believed that petty concerns over the acquisition of material things distracted the mind from the pursuit of justice. These ancient critiques of property have reverberated throughout the ages.

Celibate, Nonviolent, Vegan Anarchists

Although most readers will associate injunctions against private property with the secular theories of socialism and anarchism, a wide variety of religious traditions have also taken a critical stance toward the hoarding of more than is necessary to satisfy immediate needs. In Hinduism and Jainism (an ancient religion originating in India), the philosophy of *aparigraha* means non-possessiveness, and promotes the idea and practice of owning no more than essential for survival. Among the Jains, non-possessiveness ranks second only to the virtue of nonviolence, and in the Yoga Sutras, *aparigraha* is one of the five precepts necessary for living a virtuous life. This philosophy of non-possessiveness led men like Mohandas Gandhi to embrace a life of poverty and simplicity.

Similarly, in Buddhism, the Four Noble Truths teach that life is stressful and that craving and earthly desire cause our suffering. The Buddha proposed an eight-fold path to help end suffering, and one of these eight doctrines is "right livelihood," which includes not earning your living in a way that harms others and not attaining more possessions than strictly necessary. Buddhist teachings against selfishness and materialism resonated profoundly with later secular critiques of private property. The current (fourteenth) Dalai Lama of Tibet once explained that "[o]f all the modern economic theories, the economic system of Marxism is founded on moral principles, while capitalism is concerned only with gain and profitability. . . . For this reason I still think of myself as half-Marxist, half-Buddhist."[9] In their cenobitic monastic traditions, members of many Hindu and Buddhist communities share what little property they possess in common, a way to practice their nonattachment to both things and people.

The ancient Jewish sect of the Essenes, which existed between the second century BCE and the end of the first century CE, also lived collectively and owned their property in common. According to historians, thousands of Essenes, thought to be the creators of ancient religious texts called the Dead Sea Scrolls, lived throughout Judea.[10] The Essenes used no money, eschewed trade, and condemned the practice of slavery, which they considered against the laws of God, despite its prevalence throughout the Roman Empire. Instead, the Essenes labored together to meet their own needs in communalist lifestyles that may have presaged the traditions of later Christian cenobitic monastics.[11]

Christianity also has a long tradition of what might be called "Bible communism," practiced by devout adherents who believe that Christ preached full communal living. The basis for common forms of property comes from several controversial passages in the New Testament reflecting on the lives of Jesus's disciples shortly after his death. In Acts 2: 44–47, we learn that: "All the believers were together and had everything in common. They sold property and possessions to give to anyone who had need."[12] Evidence is provided again in Acts 4: 32–35: "All the believers were one in heart and mind. No one claimed that any of their possessions was their own, but they shared everything they had. . . . And God's grace was so powerfully at work in them all that there were no needy persons among them. For from time to time those who owned land or houses sold them, brought the money from the sales and put it at the apostles' feet, and it was distributed to anyone who had need."[13] These passages influenced millennia of Christians whose views on property conflicted with those of the church and led to their continued persecution.

In Bulgaria, the Bogomils were a dualist sect founded sometime in the tenth century. As dualists they believed in two divinities, one all good and one all evil, and they rejected ecclesiastical hierarchies, said their prayers in private homes, and allowed women to become religious leaders because, in their view, the human spirit was sexless.[14] From our vantage point today, the Bogomils were essentially celibate, nonviolent, vegan anarchists. They attracted many converts and their influence spread from the Balkans into Western Europe. In his "Treatise Against the Bogomils," a medieval Bulgarian priest declared them heretical because: "They teach their followers not to obey their masters; they scorn the rich, they hate the Tsars, they ridicule their superiors, they reproach the boyars [nobles], they believe that God looks in horror on those who labour for the Tsar, and advise every serf not to work for his master."[15] Not surprisingly, the tsar did everything possible to get rid of them and eventually they left Bulgaria and settled in the lands that are now Bosnia and Hercegovina.

The Bogomils influenced the Cathars in Italy and the Cathars/Albigensians in France, who also believed in the full equality of men and women and allowed the latter to become "Perfected Ones," the highest spiritual achievement in their religious community. The *Perfecti* were not clerics, but more like Buddhist bodhisattvas in the sense that they had achieved spiritual perfection and saw their primary purpose as guiding others to do the same. By this era, Christianity had grown from a persecuted underground sect with believers being fed to the lions to one of the most powerful institutions throughout medieval Europe. The Catholic Church owned vast lands across the continent and often collected a tithe, or one-tenth, of people's incomes, on top of the taxes already collected by local lords or kings. The Church despised the Cathars because of their rejection of authority and property, as well as their unorthodox views about women and their Manichaean dualist cosmology that recognized both divine good and divine evil. In France, the Albigensians were among the first targets of the medieval Inquisitorial courts. Like the Bogomils before them and the Beguines after them, the Church considered these communities heretical. The Cathars were ruthlessly persecuted in the twelfth and thirteenth centuries until their total annihilation in the Albigensian Crusade in 1209 to 1229 CE.

But the Catholic Church could not delete the offending verses in the Bible, and the avarice and brutality of the popes and archbishops of medieval Europe led many believers to question the role of property in Christian teachings. Even a devout man like Thomas More could not ignore the suggestion made in these verses. They echo clearly in his own 1516 text: "In Utopia, where every man has a right to everything, they all know that if care is taken to keep the public stores full, no private man can want anything; for among them there is no unequal distribution, so that no man is poor, none in necessity; and though no man has anything, yet they are all rich; for what can make a man so rich as to lead a serene and cheerful life, free from anxieties."[16] More is not only making a spiritual argument about the moral superiority of sharing property with others like Christ's disciples, he is also attempting to redefine what it means to be rich. Rather than hoarding things in excess of what is necessary to live, Thomas More proposes that all will be equally rich if they can lead "a serene and cheerful life, free from anxieties," a particularly appealing proposal for our era with its epidemic levels of stress, depression, and growing numbers of "deaths of despair."[17]

Similar to the Bogomils and the Cathars were the later medieval Anabaptist sects of central Europe, such as the Hutterites and others inspired by the doctrines of the German theologian Thomas Müntzer. Unlike Martin Luther, who chose not to challenge the feudal authority of landlords when he challenged the feudal authority of the Catholic Church, Müntzer preached equality and asserted that true Christians would live simply and share their property in common. Müntzer radicalized his followers and led an unsuccessful peasant uprising in 1524 to 1525 in the German region of Thüringen, after which he was captured, tortured, and executed. Both Thomas More and Thomas Müntzer became martyrs and their ideas lived on: their pointed critiques of medieval society and its dubious theological justifications for the accumulation of private wealth. They inspired many later generations of utopian thinkers, particularly those who understood that rejecting the moral legitimation for private property provided a necessary first step for the liberation of those people who found themselves reduced to the status of property.

The Rich Getting Richer

Like John Locke, most classically liberal philosophers believed private property a necessary evil to live in a civilized world. Why would anyone work hard, they asked, unless he could benefit from the fruits of his labors and pass the accumulated fruits on to his children? At the same time, the enclosure of once commonly held lands across Britain, following the Inclosure Act of 1773, forced the peasants out of the countryside and into the factories of a newly rising class of industrialists who needed their labor. The American Revolution and the French Revolution rejected the supposedly divine right of kings and did away with the ancient regime of feudal relations. In France, the revolutionaries dispossessed the aristocracy and the clergy, and celebrated the values of liberty, equality, and brotherhood. But bourgeois revolutionaries wanted to rid the world of hereditary wealth and power to make way for their own newly earned wealth and power. Both societies upheld, and even reinforced, the rights of property, while also maintaining the political subjugation of women, enslaved people, and the non-propertied classes. The contradictions emerging from the upheavals of the French Revolution and subsequent Napoleonic Wars gave birth to an entirely new set of critiques of private property from a wide variety of utopian socialists, communists, and anarchists, many of them either directly or indirectly concerned with the emancipation of women.

Very few people realize that the English philosopher and polymath John Stuart Mill referred to himself as a "socialist" in his posthumously published autobiography despite being one of the heroes of classical liberals and libertarians. This principal proponent of the ideals of free speech, personal autonomy, and liberty believed that capitalism and its enforced regime of private property was morally inferior to some form of socialism. For Mill and his wife, the women's rights advocate Harriet Taylor Mill (both contemporaries of Marx and Engels), the word "socialism" denoted the opposite of individualism rather than a system of government whereby the state owned all productive enterprises on behalf of the workers. The Mills disdained self-interest as the driving force of the economy and believed that socialism would ultimately prevail.

They were also realists. In John Stuart Mill's landmark *Principles of Political Economy*, he accepts "that the energies of mankind should be kept in employment by the struggle for riches, as they were formerly by the struggle for war, until the better minds succeed in educating the others into better things, is undoubtedly more desirable than that they should rust and stagnate. While minds are coarse they require coarse stimuli, and let them have them."[18] Writing in the nineteenth century, Mill believed his compatriots incapable of the kind of moral fortitude necessary for any form of socialism to work; instead, he argued that the unbridled pursuit of wealth was at least an improvement on the once ubiquitous tendency toward violence and warfare. Our "coarse" minds required the coarse stimuli of capitalism until "better minds" succeeded in educating others into whatever Mill considered "better things"—another tall task for our formal school system. More important, where Mill agreed that Adam Smith's ideas about the "Laws of Production" might be immutable (that is, that there is scarcity, competition for resources, and that prices are set by the workings of supply and demand), he saw no reason why the wealth accumulated under these laws needed to remain in the hands of the few. Mill argued that the "Laws of Distribution" were matters of social convention, and that wealth could and should be distributed more equitably across society.

Mill's ideas emerged in the aftermath of the French Revolution and in dialogue with a group of far more radical theorists who preceded him. One of these important thinkers on the question of private property was the Englishman William Godwin, who many consider to be the father of modern anarchist thought. He was the husband of the feminist Mary Wollstonecraft and the father of Mary Shelley, author of *Frankenstein*. Godwin was an enormously popular and influential journalist and philosopher in his day. As the revolution raged in France, he published his *Enquiry Concerning Political Justice and Its Influence on Morals and Happiness* in 1793. His book attacked not only private property, but also the monarchy, monopolies, and marriage as political institutions that stymied the progress of humanity. Appealing to reason rather than to religious texts, Godwin's critique of property and his utopian imagining of how an ideal anarchist society might work in practice influenced a subsequent generation of anarchists such as the Frenchman Pierre-Joseph Proudhon and the Russian Peter Kropotkin.

Once again, I must return to Proudhon's distinction between possessions and private property so I can more clearly elaborate the difference between the socialist and anarchist critiques of the latter, because each leads to different strategies for the pursuit of women's and workers' emancipation. There is an essential difference between me owning the house in which I live and me owning a wide variety of properties that I rent out to less fortunate others who cannot afford to own their homes. Maybe I came into these properties through inheritance, or maybe I bought these properties with money that I saved from working hard and being frugal, but Proudhon would always see these properties as the result of a historical process whereby a small minority dispossessed the majority *from lands once held in common* and then used the violent power of the state to legitimate their ability to charge rents for something that was once free. The enclosure of common lands, laws against vagrancy and squatting, and the lack of social housing options (which predate the Industrial Revolution in Europe) compels people to rent their dwellings at market prices, which fluctuate based on supply and demand. Landlords benefit from a system that denies access to affordable housing because it keeps rental units scarce and therefore rents high.

Similarly, having money saved to provide for my personal needs in the future is different from having money saved for the purpose of lending money to poorer people and charging them a fee to use my money, which is basically what banks do with our money when we deposit it in a bank account. If working people had access to public housing, or jobs that paid enough for them to own their own homes, there would be fewer mortgages. Since many investors now buy mortgage-backed securities (a financial instrument that bundles multiple mortgages so that investors get a portion of the interest payments that borrowers make to banks), fewer mortgages would ultimately mean fewer mortgage-backed securities, which would mean one less investment vehicle for those with surplus savings. If you spend a moment to think about it, wealthy investors stand to benefit at least twice from the lack of affordable housing. If they own investment properties, they can charge higher rents. With the profits that they earn from rents they can buy mortgaged-backed securities. This allows them to make money off of former renters who cannot afford to buy their homes in cash, often because they have spent most of their incomes paying rent. This places a tremendous strain on families trying to keep a roof over their heads and increases the cost of having children in societies where the ideal is for parents to live with their own kids in nuclear families within the walls of a single-family home.

When I bought my first house in 2003, I didn't have enough money to buy it in cash. I applied for a thirty-year mortgage at my local bank, and they approved me. I paid some initiation fees and signed a contract saying that I would return the borrowed money plus a certain amount of interest over the next three decades. The initiation fees and the interest payments were the price of borrowing the money I needed to buy the house, and the bank held partial ownership in that house as collateral. But within less than a month, my bank had sold my mortgage to another bank. That bank then sold my mortgage to a third bank. For the first time, I understood that my mortgage debt was a valuable commodity. As long as I made my payments, the bank that owned it would earn a lot of money from me.

Here's how it works. Let's say a single-family house costs $300,000. A rich person can pay $300,000 in cash, but (as discussed above) a poorer person will need to borrow money from a bank. If they borrow $250,000 with a fixed thirty-year mortgage of 5 percent, and they take the full thirty years to pay off this mortgage, they will pay about $233,000 in interest to the bank, not considering any tax deductions. The bank will keep a portion of this money as its fees and profits, and the rest of it will be paid out to depositors and to the wealthy people who bought mortgage-backed securities, which the banks created by lending out their depositors' savings and then selling those mortgages on to mortgage aggregators. It's meant to be confusing. The point is that the exact same house costs $300,000 for a wealthy person and approximately $533,000 for a poorer one, and that this whole system further exacerbates inequalities by facilitating wealth transfers from the poor to the rich.

Proudhon also wants us to pay attention to the historical processes of dispossession that led to the unequal distribution of resources in the first place. Obviously, he includes things like slavery and enclosure, but this could also include landlords lobbying against the creation of public housing, co-living, or zoning laws that specifically prohibit the construction of cohousing communities or multifamily dwellings in more affluent neighborhoods. These injustices then get passed on from one generation to the next. Between 1989 and 2016, American households inherited $8.5 trillion in wealth, and a further $36 trillion will be transferred from parents to their heirs in the next three decades.[19] In the UK, 28 percent of all wealth is inherited.[20] Even a free-market libertarian hero like the philosopher Robert Nozick, author of the 1974 book *Anarchy, State, and Utopia*, said that, "If past injustice has shaped present holdings in various ways," we must correct for these past injustices before we can proceed to embrace his imagination of a minimalist state. Nozick further accepts that these "past injustices might be so great as to make necessary in the short run a more extensive state in order to rectify them."[21]

Who Owns Wikipedia?

Let's consider the case of Wikipedia, a modern utopian project that aims to give the sum total of all human knowledge to the world for free, to remove information from the realm of commodities. The *Encyclopaedia Britannica*, which first started its print publication in 1768, cost $1,400 for the full thirty-two-volume set when it finally ceased its print publication in 2012 after 244 years.[22] In 2022, if you wanted to access the full digital version of *Encyclopaedia Britannica* online, including the "exclusive content" and without all of the ads and pop-ups, you could subscribe to Britannica Premium for $74.95 a year.[23] Institutional subscriptions cost more. Wikipedia manages to create similar content in multiple languages and disseminates it freely on the internet. On its fifteenth anniversary in 2016, Wikipedia was averaging more than 18 billion page views per month.[24] Wikipedia is completely free from advertising and is maintained by an army of volunteer Wikipedians who create, edit, and update the articles on the site, donating their labor to what they see as a worthy cause. Users also donate to the nonprofit Wikimedia Foundation, which supports the infrastructural costs associated with its maintenance.

Now imagine if Wikimedia's founder, Jimmy Wales, had decided in 2016 to paywall all Wikipedia pages for two cents per page viewed. In that case, Wikipedia would earn $360 million per month, or $4.3 billion per year. With the revenue earned, Wales could pursue two options: to pay all of the Wikipedia editors a sum in proportion to their contributions to the site or to keep all of the money for himself because it was his idea in the first place. If Wales pursued the second option, he would be expropriating for himself and his three daughters all of the wealth that was created collectively by the Wikipedian community.

Now let's assume a counterfactual scenario in which Jimmy Wales and Wikipedia had actually hired and paid content editors and fact-checkers from the beginning. Let's assume that editors got paid a certain hourly wage, but that at the end of the day, Jimmy Wales still makes billions of dollars in profit above and beyond what he pays the Wikipedia editors, the costs necessary for maintaining the site, and other associated business expenses. Would this be considered fair? Of course, in our free-market societies this is the basic business model of most enterprises. Employers earn profits by paying their workers less than the value those workers create, in this case, individual Wikipedia articles. And you might argue that this is fine if the workers agree to do this freely.

But socialists, communists, and anarchists will be the first to point out that most workers really don't have a choice. By depriving people of the once–collectively owned property, especially land, by which the poor could have grown their own food and met their basic needs, most workers are forced to sell their labor to anyone willing to buy it and at basically any price unless the state intervenes and sets things like minimum wages. The only difference between these two examples is that in the first scenario the Wikipedians volunteered their labor believing that they were doing so for the good of humanity, and then Wales cheated them by privatizing the fruits of their collective work. In the second scenario, the Wikipedians agreed to sell their knowledge for a fixed price because it seemed the best means of sustenance among the options available to them. Wales benefited from their desperate position by accruing to himself the sums he earned in excess of the wages he paid them and the costs necessary to run the website.

It is against this second type of expropriation of the value that workers create for the owners of productive property (sometimes called "the means of production") that the communists and anarchists railed. Peter Kropotkin, the Russian prince who became an anarchist, argued that humanity's progress toward a more advanced and harmonious state of collective living, where everyone could have their basic needs met, was impeded by the state's violent protection of private property rights. If the dispossessed Wikipedians in my counterfactual example marched to Jimmy Wales's home with pitchforks, it would be the local, *taxpayer-funded* police who would protect his private property. Similarly, it is taxpayer-funded courts and judges whose dedication to upholding the law often also uphold the property interests of economic elites. Kropotkin proposed that in order to ensure the well-being of all people in society, and not just those clever (or dishonest) enough to come up with schemes to accrue to themselves the value produced by the labors of others, the state—and its monopoly of legitimate violence—must be abolished. All productive property should be returned to common ownership, not including personal possessions.

The big distinction between the anarchists and the communists in the nineteenth and early twentieth centuries was that while both imagined a final utopian world with no state, no laws (since laws need someone to enforce them), and no private productive property, the communists imagined an intermediate stage that they called "socialism," wherein the state would own all of the productive property on behalf of the non-propertied classes. Anarchists like Kropotkin argued that this intermediary stage would inevitably lead to a form of authoritarianism that impinged on personal liberties. He therefore advocated for the most minimal government structure necessary to maintain collective ownership.

But theorists such as Marx and Engels believed it impossible to move from capitalism to the ideal statelessness envisioned by the anarchists without first having a worker-controlled state able to forcibly return to the masses the productive property unfairly seized by the wealthy. While communists more or less agreed with the anarchists on the ideal end goals of their utopian society, one without private property or the state necessary to protect it, they disagreed on how to get there. Basically, in my imagined example where Jimmy Wales had privatized Wikipedia, Marx and Engels would want the government to nationalize Wikipedia on behalf of its editors and its readers, at least in the short term. Kropotkin and other anarchists would want to immediately return Wikipedia to the decentralized, volunteer-based, and freely disseminated project that it is today.

Producing the Producers

All of this relates back to women and the family because the owners of productive property often earn profits from the work of other people's grown children (in this case those that grow up to edit Wikipedia). The production of those children is a necessary part of the system, but future laborers don't just roll off of an assembly line ready to work. They require years of nurturing and maintenance. The owners of productive property essentially get a valuable asset without really having to pay for its production. And when future workers are feared to be in short supply, bodies with wombs can themselves be reduced to a form of productive property. Women who desire bodily integrity can present a profound threat to the economic system if they refuse to gestate and deliver new babies. It should be no surprise that states often attempt to limit access to birth control or outlaw abortion when birth rates start falling, such as in the USSR between 1936 and 1955, in Ceauşescu's Romania between 1966 and 1990, and in an increasing number of US states today.

From a feminist perspective, the most influential text regarding the way that productive property held in common would benefit women specifically is Friedrich Engels's 1884 book, *The Origin of the Family, Private Property, and the State*. After Karl Marx's death in 1883, Engels found his coauthor's notes on an 1877 book by the anthropologist Lewis H. Morgan, *Ancient Society*. Engels presumed that Marx intended to write a full-length treatment of Morgan's work and took the task upon himself, producing what some consider to be the first work of feminist economics. Engels's detailed and complicated arguments have met with much controversy over the years, but in a nutshell, he asserts that women's inferior position in society is not a natural state of affairs, but rather one that arose specifically as a result of the creation of private property.

He argues that preagricultural societies revered women as mothers and tended to be matrilineal and matrilocal. It was only after humans abandoned their hunting-and-gathering lifestyles and settled into agricultural communities that could produce more food than was necessary to meet their basic caloric needs that women's reproductive capacities became valuable for their ability to create future workers. "The overthrow of the mother right was the world historical defeat of the female sex," Engels writes. "The man took command of the home also; the woman was degraded and reduced to servitude, she became the slave of man and a mere instrument for the production of his children."[25] In this view, a return to the collective ownership of productive property, where people share surpluses equitably among all members of the community, would restore what Engels imagined to be women's previous position in society.

Just because it sounds good, doesn't mean it's right. As I discussed earlier, recent archaeological and anthropological evidence challenges Engels's assumptions that human history can be marked out in defined stages or that humans are "naturally" one way or another. It's increasingly believed that greed and the desire for private property did not develop in some direct teleological way as we moved from hunters and gatherers to settled agriculturalists, but that there have always been competing political and economic formations, reflecting a diversity of human civilizational projects.[26] While debates continue to rage around the origins of private property and inequality, or whether we should even be asking these questions in the first place, there remain many communities around the globe continuing the various spiritual and secular projects to live in pocket utopias where property and incomes are shared in common among people living in groups beyond the consanguineous bonds of the family.

Bible Communists

Some of the oldest continuous communities who share property in common today are the theological descendants of the central European Christian Anabaptist sects inspired by Thomas Müntzer and the Radical Reformation in the era of the German Peasants' War in the sixteenth century. Founded by Jakob Hutter, the Hutterites organized their first communes in 1528, but like other sects considered heretical, the Roman Catholics persecuted them for their beliefs. The Hutterite communes initially manufactured goods, but took up farming when forced to flee their factories in central Europe. They settled in Russia in the eighteenth century and eventually came to North America. Today, there are about fifty thousand Hutterites living in colonies of up to 250 people each in the United States and Canada.[27] Linda Maendel, a contemporary Hutterite, explained in an interview for the website Amish America that her Canadian community of 120 adults and children chooses to live "communally because we believe that's what Acts Chapter 2 teaches and also because we feel that is the ideal way to show love for your fellow man as taught in the New Testament. Community of goods simply means that we do not have personal bank accounts. Nor is there any need for it as our needs are supplied by our colony and we take care of our own from the cradle to the grave."[28]

Another example of a communal Christian sect are the Shakers, a religious community founded by an Englishwoman around 1747 and established in the United States in the 1780s. Historically, the Shakers lived in largely self-sustaining colonies and held all property in common. Like the Bogomils and the Cathars before them, the Shakers allowed women to take on roles as prominent religious leaders. They also emphasized simplicity and modesty in their way of life, rejecting the customs of patrilineality and patrilocality through the practice of celibacy.

The Shaker communities initially sustained themselves by attracting converts and taking in orphans, abandoned children, and women who became pregnant out of wedlock. Their belief system "leads the Shaker quite naturally to the pooling of goods" because "the Christian's task is to live in the present moment and not to store for tomorrow the bread that comes from heaven."[29] In a 2019 interview for the *Portland Press Herald*'s Maine Voices Live series, Brother Arnold, who joined the Sabbathday community as a twenty-one-year-old in 1978, explained: "The giving up, you know, it's not as dramatic as you think it is. It's pretty easy, really, not to own anything. It's very easy. We don't own anything, but we all own everything together."[30]

But lifelong celibacy proved unattractive to many potential adherents. Without children of their own, the Shaker colonies dwindled, and today there is only one extant Shaker community on Sabbathday Lake in New Gloucester, Maine. Founded in 1783, it sustains itself through tourism and the production of specialty foods, crafts, bowls, baskets, and chairs. When I visited Sabbathday Lake in March 2022, the whole village was still closed to outside visitors because of COVID-19. I met Brother Arnold briefly as he made his way to the barn and got his permission to wander around the village and take some photos, but the place felt abandoned: Brother Arnold and Sister June were the last two Shakers living in the community.

Figure 5.1. The Sabbathday Lake Shaker Village closed for COVID-19.

Another contemporary religious community that owns all of its property in common is the Bruderhof. Originating in Germany in 1920, the Bruderhof colonies are self-sustaining, growing most of their own food and maintaining small manufacturing enterprises. New members who wish to join donate all of their savings and inheritances to the community; in exchange, the community guarantees all of their basic needs for the future. Today there are about three thousand people living in twenty-nine communally owned settlements in Australia, Austria, Germany, Paraguay, South Korea, the United Kingdom, and the United States. They actively promote their unique vision of Christianity: "Love your neighbor. Take care of each other. Share everything. We at the Bruderhof believe that another way of life is possible. We're not perfect people, but we're willing to venture everything to build a life where there are no rich or poor."[31]

The Bruderhof colonies maintain a gendered division of labor. One community in East Sussex in the UK runs a successful company called

Figure 5.2. 1880 drawing of the Shaker village at Sabbathday Lake.

Community Playthings, which makes all-wood furniture, play equipment, and environments for children. All members of the colony share equally in the profits. Both men and women work in the enterprise: the men make the furniture and equipment, while the women run the sales division. When a journalist for the British newspaper *The Guardian* visited this community and observed that it was women who still did the cooking and child minding, while the men chopped the wood, a resident named Rachel responded, "I don't mind that; I choose that as a Christian. My view is that men and women have different roles, but neither is superior."[32]

What these religious communities demonstrate is that experiments with communal living do not have to be secular or progressive, despite the negative stereotypes associated with them in the West. The sharing of property in common is also fully compatible with leading a rather traditional family life: the Hutterites and the Bruderhof formally embrace patriarchy (as well as patrilineality and patrilocality), but individual wives are not economically dependent on their husbands or isolated from other women. If anything, women living in these communities may have more economic power in their relationships than women living in traditional nuclear families. The gendered division of labor results in fewer economic inequalities between husbands and wives because they all share equally in the redistributed wealth produced by their collective labor. Also, since property is shared in common with others, all children who choose to stay in the community as adults will receive an equal share of the community's resources. This disrupts the role that individual nuclear families play in the differential intergenerational transfer of wealth and privilege.

Taxing Utopia

So how do these communities run their collective treasuries, and what are the legal and logistical hurdles they face? One might think that the laws in capitalist countries like the United States would make it difficult to buy a piece of land and set up a self-sustaining commune where no one has bank accounts. But it's much easier than you think. Communities like the Hutterites, the Shakers, and the Bruderhof are established and taxed under a little-known section of the IRS code. All nonfamilial income-sharing groups qualify for a special tax exemption under section 501(d) reserved for "religious or apostolic associations or corporations which have a common treasury or community treasury," which means that most community members earn too little to pay federal income taxes.[33] In 2022, the annual standard deduction for earned income was $12,950 for a single adult so, depending on the number of members in the "apostolic association," the total amount of revenue, if divided equally among the members, would have to exceed $12,950 per person for the community to owe any income taxes.[34] A 2016 article called "Taxing Utopia" describes the unique historical context of this exemption:

> Nineteenth-century American religious movements challenged many aspects of American society. Although their challenges to mainstream America's vision of sex and marriage remain the best-known aspects of many of these groups, their challenges to traditional American economics are just as important. Eschewing individual ownership of property, many of these new Christian movements followed the New Testament model of a body of believers that held all property in common.
>
> In the early twentieth century, these religious communal groups had to contend with something new: an income tax. Communalism did not fit into the individualistic economic system envisioned by the drafters of the income tax.[35]

After several controversial lawsuits by the Israelite House of David (a Christian communal religious society based on doctrines of an eighteenth-century British "prophetess," Joanna Southcott) and two Hutterite groups against the Internal Revenue Service, Congress specifically drafted a special provision to deal with religious groups in the Revenue Act of 1936. Under this new provision, income-sharing groups could engage in farming, manufacturing, or any form of service work, as long as proceeds were distributed equitably among all adult members of the community to cover their everyday expenses. To qualify as a 501(d) organization, the community must be registered as a corporation; it must have a shared set of values, beliefs, or principles; the communal money must be used specifically for the benefit of its members; and those members must include their share of the collective income in their gross income for tax purposes. Contributions to 501(d) organizations are not tax-deductible, and they can engage in political work without losing their tax status (unlike churches or other religious organizations).

There have been attempts to challenge this provision in the tax code. One legal scholar noted that:

The most common criticism of this option is that it promotes socialism, or that it is just a utopian, hippy ideal that cannot exist in reality. The reality is, however, that thousands of intentional communities already exist, whether structured as 501(d)s or something else, and their business ventures coexist alongside more "capitalistic" business organizations. In any event, it seems unlikely that a small segment of society choosing alternative living arrangements will alter the market values of the entire nation; indeed, this is not even the intent. Instead, those who truly want to live off the land in a communal environment, away from the political circus, have the legal protection of a 501(d) organization if they so choose.[36]

Fearing that income-sharing groups might promote socialism or "alter the market values of the entire nation," some conservatives have argued that this tax status should only apply to religious communities because apparently Bible-inspired communalism is more acceptable or less of a threat than other forms. But the courts have upheld that any shared belief system that informs the collective ownership of property will qualify a group for the exemption. In 1986, in *Twin Oaks Community, Inc. v. Commissioner, 87 T.C. 1233*, the Tax Court also ruled that members of 501(d) organizations did not have to take a vow of poverty or to irrevocably donate all of their property to the organizations before joining.

In the United States at least, the legal status of "apostolic associations" under the tax code makes all women in an income-sharing community the full equals of men and promotes income equality between the sexes, despite whatever other patriarchal structures the community might have in place. In mainstream society, by contrast, a married woman who stays at home and does the cooking, cleaning, and childcare for her employed husband has no personal income and she makes no pension contributions to Social Security. She most likely receives her health insurance through her husband from his employer, and it is only upon divorce that the courts award her a portion of the property accumulated during the length of the marriage in recognition of her nonmonetary contributions to their joint household. Ironically, because of their legal structure, many of these more orthodox religious communities require that women receive an equitable share of the community-held resources, provide equal access to the health insurance plan organized by the community, and support their elderly residents equitably out of their common treasury. Income-sharing arrangements are particularly helpful to unmarried women and widows who also receive an equal share of the community's resources.

Communards and Ecovillagers

Around the globe today, there exists a growing network of people bound together by their critiques of materialism, their desire for more egalitarian societies, and a commitment to environmental sustainability. According to the Intentional Communities Directory in April 2022, there were 222 communities in its database that described themselves as "communes," meaning that members share almost everything. These included the "1st Indigenous Ecovillage" in Amazonas, Venezuela; "La Poudrière" in Brussels, Belgium; and the "Ecovilla Gaia" in Buenos Aires, Argentina. The Global Ecovillage Network (GEN) is also an umbrella organization promoting self-sustaining communities of people dedicated to preserving and regenerating the environment.[37] In their database in April 2022, GEN includes 238 intentional ecovillages, 138 religious or spiritual ecovillages, and forty-nine that are listed as traditional or Indigenous. Since communards prefer the terms "ecovillage" or "intentional community" over the more pejorative term "commune," because the latter conjures images of "cults" and drugged-out hippies, it's difficult to determine exactly how many "ecovillages" are fully income-sharing communities.[38]

Where earlier generations of communards sought to get closer to God or live a more harmonious spiritual life, today, environmental concerns and the desire to challenge traditional gender roles and family structures often draw people toward experiments in communal living. As of 2022, Western Europe hosted the highest concentration of ecovillages. Many communities grow their own food and engage in sustainable native forms of agriculture called permaculture. One example of a full-income-sharing community is the Tamera Peace Research & Education Center, which was founded by a group of Germans in 1995, based on an earlier community founded in 1978. Today, Tamera includes more than two hundred people who are "working towards autonomous decentralized models for a post-capitalist world" on 335 acres of land in southwestern Portugal.[39] The community works on a gift-based economy outside of the monetary system, and 59 percent of their income flows from visitors and students who come to the community to learn about their work. Another 35 percent comes from various donations.[40]

Their vision of a future world is that of a "a post-patriarchal civilization free of violence and war." Tamera's education center promotes a particular form of environmentalism that combines the restoration of nature and the reversal of the effects of climate change through practical permaculture and rainwater retention methods with utopian visions about the future of "a new planetary community" called Terra Nova. Faced with what they see as the impending global catastrophe of an anthropogenic mass extinction event, the residents of Tamera work to create "a global system of self-sufficient communities" that will flourish after capitalism and nation-states collapse.[41] You might call them extreme green preppers.

In Japan, the utopian community of Atarashiki-mura has existed in one form or another since 1918, and the Yamagishi Association is a federation of more than thirty different leaderless, income-sharing communities across the archipelago that began in the 1950s, including many that incorporate spiritual aspects of traditional Japanese Shintoism into their collective pursuits.[42] The income-sharing and nonconsanguineous Konohana Family in Fujinomiya was founded in 1994 and includes almost a hundred adults and children trying to live sustainable, self-sufficient lives in the foothills of Mount Fuji, and "reviving utopia for modern society."[43] The Konohana Family calls itself a "village of Bodhisattvas" and roots its commitment to environmental protection in the doctrines of both Buddhism and Shintoism. In recent years, Chinese millennials can also choose from a small but growing collection of back-to-the-land-type intentional communities as they flee grueling work schedules and burn-out in the country's urban areas.[44] These communes include the "Southern Life Community" and "Another Community," both founded in 2015.[45]

The Israeli kibbutz represents another long-lived example of an income-sharing community, both in its religious and secular varieties. Although the number of full income-sharing kibbutzim began declining in the 1980s, the kibbutz movement enjoyed a small revival after the global financial crisis in 2008.[46] In 2015, 29 percent remained fully committed to the cooperative model.[47] By 2020, Dr. Shlomo Getz of the Kibbutz Research Institute at the University of Haifa found that there were forty-five fully income-sharing kibbutzim left, including the Kibbutz Hatzerim where I lived and worked back in 1990. This accounted for less than 20 percent of all remaining kibbutzim. The rest followed a hybrid model with only some cooperative aspects.[48] At the same time, some of the children of kibbutzniks who left to pursue higher education and "normal" life in Israel's bigger cities have begun moving back into their natal communities once they have their own children. Many kibbutzim now have wait lists for these returnees.[49]

Even more interesting are the new urban kibbutzim, where young people live together in high-rise buildings, share their property, and pool their incomes in ways not so different from the urban ecovillages emerging in European cities such as Magdeburg, London, Berlin, and Barcelona.[50] These new urban kibbutzim are generally secular and socialist and include communities such as Mishol, which had about a hundred members and was still growing in 2019.[51] Mishol is also an educational nonprofit organization, and its members teach in local elementary schools in their surrounding communities. Many of Mishol's members grew up on traditional rural kibbutzim and are keen to reimagine what communal life could look like in an urban setting. Rather than withdrawing from the world to build their own utopias, members of Kibbutz Mishol claim that they want to bring their utopian practices to the world.

"Probably Bathrooms Are the Most Difficult to Share"

In the United States, Twin Oaks in rural central Virginia was founded in 1967 by some graduate students who read B. F. Skinner's utopian novel, *Walden Two*, and decided they wanted to live collectively. The secular community has survived for over fifty years, tucked far away from the mainstream of American society. The community grows food, but they also weave handmade hammocks, make tofu, index books, and sell seeds and plants for income. The one hundred or so members of the community must work an average of forty-five hours per week, although this fluctuates depending on the number of visitors. Other than a few hours of washing dishes, which everyone must do, they are free to choose where and when they want to work as long as all of the necessary labor gets done. All domestic work (childcare, cooking, cleaning, etc.), as well as taking on leadership roles within the community or engaging in political activism outside of it, are recognized as labor hours that count toward the weekly quota. The labor requirements of older residents taper off as they age: "Every person over the age of 49 may take one pension credit (credit without doing any work for it) per week for every year of age past 49."[52] In exchange for their labor, members are guaranteed work, shelter, food, and health insurance, as well as access to the community's shared amenities. Each member also receives a personal allowance of about $100 per month to purchase things not produced by the community: coffee, chocolate, cosmetics, and other personal items. Members earn an annual two-week vacation and can also apply for extended personal leaves.

Residents of Twin Oaks share major appliances and equipment, which keeps living expenses low. Rather than having eighty individual refrigerators, washing machines, or dishwashers, the community has invested in higher-quality items with longer life spans, cutting down on their carbon footprint. Twin Oaks maintains a car cooperative that allows members to rent vehicles when needed. They also practice a form of wardrobe communism like me and my daughter. "Oakers" maintain a special room of "community clothes" that is a shared wardrobe that any member can borrow from. Residents return dirty clothes to a communal laundry and the washing, mending, hanging, and sorting of the clothes is done by those who receive labor credits for their work. Clothes are organized by type and size. No one is prohibited from having private wardrobes, but clothes owned individually must be laundered or mended by their owners in their free time.

Similarly, the community maintains a fleet of shared bicycles that get repaired in an on-site bike shop. People can keep their own private bikes if they choose, but they must "pay" for repairs in the communal bike shop by working extra hours. Individually owned goods also circulate through the process of "freecycling." All children share toys and books, receive education, take music lessons, and can range freely over the shared 350-acre property. Older residents benefit from community support and palliative care when necessary.

Former members of Twin Oaks acknowledge the challenges and drawbacks to being an Oaker. The community maintains several large collective houses, some designed for more traditional families, and others are home to polyamorous groupings who reject what they consider the confines of a monogamous lifestyle. Oakers reside with one or two "Small Living Groups" (SLGs) of ten to twenty people each, which function as a sort of surrogate family. Daily interpersonal interactions between residents can be harmonious or acrimonious, just as they are in any normal household, but on a much larger scale. Rather than one partner leaving the cap off of the toothpaste or taking too long in the toilet, Oakers have to deal with the personal habits of up to twenty other people. "Folks complain about sharing kitchens and bathrooms—probably bathrooms are the most difficult to share," explained Kristen "Kelpie" Henderson, who has been living in Twin Oaks since 1991, in an email to me in March of 2022.

Like many cohousing communities, Twin Oaks has clear protocols for conflict resolution between residents, and members strive to make all decisions by consensus. This focus on consensus can be intensive and time-consuming and extends into even the most personal aspects of members' lives. Oakers wishing to have children must seek permission from the community because each child born is another mouth to feed out of their shared resources, although those wishing to have more children are free to leave at any time.[53] And then there is the problem of not being able to accrue personal savings. Although members are not required to give up any of their assets when they join, the legal status of Twin Oaks as an "apostolic association" means that they receive no payment for their labors during their time in the community if they decide to leave, no matter how long they have worked there. Former members have filed lawsuits against Twin Oaks, which has considerable annual revenues from the sale of its hammocks and tofu, as well as its book indexing services. But the law generally protects income-sharing communities from such suits because people must voluntarily agree to these terms when they decide to join. People are free to come and go as they please, but the only thing you can take from the community are your personal possessions and whatever is left of your monthly allowance. Only preexisting "petty personal property" can be brought in and used at Twin Oaks—that is, phones, computers, furniture, bedding, and clothing. Televisions are not allowed, and private cars must be put into the car collective or stored off-site.[54]

Despite these drawbacks, for years after the global financial crisis Twin Oaks had a wait list, but closed itself to outsiders in 2020 because of the pandemic. In 2022, Twin Oaks maintained a "priority list" of people who had been accepted but were waiting to join when space became available. Sometimes members will take leaves of absence and they are often replaced by young people who plan to stay on for a year or two. The high turnover of members is accepted as part of the challenge of living in a community that has endured for more than half a century. Outsiders are often curious to experience a different form of life and may not fully appreciate the challenges until they get there. "We operate like a small school that way, but without semesters," writes Henderson.

Oakers know that this type of communal living is not for everyone, and prospective members must complete a three-week visit meeting all labor requirements, undergo a medical exam, attest that they have not attempted suicide in the last year, and be accepted into the community by its existing members before they can join. Reflecting on her more than three decades at Twin Oaks, and the two now-grown sons she raised there, Henderson explained to me: "I find it much easier to live in a group where people are sharing, and I think most Oakers find that to be true. The kids love it here. It's quite a bit safer to grow up here than in suburbia. Both my boys are happy and well-adjusted. My younger boy went to college at UVA [University of Virginia], and has remarked several times that people have too much money there. I think he's probably right."

Toward a Real Sharing Economy

Whether as kibbutzniks, Bible communists, or the secular residents of other income-sharing communities, people around the world continue to organize their personal relationships with private property in ways not so different from the followers of Pythagoras at Kroton way back in the sixth century BCE. Social scientists have taken note and started asking questions. A growing body of empirical evidence points to high self-reported life satisfaction among people who live in property-sharing communities. One 2004 study revealed that while people living in communities with shared treasuries had less economic capital, their lack of material resources was more than compensated for by what the authors called "social," "human," and "natural" capital, meaning that community residents benefited from healthier and more stable social relations, more opportunities to develop their unique skills and talents, and more time spent in nature.[55]

A 2018 study of 913 residents in intentional communities in the United States and Canada found that residents reported levels of personal well-being that were among the highest ever recorded in a multinational comparison group that included thirty-one other representative studies.[56] Although you have to consider the selection bias inherent in surveying people who have chosen to live in intentional communities, the authors of the study believed that their findings supported "the contention that sustainability, in the form of a communal lifestyle of a low ecological footprint, may be promoted without forfeiting well-being."[57] As in cohousing communities, it may also be that women particularly benefit from living in intentional communities, where their domestic labors are valued as work and where shared chores create time savings through economies of scale.

Obviously, it isn't easy to measure comparative individual well-being in different types of living arrangements because there are so many confounding factors. It's also true that people who freely choose to share their possessions in common are a self-selected minority who might be predisposed to be happier with their life choices. Not all of us can upend our lives to join an ecovillage right away, and I imagine that many of us wouldn't want to. The goal of accumulating personal wealth and property motivates many people raised in capitalist societies. Of all the utopian experiments discussed in this book so far, I know that communal ownership and income sharing may be the least appealing, particularly for more mature readers who may have spent decades in the dogged pursuit of some semblance of financial stability.

I also understand that economic independence can be very empowering because it opens up a more diverse set of life choices, especially for women in countries with minimal social safety nets. But it's important to recognize the depth and diversity of different historical critiques of materialism. From Plato to the Buddha, from the Bible to *The Communist Manifesto*, many philosophical traditions, religious teachings, and political movements have pointed to our collective obsession with possessions as the root of our discord, division, and discontent. Learning about ecovillages and intentional communities might help us all better reflect on our own attitudes to property and the role it plays in determining the character and quality of our interpersonal relationships.

And you don't have to run off to a commune to make a difference. There are plenty of ways to "resist in place," to borrow a phrase from the artist Jenny Odell.[58] Even small steps can help us build stronger communities, lighten our carbon footprints, and reduce the lingering effects of patriarchal property relations in our domestic lives. Many utopian groups have experimented with setting up "free stores," where people can drop off goods they no longer need, to be shared freely with their communities. Once organized by anarchists in San Francisco in the 1960s, free stores were staffed by volunteers and thrived as alternative spaces long before the online freecycling networks that exist today. Across the United States, there are also tens of thousands of "Little Free Library" boxes planted in people's front yards, where neighbors share their books.[59] Many of our communities already have public libraries that provide collective access to books, music, movies,

Figure 5.3. Free book exchange in Pennsylvania.

games, computer stations, Wi-Fi, heat, and air-conditioning. Why not expand these practices to include toy libraries or tool libraries? We could have shared pools of kitchen items or landscaping equipment.

In some ways we already see steps being taken in this direction by start-ups in the so-called sharing economy; businesses like Zipcar, Citi Bike, HomeExchange, and Rent the Runway are finding ways to monetize either our desire to have less stuff or, more cynically, our inability to afford all of the stuff we want on our shrinking incomes in the precarious gig economy. But to the extent that young people avail themselves of these new services, they are accustoming themselves to the idea that property can be shared in common even if, for now at least, that sharing must be mediated by a for-profit company. The sharing economy may normalize communal property in otherwise competitive societies obsessed with material accumulation.

Of course, there will always be a high social cost associated with living outside of the mainstream, and of organizing our private lives in ways that flaunt the expectations of our parents, friends, colleagues, and neighbors. It's hard to be different. But if it turns out that many of us would live less stressful, healthier, more equitable, and sustainable lives in communal domestic arrangements or in sharing our resources with others, why has there been so much resistance to these forms of being in the world over the millennia? Could there be one last institution in our societies that stands in the way?

Many utopian thinkers, beginning with Plato, seemed to believe so. This institution makes it feel natural to share my clothes with my own daughter but not with anyone else. This institution perpetuates patrilineality and walls us off from our neighbors and friends. This institution renders it difficult to raise our children in common or reimagine our schools as more than crass sorting mechanisms that might give our own kids an advantage over others. To unfetter our imaginations and consider ways we can bring different utopian visions into our everyday lives, we must think critically about the role of the nuclear family.

CHAPTER 6

Shall I Compare Thee to a Violent Ape?

Why Our Families Are Nuclear

Ihail from a long line of complicated families. My great-great-grandmother was a young widow from the Balearic Islands in Spain who settled on a small farm in Puerto Rico. She ventured alone to the island, then a Spanish colony, where she gave birth to my great-grandfather Gregorio, who grew up to fight in the Spanish-American War of 1898. Gregorio married, and he and his wife, Rosa, took over the farm and had fourteen children together. My grandmother Cristina was number twelve. Born in 1927, she grew up subsistence farming with her extended family during the Great Depression. When my great-uncles were drafted away to fight in World War II, my grandmother and her sisters worked hard to keep the farm going, but one by one they married and moved away to follow their husbands.

On April 7, 1946, Cristina boarded a Trans Caribbean Douglas DC-4 propeller-driven airplane in San Juan. She was nineteen years old and owned exactly one pair of shoes when she landed in Nueva York. A skilled seamstress, she immediately found work in the city's booming garment industry. A year later, she was pregnant with my mom and married to a notorious philanderer who had already fathered four children with four different women. Within a few years, her husband abandoned her to care for the child alone.

Far from home, my grandmother first sent my mom, Josephine, to live with her family in Puerto Rico. When Josephine turned five, she returned to New York, but my grandmother struggled to arrange care for her. A lifelong Catholic, Cristina decided to send Josephine to board at St. Lucy's School in Newark, New Jersey. The Baptistine nuns who ran St. Lucy's became young Josephine's surrogate parents. They cared for her for eight full years. She received only sporadic weekend visits from my grandmother, who often couldn't afford the combined subway and bus fare from Washington Heights.

When Josephine aged out of St. Lucy's, she finally moved in with her mom to attend high school. My grandmother was paranoid and wildly overprotective, since Josephine knew little of the real world. Cristina hoped my mother would get married and settle down with a nice husband who could support her. Josephine met my father, a recent immigrant to the United States, at Roseland Dance City in October 1968. They went on a few dates under the watchful eyes of my mom's chaperone, and two months later, they got married. She was nineteen and he was thirty.

Figure 6.1. My parents' first wedding day.

Josephine moved to California with my father in January of 1969. They lived together for almost six months before he admitted that he already had a Brazilian wife and child living in New Jersey. This first marriage invalidated his marriage to my mother. Humiliated and furious, Josephine was planning her return to New York, when she found out that she was pregnant (with me). Fearing her mother's disapproval, Josephine decided to stay. Because it would take six months for my dad to get a divorce in California, my parents moved to Nevada, where it took only six weeks. My father remarried my mother in Las Vegas at the end of her first trimester, his previous family abandoned back east.

But my father's initial deceit proved the least of Josephine's problems. Given the deprivations of her childhood, my mother wanted more than anything else to bring up her own children in a cozy nuclear family, in a nice suburban home with a backyard and shag carpeting and chic French doors. From the outside, my family fit every stereotype of middle-class America, with both of my parents insisting we speak English at home so neither my brother nor I would "sound like immigrants." But those quaint four-bedroom McMansions on the cul-de-sac hide a lot of misery. My mother clung to her fantasies of the 2.3 kids and the two-car garage on the other side of my father's fists.

If Josephine never forgave Cristina for abandoning her to the Baptistine nuns, I harbored a resentment against my own mother for decades. She should have protected herself. She should have protected us. But she felt helpless: "He told me it was my fault, and I started believing it." The few memories I retain from my childhood in San Diego are filled with packed suitcases and tearful taxi rides to the airport, only to have my mom chicken out at the last minute and return home because she didn't want "to break up the family." I don't remember how many times the police came to our house, perhaps summoned by concerned neighbors. I know I called them once. My mom, whose own memories of this era are spotty, now thinks she dialed 911 at least twice: Once when my father pushed my little brother down the stairs. Maybe another time on the second day my brother spent locked away in a closet without food.

Before the mid-1980s, battered women and children received little support. It wasn't until 1984 that California legislation required law enforcement agencies to write up concrete policies and provide training to officers on how to deal with domestic violence. Before that, the police didn't even have the authority to temporarily confiscate a firearm in plain sight when responding to an emergency call for protection from a spouse or to issue a temporary restraining order unless a court was in session. And only after 1985 were police obliged to provide the phone number of a nearby shelter (if there was one) or to give any information about community services or legal protections.[1]

When they did show up at my house, the police always seemed annoyed. They would take my dad outside, talk to him for a while, and then leave. My mom never pressed charges. No matter how bad it got, she knew she couldn't support us on her own and she didn't

Figure 6.2. My nuclear family in 1974.

want to send us away to live with nuns. My grandmother also advised my mom to stay in the marriage; an abusive husband who paid the bills was better than one who ran away. As a Catholic, my mom also considered divorce a sin. The Church taught forgiveness. Josephine was young and my dad could be very charming. "I thought he would stop." "I didn't have a father, and I didn't want my children to grow up without a father." "I was afraid to break up the family."

It was in late 1982 or early '83, neither my mom nor I can remember exactly. I woke at night to hear my parents fighting. I heard shouting, then my mom screaming, then sort of croaking, and then gurgling. I peeked out. My brother's door stood wide open as he stared down at my mother gasping and convulsing on the floor, my father's hands around her throat. I shrieked. My father didn't seem to hear me, but my grandmother, who was visiting us at the time, came flying up the stairs calling down God and Jesus Christ and the Virgin Mary and Mary Magdalene and John the Baptist and the Holy Spirit in high-pitched frenzied Spanish. She threw the full weight of her hefty Puerto Rican body at my father, knocking him off my mom and cursing him as she pointed to me and my brother. No one called the police. Mom wore turtlenecks for weeks afterward, and Grandma Cristina finally let her daughter file for divorce.

Is the Nuclear Family a Mistake?

I recall these incidents with some trepidation; when I was growing up, these weren't the kinds of details you discussed with strangers. I share my own story here only to emphasize that the problems of the family are not merely an abstract theoretical consideration for me, but something I experienced in my own life and something that is still pervasive throughout all of our societies. Although there are more laws against, and far greater awareness of, domestic violence today, the problem persists behind the many closed doors of homes around the world. The lockdowns imposed by COVID-19 exposed the ubiquity of what UN Women called the "Shadow Pandemic," the significant rise in domestic violence when women and children were forced to isolate with abusers in single-family homes.[2] Even before 2019, UN Women estimated that a third of all women globally suffered from physical or sexual violence at the hands of an intimate partner (often called intimate partner violence, or IPV) in their lifetimes. In the United States, the Centers for Disease Control estimated that 25 percent of women and 10 percent of men were victims of IPV in 2018 alone.[3] Despite heroic efforts to staff hotlines and build shelters, the black box of the nuclear family can provide cover for horrendous levels of abuse and neglect.

Even in the absence of physical violence, the idealization of the nuclear family obscures the occasionally crushing demands of parenting. Some adults stumble into parenthood by mistake, but even the most well-meaning mothers and fathers can struggle with the massive responsibility of raising children in a society that provides little support. Since most US states consider child abandonment a felony crime, some parents grow to resent their children, and this is not including the mothers with postpartum depression discussed in chapter 3. To understand the desperation that some mothers and fathers feel, consider what happened in 2008 when the state of Nebraska passed a unique "Safe Haven" law designed to protect children from overwhelmed parents.

"Safe Haven" laws prevent infanticide by allowing new-born babies to be dropped off legally and anonymously, often at hospital emergency rooms. Most states place a thirty-day age limit on the children eligible for surrender, but Amanda McGill Johnson, the Nebraska legislator who proposed her state's new law, deliberately left this limit off. "We'd seen nationally a mother who drowned her kids in a bathtub because she was depressed. And, so, in our minds, why should only infant life be protected?" Johnson told the Canadian Broadcasting Corporation in 2017.[4]

No one was prepared for what happened next. In the 120 days after the law's passage, a total of thirty-five older children, most between the ages of ten and seventeen, were dropped off at hospitals across the state.[5] According to a social worker at one of the hospitals in Omaha, some parents walked their older children in and explained their mental health or behavioral issues before leaving them in the care of the staff. Other parents deposited their kids at the emergency room entrance and drove away. Confused children just wandered into hospitals without identification or money. After four months, the Nebraska legislature added a thirty-day age limit to the Safe Haven law, but the whole incident made people wonder how many mothers and fathers would abandon their children if the law allowed them to do so.[6]

In March 2020, just before the first pandemic lockdowns, the conservative columnist David Brooks caused a commotion with a story in the *Atlantic* called "The Nuclear Family Was a Mistake." Brooks mounted a devastating case against isolated, two-parent families and argued that Americans need to embrace the extended family forms our grandparents and great-grandparents once accepted as normal. "The family structure we've held up as the cultural ideal for the past half century has been a catastrophe for many. It's time to figure out better ways to live together," Brooks wrote.[7] It is not often that I agree with David Brooks, but he put his finger on the fragility of child-rearing arrangements that depend on potentially precarious romantic relationships between parents.

As Brooks quickly discovered by the internet furor his article inspired, questioning the family is still a third rail in contemporary Western culture, particularly in the United States. So smitten are we with the postwar vision of a heterosexual monogamous couple who raise their children in a single-family residence that any number of social ills are often blamed on the "crumbling" of this supposedly venerable institution. As one early example, consider Daniel Patrick Moynihan's 1965 report: "The Negro Family: A Case for National Action," which partially blamed high rates of urban poverty on the lack of two-parent households in Black communities. In addition to combatting racism, Moynihan called for a "national effort" to support "the establishment of a stable Negro family structure."[8]

Millions of federal dollars have been spent on "Healthy Marriage Initiatives," or what the journalist Katherine Boo once called "The Marriage Cure," trying to reduce the prevalence of single motherhood and encouraging the formation of nuclear families.[9] Fifty years after Moynihan's report, proponents continue to point to correlations between the rise in child poverty and the increase in single-parent households to support the idea that the traditional family is best for both children and the economy.[10] In a response to Brooks's article in the *Atlantic*, W. Bradford Wilcox and Hal Boyd, a senior fellow at the conservative Institute for Family Studies, argued that the nuclear family "remains the stablest environment in which to raise children" and that "it takes a village—but of *married* people—to raise the odds that a poor child will have a shot at the American dream."[11] But what if the nuclear family is part of the problem rather than part of the solution?

Before we dive into the next sections, I want to stop and acknowledge that you may feel a bit uneasy about where we're about to go. Readers who have open minds for things like cohousing, collective childcare, or ethical education might draw a firm line at shaking up the family. I know that many of you were raised by decent and loving parents who did their best to nurture and provide despite the challenges. I also understand that the family can shelter us from the hyper-individualistic cruelty of our dog-eat-dog economies; it is often the only place where we receive unconditional and non-transactional love and affection. And for those among us who are already parents—or who wish to become parents in the future—creating this environment of protection and care often gives life a certain meaning and direction, even when we know that this meaning and direction is at least partially rooted in the general societal expectation of parenthood at a particular stage of our lives.

And when it comes to the question of monogamy, many intuitively resist the idea that people can be "polysecure," to borrow the title of psychotherapist Jessica Fern's 2020 book, meaning that we can be securely attached to more than one partner at the same time.[12] Even the anti-religious Mr. "Imagine no possessions" considered himself a very "jealous guy" where his wife, Yoko Ono, was concerned. In his final years, the unconventional John Lennon lived a rather conventional life in a monogamous nuclear family with his wife and son. Vladimir Lenin, too, embraced a traditional domestic arrangement with his wife, Nadezhda Krupskaya, although the couple never had children. And when Lenin's fellow Bolshevik, Alexandra Kollontai, questioned the role of monogamy and the "bourgeois" nuclear family in building the world's first worker's state, he shut her down and insisted that the revolution had more important problems to deal with than the reorganization of intimate life along socialist lines. Utopian thinkers have often faced both ridicule and resistance to their nonconventional ideas about love and sexuality because people find it difficult to consider these topics dispassionately.

I get it. I understand the resistance. You might think that the nuclear family is *natural*: either the inevitable outcome of our evolution, or the obviously best way of doing things, or even divinely commanded. Despite the difficulties of my own childhood, I, too, grew up believing that two parents with their kids in a nice suburban house was the ideal. But even loving, stable nuclear families still strain under the stress of all they are expected to be and do for each other. This is why I'm going to take two chapters to build a case for why we will all be better off if we open ourselves up to dreams for reimagining the nuclear family, beginning with a dive into our prehistory to explore how and why the nuclear family may have evolved, before proceeding on to a brief overview of creative alternatives.

Those who tout the nuclear family as the "stablest environment" for raising the next generation lack imagination; more important, they seem to assume that certain features of our societal structures are fixed and unchangeable. The modern nuclear family coexists with atomistic, individualistic societies defined by drastic inequalities in wealth and well-being as well as increasing levels of precarity and fewer social safety nets. The question I want to explore in the next two chapters is how a different set of underlying circumstances might change what we consider to be the "stablest environment" for creating happy families.

Utopian family abolitionists often mean different things by the word "abolition," and I choose not to use this word because it causes confusion and puts people on the defensive. It sounds to some like a nefarious state shall swoop in and declare the family illegal. Others might bristle at the equivalence of "family" and "slavery" that the use of the term "abolitionism" implies. Rather than family abolition, I explore visions of family expansionism that allow us to each arrange our domestic lives free from the meddling of state or religious authorities. This is ultimately a utopian call for a world in which we can choose our own definitions of family; to liberate the concept of "family" from the stranglehold of millennia worth of dogma and crass social engineering.

The Evolutionary Lessons of Chimpanzee Testes

Throughout history, people have believed that the specific ways they organize their private lives reflect the way that human private lives *have always been organized*. But within the scholarly worlds of history, anthropology, archaeogenetics, psychology, and evolutionary biology, a broad consensus suggests that there is nothing inevitable about the traditional picture of the nuclear family consisting of a monogamous pair who provides virtually all of the care and resources for their biological offspring. This vision of nuclear family as a solo economic, social, and parenting unit is a relatively recent invention.

Surveys of our evolutionary ancestors reveals that biparental care—where the two biological parents raise the children—is far from universal. When we look at currently existing nonhuman primates, we also find a spectrum from independent to cooperative rearing of offspring. At one pole sit the orangutans and chimpanzees, where mothers display extreme possessiveness toward their young, shunning all attempts by other group members to take or carry their infant after birth. At the opposite pole sit marmosets and tamarin monkeys. According to anthropologists and primatologists Sarah Blaffer Hrdy at the University of California at Davis and Judith M. Burkart and Carel P. van Schaik at the University of Zurich, these primate "mothers voluntarily permit access to their infants and many group members are actively engaged in active care and provisioning of infants, thereby increasing their growth and survival."[13]

This variety among our distant cousins doesn't tell us where our direct evolutionary ancestors lay on this spectrum, but it's worth noting that humans differ from other primates in a number of key respects that would make the cooperative rearing of young even more beneficial. First, humans have shorter birth intervals than other primates (that is they have their children much closer together and so often have multiple children of different ages to look after at the same time), which makes it likely that older children helped their mothers look after their younger brothers and sisters.[14] Second, unlike other primates, human infants are essentially born premature and require intensive care and nurturance over an extended time. The archaeological and anthropological evidence indicates that our human ancestors solved this problem through cooperative breeding, meaning that human young were tended to by other providers, often kin, but not always.[15]

This history of alloparental care makes sense when you consider that human females have a uniquely long postmenopausal life expectancy, something not true of any other primate species.[16] Post-fertile women are usually grandmothers who help their daughters raise the subsequent generation. Hrdy, Burkart, and van Schaik even propose that, "Engaging in routine allomaternal care and provisioning was the impetus behind the emergence of prosocial dispositions and thus, eventually, uniquely human cognition."[17] In other words, the practice of cooperative breeding among our early hominin ancestors (that is, the group that includes modern humans, now extinct human species like the Neanderthals, and all our immediate forebears) may be responsible for our unique capacity for social collaboration. This then evolved into language, cultural intelligence, religious belief, and eventually the ability to organize complex nation-states.[18] The cooperative care of highly dependent human infants born in rapid succession may have determined a big part of what made humans human.

Anthropologists, primatologists, and biologists have also gathered interesting evidence from the study of nonhuman primates around the evolutionary origins of monogamy.[19] Here we see a variety of models for what we might call ape families, with two extremes being most notable. On one side we have the gorillas, who are generally polygynous:

one alpha male keeps a harem of females. As male gorillas mature, they can stay in their own natal group and hope to replace the alpha male, or they can strike out on their own and try to lure females away from another alpha male. If a young male succeeds in acquiring a harem of females, his first action as a new alpha will often be to kill the babies of the old alpha. The murder of their infants makes the females fertile again, because, as with humans, breastfeeding suppresses fertility for some period of time. The new alpha male can then ensure that all new infants born will have his genes, which gives him an evolutionary advantage. In contrast, having her offspring killed is not ideal from the evolutionary standpoint of the female gorillas, so females will attempt to choose the strongest male they can find as a mate to protect their young from infanticide. If females have an incentive to breed with the biggest and strongest males, genes for size and strength will be selected for over time, causing high levels of sexual dimorphism (in this case, the much bigger body size of males relative to females): exactly what we find in gorillas where males are literally twice the size of the females.

At the other extreme, chimpanzees mate in large groups with many males and many females, and female chimpanzees mate with multiple sequential males during ovulation. Infanticide is discouraged by multiple mating, since males may be less inclined to kill babies that might be their own.[20] There also exists little evolutionary advantage for females to seek out the biggest and strongest males, so genes for size are not selected for over time, and male and female chimpanzees are generally the same size. But chimpanzee males can gain an evolutionary advantage in a different way. With multiple mating, the sperm of rival males competes to fertilize the eggs, and the more sperm an individual male produces the better the chance of fertilization. Since larger testes produce more sperm, males with large testes are selected for over time. And we can see the results, for a single chimpanzee testis is almost as large as a chimpanzee brain! By contrast, gorilla testes are tiny in relation to their body size.

Neither the gorillas nor the chimpanzees are monogamous, since the gorillas have a polygynous harem and the chimps are, by human terms, promiscuous. In fact, sexual monogamy is relatively rare among nonhuman primates. The anthropologist Christopher Opie and his colleagues in psychology and evolutionary biology argue that, where monogamy has evolved, it did so specifically as a response to the risk of male violence and infanticide.[21] The family of apes called gibbons, for example, form relatively monogamous pairs and raise their infants away from other males and females. In effect, the male guarantees the paternity of his mate's offspring by removing her from the presence of other gibbons, and she accepts this exclusive coupling to ensure safety for her babies from potentially murderous rival males. Without the support of her wider alloparental network, the female then relies much more heavily on the male to help provide for the offspring. Whereas non-monogamous primate females have developed a variety of strategies to protect their young from infanticide, including forming protective groups with other mothers, females among the monogamous primates rely primarily on fathers to help protect and provision their young.

Some scholars dispute the idea that monogamy emerged as a response to male infanticide. They argue instead that monogamy in primates evolved because of either the fitness advantages of biparental care or because of the tendency of fertile females to range over a larger territory, which makes it more difficult for a male to guard more than one female at a time.[22] But by correlating a range of behavioral traits against the evolution of monogamy in 230 primate species, Opie and his colleagues insist that the risk of male infanticide came first. They assert that paternal care and dispersed female ranging emerged as "secondary responses to . . . the appearance of monogamy,"[23] whereas "it was only infanticide that reliably preceded monogamy [in primates] and could therefore be implicated in its evolution."[24]

So, what about humans? Gorillas, chimpanzees, and gibbons are our distant cousins, but what were the mating practices of our more direct evolutionary ancestors? Unfortunately, we don't really know for sure, for the empirical data is sparse and points in different directions.[25] Human males are generally bigger than human females, but not by that much; that is to say, sexual dimorphism in humans is relatively small. This suggests that our evolutionary ancestors probably didn't live in gorilla-type harems with one alpha male, although there must have been some male-male competition and some female choice. If Christopher Opie and his colleagues are correct about the evolutionary origins of monogamy in nonhuman primates, then the threat of male infanticide may also have triggered a proclivity toward monogamy among humans as well. In the face of male violence, mothers may have traded sexual fidelity for protection of their young. Fathers then offer the exclusive investment of their resources to help raise the offspring they sired, but must isolate the mothers in order to guarantee paternity.

But are humans "naturally" monogamous? Human male testes are not nearly so big as chimpanzee testes, even in absolute terms, let alone in comparison to the size of their bodies. On the other hand, human testes are larger than gorilla testes, again, even in absolute terms. This suggests that although our ancestors did not mate like promiscuous chimpanzees, there was some level of multiple mating going on. In the absence of exclusive paternal investments, cooperative breeding would have been essential for human survival as one mother alone cannot possibly meet the caloric needs of multiple offspring. The anthropologists Karen Kramer and Andrew F. Russell provide evidence which suggests that early humans were breeding cooperatively before the advent of monogamy tipped the scales in favor of biparental care. This means that monogamy evolved in response to a specific set of circumstances, and that these circumstances did not equally affect all human populations.[26]

Unlike different species of other primates, humans have maintained a remarkable flexibility throughout our evolutionary history. This is why we find such a diversity of mating practices and marriage customs around the world.[27] Human males—today, as in millennia past—have a competing set of strategies to maximize their fitness. They can impregnate as many females as possible, hope that rival males do not harm their offspring, and trust that others will help the mother feed and care for the children. Generally speaking, if he takes the playboy route, a father will invest few of his own resources in raising his children because he cannot assure his paternity. Instead, fathers rely on the resources and care provided by the mother and her alloparental network. Quantity over quality. Alternatively, would-be papas can choose to stay with one female, investing his time and resources to ensure the survival of only a few children, which he assumes to be biologically his own. Quality over quantity.

These different male strategies allow for a variety of mating practices. In human societies where there is less monogamy and paternity is not guaranteed, such as among the matriarchal Mosuo, who practice "walking marriage" as discussed in chapter 1, human females live nearer to their maternal kin, and human males invest their energy and resources in their sister's children—who carry 25 percent of their DNA. In these societies the role of *maternal uncle* is much more revered than the role of father. Heterosexual relationships can begin and end without any detrimental effects on the children because of the persistence of cooperative breeding. These societies tend to be more matrilocal and matrilineal.

But fathers enhance their reproductive fitness when they invest in their own biological children, which carry 50 percent of their DNA, rather than the 25 percent they share with their sisters' children as uncles. In societies where strict codes of sexual fidelity or female sequestration inhibit women from having extramarital partners, males redirect their energies away from their nieces and nephews and toward their own offspring. But this second strategy requires greater policing of female sexuality. The desire to ensure paternity can, in many cases, lead to the isolation of females from their maternal kin. As females are cut off from access to wider alloparental networks, often by being physically separated from others by the walls of a dwelling, they rely increasingly on the resources provided by their sexual partners. There may be a move away from cooperative breeding and toward exclusive maternal or biparental care.

But these changes are not universal. Persistent shortages of men due to warfare could encourage polygyny (one husband with more than one wife), just as a paucity of potential brides or a scarcity of resources might lead to polyandry (one wife with more than one husband). In some Himalayan cultures, where arable land is limited and resources are scarce, a woman having multiple husbands works as a natural form of birth control, which keeps populations necessarily small.[28] Among the Indigenous tribes of the Amazon, some assign what is called "partible paternity" to a woman's sexual partners. This means that children have multiple fathers to help with protection and provisioning in case any one of them dies.[29] A key question is to understand why some human populations moved more in the direction of monogamy and biparental care while others persisted with mating practices that allowed for the preservation of cooperative breeding.

Though the evolutionary picture is murky and contested, a general outline comes into view. Our ancestors were by no means always monogamous. Where monogamy did evolve, it may have done so for darker reasons than you'd expect. The nuclear family is not evolutionarily inevitable. Our contemporary mating practices are not "natural" or "unnatural," "right" or "wrong." Instead, the diversity, flexibility, and creativity around how we love, lust, marry, and raise our young has allowed humans to adapt and change over our evolutionary history. Family forms can respond to different demographic, environmental, or economic contexts, leading researchers on the evolution of human family forms to conclude that: "The cross-cultural empirical record supports that the family is a highly flexible social organization that is transiently, culturally and ecologically adaptable, a dynamic less transparent from traditional positions on patrilocality, patrilineality, and male parental care."[30]

The Many Great-Grandsons of Genghis Khan

From a historical perspective, we also know that many cultures favored polygamy over monogamy, especially for political elites. We know, for instance, that polygyny was deemed normal in the books of the Old Testament. God tells Moses that if a man "marries another woman, he must not deprive the first one of her food, clothing and marital rights," suggesting it was perfectly fine to take more than one wife, so long as you still took care of the first one.[31] King Solomon was said to have had "seven hundred wives of royal birth and three hundred concubines."[32]

While we might doubt the historical accuracy of scriptural reports about people like Solomon, we have more concrete evidence concerning other polygynous men. In 2003, a shocking article in the *American Journal of Human Genetics* announced that sixteen million men, or about one out of every two hundred men on the planet, were the direct descendants of Genghis Khan. The Mongol leader supposedly had six wives and over five hundred concubines, and the researchers found traces of his Y-chromosomal lineage in 8 percent of the men living in sixteen different populations distributed across a massive geographic territory delimited by the Caspian Sea in the west and the Pacific Ocean in the east.[33]

The Ottoman sultans, too, were famed for their concubines; the harem at Topkapi Palace in Istanbul has over three hundred rooms. In the nineteenth century, Joseph Smith, the founder of the Church of Jesus Christ of Latter-day Saints, married more than thirty women, and his successor, Brigham Young, had over fifty wives.[34] More recently, a man named Ziona Chana died in northeast India in June of 2021, leaving behind what was considered "the world's largest family."[35] Chana had thirty-nine wives, ninety-four children, and thirty-three grandchildren, for a total of 166 family members at the time of his death at the age of seventy-six. Such large numbers of wives are wildly out of proportion with anything we see in the polygyny of our evolutionary cousins. Gorillas, for example, tend to have three to six females in their harems.

Polygamy is also still practiced by consenting adults in cultures around the world, either formally, where it is legal, or informally, where it is banned. After an examination of international census data between 2010 and 2018, the Pew Research Center found that 11 percent of the population in sub-Saharan Africa lived in a household with more than one wife. In Burkina Faso, 36 percent of households were polygamous. In Mali, the figure was 34 percent. In Nigeria, 28 percent of the total population resided in a polygamous family, although this aggregate figure hid a large disparity between the Muslim population in the north and the Christian population in the south, where monogamy remained the social norm. In countries like Italy or France, where a husband can legally only wed one wife, many men also openly keep mistresses. This is socially acceptable. In 1996, the widow of French president François Mitterrand, Danielle Mitterrand, invited her husband's longtime mistress, Anne Pingeot, to stand beside her at his funeral.[36]

There could be good reasons for a woman to enter into a polygynous marriage, where she is but one of a number of wives. If patriarchal customs ensure that women have few opportunities to support themselves financially, individual women may quite rationally choose to become the second, third, or fourth wife of a rich man (or become his mistress, concubine, or sugar baby) in societies with high levels of wealth inequality. To put it another way: if some males are much wealthier than others, and if a woman cannot survive without being attached to a man, then she might accept a polygamous arrangement where her portion of shared resources from a relatively wealthy male could be greater than having exclusive access to the resources of a relatively poorer one. According to the economist Gary S. Becker, a wide variance in men's ability to provide for their families is a predictor of polygyny, and so polygyny would tend to increase with inequality unless the society enforces monogamy.[37]

Of course, many countries, particularly in the West, do effectively impose monogamy, a social custom that some argue comes to us from ancient Athens.[38] In the cultural world of the Athenians, the protection and perpetuation of the wealth and status of the individual *oikos*, the private household, necessitated the production of legitimate heirs. Young teen girls were married off to their husbands to produce sons who could carry on the father's name and inherit his wealth.[39] In classical monogamy, partners theoretically wed as virgins and had exclusive sexual relations for their entire lives. Divorce was prohibited, and remarriage only permitted after one partner died. In practice, classical monogamy rested on a sexual double standard whereby virginity and

fidelity were required for women, but men continued their sexual relations outside of marriage with concubines, prostitutes, or enslaved
people.

Still, Greek men of all social classes were only allowed one legal
wife. Some scholars believe that monogamous marriage gave ancient
Athenians a distinct cultural advantage over the contemporaneous societies surrounding Greece that allowed for polygyny.[40] The argument
runs like this: because polygynous societies create a class of bachelors
who may be permanently shut out of the marriage market (even if only
a minority of marriages are polygynous), intra-male competition for
a limited number of potential wives increases. This competition leads
to greater divisions in society. Rather than cooperating, for instance,
in defense of their city, unmarried men might spend their time seeking
to undermine their compatriots as they search for a wife, weaken-
ing their defenses to outside invaders. By enlarging the chances that
each would-be husband could find a wife, the Athenians supposedly
promoted social cohesion and reduced male violence. This may have
provided them an advantage over their more fractious neighbors.

Anthropologist Laura Fortunato offers a different reason for the
rise of monogamy in the West: monogamous marriage ensured the
"monogamous transfer" of a father's resources in areas where "intensive agriculture led to scarcity of land," made worse by the "depletion
in the value of estates through partitioning among multiple heirs."[41] In
other words, because agricultural land becomes less productive when
divided into smaller and smaller plots, monogamy reduced the number of potential heirs by limiting the number of wives a man could
father legitimate children with. The reduced value of divided land also
precipitated the legal practice of primogeniture in many agricultural
societies, whereby the firstborn son of a father inherits a majority or
all of his wealth, even in societies where a husband had more than
one wife, whether simultaneously or in succession. While a handful of
societies practiced ultimogeniture, where the last-born child inherits
the wealth, it was far less prevalent than the practice of primogeniture.

In the Middle Ages, the doctrine of primogeniture often led second
and later sons to join the Church, since they stood to inherit little or

nothing of their father's wealth. If a wealthy firstborn son died without leaving a male heir, his money and properties automatically transferred to his younger brother, and thereby regularly to the Church. This led the historian Laura Betzig to propose that part of the reason the Catholic Church strictly enforced monogamous marriage was to further its own financial interests. The condemnation of polygamous marriage and the prohibition on divorce reduced the chances that a firstborn son would produce a male heir.[42]

Although this did not prohibit extramarital affairs, it did prevent the issue of these affairs from inheriting their father's titles and property. Henry VIII had a son by his mistress, Elizabeth Blount, in 1519, and even recognized him as his son in 1525. But as an "illegitimate" son born out of wedlock, Henry FitzRoy could not be Henry VIII's heir. None other than Martin Luther himself argued that it would be better for Henry VIII to take a second wife than to abandon his first, because the Bible sanctioned polygamy but prohibited divorce.[43] But Henry VIII banished Catherine of Aragon, his wife of twenty-four years, and was willing to dissolve the monasteries, break with papal authority to create the Church of England, and behead his opponents (ahem, thou shalt not kill?), all because he wouldn't dare to marry two women at the same time.

With the Church decisively behind monogamy (despite certain passages in the Old Testament discussed above), the religious ideals and legal structures supporting the expansion of universal monogamy accompanied missionaries as they set out for other continents and hitched a ride with white colonial administrators trying to force Indigenous populations to adapt Western "civilizing" mores. As some non-Western societies endeavored to replicate European social institutions in the hope of emulating their economic success, they also passed laws prohibiting alternative forms of marriage: Japan outlawed polygyny in 1880, China in 1953, India in 1955, and Nepal in 1963. Despite this, data from the 1969 Standard Cross-Cultural Sample, a global survey of preindustrial societies, revealed that 85 percent of those societies still allowed for polygyny. Political and economic elites practiced polygamy, while monogamous marriage remained the norm for most poorer men in society who could not afford more than one wife, if they could afford to have a wife at all.[44]

In North America, the expectation of one husband and one wife defined what the Indigenous scholar Kim TallBear calls "white settler sexuality." According to TallBear, the Dakota people once embraced a fluid sexuality that allowed for multiple partners beyond the bonds of traditional monogamous marriage, similar to the Inuit who seasonally gathered in the winter months to build great meetinghouses, shared their wealth in common, and swapped husbands and wives with others.[45] "As part of efforts to eliminate/assimilate Indigenous peoples into the national body, both the church and the state evangelized marriage, nuclear family, and monogamy," writes TallBear, arguing that Indigenous peoples in North America have endured unrelenting criticisms for their "bad" or "broken" families when they failed to live up to a cultural ideal that was imposed on them from the outside. The full coercive powers of the Canadian and American states upheld the monogamous nuclear family as a key to "civilizing" and "whitening" their Indigenous populations, as evidenced by the residential schools where many Indigenous children were sent.[46]

Legislating Monogamy

Governments can socially impose monogamy in a wide variety of ways. They can require marriage licenses and can refuse to issue more than one (although my own father avoided this particular prohibition by marrying his first wife in New Jersey and his second in New York). States can also provide special social benefits that are specifically favorable to married couples or write tax codes to encourage marriage by financially penalizing single people. But when reviewing the history of monogamy, it's always worth remembering that the American government once viewed non-monogamy as such a threat that it threw people in jail for it.

The members of the Church of Jesus Christ of Latter-day Saints (the Mormons) were white, patriarchal Christians who also rejected the cultural norm of monogamy in nineteenth-century America. In the United States, most of the laws criminalizing non-monogamy result directly from congressional acts and Supreme Court decisions regarding the Mormon practice of "plural marriage," which the Mormons saw as living in accord with the divinely ordained polygynous marital relations of the Old Testament. Although the Mormons claimed that plural marriage enjoyed constitutional protection as the free exercise of religion, the 1878 *Reynolds v. United States* Supreme Court decision found that religious beliefs could not excuse this "crime."[47] "Polygamy," the all-white, all-male Court opined, "has always been odious among the northern and western nations of Europe, and, until the establishment of the Mormon Church, was almost exclusively a feature of the life of Asiatic and of African people."[48]

Following the *Reynolds* decision, President Chester Arthur signed into law the 1882 Edmunds Anti-Polygamy Act, which made plural marriages a felony crime in all federal territories and forbade convicted polygamists from voting, serving on juries, or holding public office.[49] Under this law, over a thousand Mormon husbands were sentenced to prison terms. Despite this, Mormons continued to marry multiple wives, citing the protections of the First Amendment, which allowed citizens to practice their religion as they pleased, so long as they did not contradict public morals or compelling state interests.

But the federal government was committed to stamping out polygamy. In 1885, President Grover Cleveland fulminated against plural marriage in a passionate State of the Union address.[50] After comparing the monogamous mothers of the land ("who rule the nation as they mold the characters and guide the actions of their sons, live according to God's holy ordinances, and each, secure and happy in the exclusive love of the father of her children, sheds the warm light of true womanhood, unperverted and unpolluted, upon all within her pure and wholesome family circle") with the "cheerless, crushed, and unwomanly mothers of polygamy," Cleveland asserted that monogamous husbands were "the best citizens of the Republic." Faced with the growing wealth, power, and influence of the Mormon church, Cleveland sought to establish monogamy as a core precept of American national identity, proclaiming: "The man who, undefiled with plural marriage, is surrounded in his single home with his wife and children has a stake in the country which inspires him with respect for its laws and courage for its defense."[51] Polygamy apparently posed a dire threat to national security.

After a series of ongoing legal challenges, the Supreme Court found against the Mormons in the 1890 *Late Corp. of the Church of Jesus Christ of Latter-Day Saints v. United States.* "The organization of a community for the spread and practice of polygamy is, in a measure, a return to barbarism," the decision read. "It is contrary to the spirit of Christianity, and of the civilization which Christianity has produced in the western world."[52] In 1890, the mainstream Mormon Church abandoned its practice of plural marriage, but some communities remained committed to their Old Testament interpretation and faced felony charges and continued imprisonment. Even cohabitation between one man and more than one woman was illegal under the terms of the now upheld Edmunds Act. It was not until 2020 that Utah finally decriminalized polygamy among fully consenting adults and focused its law enforcement efforts only on those plural marriages that involved coercion, deception, or the betrothal of underage girls.[53] To be clear, I'm not suggesting we model our future families on patriarchal polygamy, but rather emphasizing that it has been a common way of organizing societies across the world, and is no more natural or unnatural than the monogamous nuclear family.

Today, no US state allows polygamy in the sense of giving legal sanction to marriages involving more than two people. But after the 2003 *Lawrence v. Texas* Supreme Court decision guaranteeing the "right to privacy" regarding sexual relations among consenting adults, the state imposition of monogamy (and heterosexuality) has relaxed in the United States (for now). And yet, the idea persists that the monogamous nuclear family is the correct way to organize our private lives. We can see the clearest evidence of the continued power of this cultural ideal when we examine contemporary Western scholarship that advocates for socially imposing universal monogamy on non-Western cultures today.

Angry Bachelors

In 2023, among some segments of the population in the United States, the idea of non-monogamy still feels "contrary to the spirit of Christianity, and of the civilization which Christianity has produced in the western world," as the Supreme Court opined in 1890. It's not just immoral, but also vaguely dangerous. But with few contemporary legal challenges to monogamous marriage, arguments defending the superiority of monogamy mostly find their expression in debates regarding the relative underdevelopment of African and Middle Eastern polygynous societies. In these discussions, we can excavate some of the deeper fears that still inform the resistance to various forms of non-monogamy in the West today, particularly when thinking about the relationship between marriage customs and societal inequality.

These contemporary warnings against the dangers of polygamy take a form that might have seemed familiar to the ancient Greeks. A 2015 article in the *Emory Law Journal* attempting to understand the underlying causes of Islamic terrorism focuses on the social consequences of a society with too many bachelors shut out of the marriage market because high-status men are hoarding wives. "[T]errorist groups understand the threat posed by large numbers of unmarried men," political scientist Rose McDermott and medical social worker Jonathan Cowden write. They argue that one important explanation for high levels of "political violence" in Islamic societies results from the continued practice of polygyny.[54] Their proposed solution to the problem of terrorism is to legislate monogamy.

A 2012 review for *Philosophical Transactions of the Royal Society* surveyed a wide variety of studies that also purportedly demonstrated the many negative social effects of polygyny in countries where the practice remains prevalent, including reduced economic productivity and GDP per capita.[55] Empirical evidence supports the claim that decreases in polygyny can increase women's status in an otherwise patriarchal society, particularly by reducing the spousal age gap. But what these studies really concern is violence, crime, and instability, as well as the poor productivity and political chaos perpetrated on societies by large populations of unmarried men. Anthropologists Joseph Henrich and Robert Boyd together with the biologist Peter J. Richerson argue that, in the aggregate, human societies that legislate universal monogamy benefit from an array of positive outcomes. Controlling for socioeconomic status, Henrich, Boyd, and Richerson show that married men commit fewer crimes and are more productive in economic terms. "Instead of engaging in risky status-seeking endeavours," the authors write, "low-status males would be more likely to marry, thus becoming risk-averse and future-oriented, and focus on providing for their offspring in the long run."[56]

But there's also another ugly possibility: that the "low status males" would just transfer the violence they would otherwise have perpetuated on society onto their wives and children. A relative reduction of crime in the public sphere may result in a concomitant increase of violence in the private sphere, which is exactly what happened in many countries during the COVID-19 lockdowns: as assaults and robberies declined, intimate partner violence skyrocketed.[57] Socially imposed monogamy may just hide the problem behind closed doors, and too often, women and children can become the sacrificial lambs. Having a wife and children may make a man more risk averse (and evidence suggests that it reduces his testosterone levels), but it does not automatically increase a man's social standing.[58] My own father (who died over twenty years ago) was a status-obsessed immigrant driven to acquire all of the material accoutrements of success. He was often frustrated and angered by his circumstances, and I sometimes wonder what violence he might have unleashed on others if he didn't have an outlet at home. "He never did it in front of other people," my mom says. "He only did it when no one else could see."

It may also be that the relative prevalence of polygamy correlates with male violence but is not its primary cause. The view that monogamy "solves" male violence assumes that male violence is somehow inevitable and not a specific response to other societal factors—such as an underlying culture of patriarchy or economic inequality—which could be changed in other ways.[59] In a thirty-year survey of studies trying to understand the significant gap in life expectancy between members of different social classes, epidemiologists Richard Wilkinson and Kate Pickett noted that homicide rates increase with greater levels of income inequality.[60] A different 2002 study on the relationship between "Inequality and Violent Crime" examined homicide rates for thirty-nine countries and robberies in thirty-seven countries. The authors found that both within and between countries, crime rates are positively correlated with inequality, and that "this correlation reflects causation from inequality to crime rates, even after controlling for other crime determinants."[61] In 2018, the *Economist* magazine charted "the stark relationship between income inequality and crime,"[62] and in 2021, a scholarly paper in *Nature* modeled how increases in income inequality quickly undermine social cohesion by increasing the potential rewards of criminal activity for those who have fallen beneath a certain "desperation threshold."[63] These and many other studies suggest that economic inequality may be a crucial factor driving increases in societal violence, as so well observed in Eastern Europe after the collapse of state socialism in the 1990s.[64]

We also know that men are responsible for the vast majority of violent crimes. In 2019, the United Nations reported that men commit 90 percent of homicides worldwide.[65] As a result, growing social disparities may effect men in ways that are particularly dangerous for the communities in which they live. But rather than attempting to rectify the economic factors which drive increased violence, proponents of the monogamous nuclear family propose that the social institutions that regulate the private lives of *all* members of a society must be primarily organized to suppress or eradicate the apparently ever-present threat of angry bachelors who might be inclined to challenge the status quo. It's possible that the monogamous nuclear family, governed by the twin traditions of patrilocality and patrilineality, developed as a specific adaptation to the needs of unequal societies where a small group of elite men wished to protect their disproportionate wealth both from external invaders and internal revolutionaries.

In other words, if the evolutionary biologists, psychologists, economists, and anthropologists are correct, the world we inhabit today may be at least partially an adaptation to the destabilizing effects of status competition in unequal societies. The social, emotional, and physical isolation that characterizes modern family life is perhaps a specific response to the ubiquity of male violence, and the desire of wealthier "high status" men to control the threat of that violence from the "low status" men that they exploit. If this is the case, then socially imposed universal monogamy requires all members of society to organize their private lives so that one group can be placated out of misbehaving. It is a Band-Aid for the much deeper wounds of patriarchy and inequality.

And there is another issue directly related to women's roles in society. As women become economically independent enough to remain unmarried, as is so well-documented in Rebecca Traister's 2016 book, *All the Single Ladies*, should we also expect a rise in violence committed by "excess" males?[66] And will women be blamed for this: lesbian and bisexual couples demonized on religious grounds, single mothers criticized for raising their kids in "broken homes," and women who freely choose to remain unattached vilified as selfish spinsters? Would these various forms of social shaming reduce opportunities for women to freely choose their own paths in life? Can we also expect growing attempts to roll back women's rights, the passage of new laws to reverse or further constrain their reproductive freedoms (such as the 2022 reversal of *Roe v. Wade* in the United States), or new policies or cultural messages encouraging them to stay home as dependent wives? For those who fret about the socially destabilizing violence of too many unhappy bachelors, don't single independent women with full bodily autonomy pose as much a threat as wife-hoarding polygynous men?

For millennia, women and girls—*who are not the source of the problem*—have been cut off from their kin networks; bartered, traded, or sold; rendered dependent on their fathers and husbands by legal codes and religious injunctions depriving them of opportunities to support themselves; and prevented from exercising basic control over their own bodies, so that one class of men can hoard resources that might otherwise be shared. Once these underlying dynamics are exposed, it is only reasonable to begin wondering whether there might be a better way of doing things. This is why utopians have long considered the nuclear family an important site for challenging the political and economic structures that produce status and resource hierarchies in the first place. It is to their alternative visions of domesticity that we now turn.

CHAPTER 7

You and Me and Baby Makes Misery

Expanding Our Networks of Love and Care

The economic fallout of my parents' divorce was devastating. My father fled the country and stranded my mom with two kids and three mortgages on our suburban San Diego abode. He also skipped out on massive credit card bills, for which debt collectors harassed my mom for years trying to find him. Without child support or alimony, Mom struggled to keep us afloat. Both she and I had multiple jobs: my first a paper route I did on roller skates at fourteen. With my maternal extended family in New York or Puerto Rico, my mother had little assistance beyond the heroic efforts of my grandmother. When conditions deteriorated further, I left home in March of my senior year of high school. Alone, and with about sixty bucks in my pocket, I made my way to the Greyhound station downtown, contemplating the long-distance bus schedules for the next day. But I needed a place to crash for the night, so I found a pay phone and dialed my English teacher.

I had my first class with Mrs. Betty Olson at Marston Middle School in 1983 and when she transferred to teach at Clairemont High School I had her again for freshman English when I was fourteen. Mrs. Olson loved Shakespeare and introduced me to the diverse pleasures of the Bard by lending me her unabridged vinyl audio recordings of *Twelfth Night*, *As You Like It*, and *Romeo and Juliet*. She also encouraged her students to write weekly "reaction papers," granting extra credit for reflecting on the world around us through the prism of the books we read for class. In the first year after my parents' divorce, as I returned home daily to a near-empty refrigerator; a hungry, angry younger brother; and a stressed, depressed, and overworked mother, I poured much of my teenage angst onto the pages of Mrs. Olson's assignments.

Just before my fifteenth birthday, I transferred into a special magnet program, and the following academic year, Mrs. Olson became that program's codirector. Because we didn't have scheduled classes and studied independently, I had many opportunities to work with her on various projects, especially on extended writing assignments. In the fall of my final year of high school, it was Mrs. Olson who asked me, "So where are you thinking of applying?"

When I rattled off a list of different employment possibilities, she marched me straight into the career center to meet with a guidance counselor, who convinced me that I would qualify for financial aid if I wanted to go to college. I decided to apply to exactly one school— the University of California at Santa Cruz—because I thought it was funny that their mascot was the banana slug. Mrs. Olson gave me her home phone number and promised she would help me with my application. She paid for my SAT exam. She read multiple drafts of my admissions essay, helped me organize my letters of recommendation, and even paid the postage on the envelope I sent in just days before the deadline. And it was Mrs. Olson who pulled herself out of bed and drove to the Greyhound station at around eleven o'clock one night in the spring of 1988.

Until I left for Northern California in September, I lived with Betty Olson and her husband, Thomas Paul, a retired naval hospital corpsman and a consummate talk radio addict. With their children grown and gone, the Olsons opened their home to me, caring for me like one of their own. Mrs. Olson took me to my first professional plays: *A Midsummer Night's Dream* in the round at the Old Globe theater in Balboa Park and Anton Chekhov's *The Seagull* at the La Jolla Playhouse, and encouraged me to read books by Isabel Allende and Gabriel García Márquez, sparking a new love for Latin-American magical realism. She bought me a blue satin dress and some rhinestone jewelry for my senior prom. But most important, the Olsons never fought, never raised their voices, and never once made me feel unwanted, unwelcomed, or unloved. "All happy families are alike; each unhappy family is unhappy in its own way," is the first line of Tolstoy's *Anna Karenina*. But I never even understood the concept of a happy family until the Olsons took me in.

And yet, the Olsons were *not* my family. To this day, I marvel at their generosity and kindness; they were probably the two most influential adults in determining the course my life would subsequently take. I don't know what would have happened to me if I had taken that Greyhound bus, or not gone to university, or never learned that all families were not as violent and miserable as mine. How many kids, I often wonder, are still trapped between unhappy parents in dysfunctional marriages worried about "breaking up the family"? How much safer, healthier, and more connected would we all feel if we could accept a plurality of family forms because we lived in a more equitable world? We could be raising our children cooperatively in dwellings designed to enhance rather than inhibit social connections. We could be more sustainably sharing our resources and teaching our children to value collaboration over competition. We could be living in wider lateral networks of love, care, and support, fighting the scourges of loneliness, anxiety, precarity, and the many stresses associated with modern life. Most of us are not.

Now that we've explored a broad outline of how we got to the monogamous nuclear family, we're ready to start examining the challenges being mounted against it. Even though it is clearly breaking down in the face of the changing social and economic demands of the twenty-first century, it remains a powerful ideal and has many fierce defenders among traditionalists. To understand its persistence, we have to ask ourselves some uncomfortable questions: Are we still perpetuating the monogamous nuclear family out of the illusion that biparental care is optimal, out of the fear of potential male violence or the perceived need for male resources, or because our religious traditions and state institutions define it as "normal"? Are we clinging to an outdated model of the family that served specific economic purposes because we are on autopilot? Or because we feel uncomfortable deviating from society's expectations of how we should or shouldn't arrange our most intimate lives? And what would a better kind of family look like anyway?

The Real Housewives of Ancient Sparta

As with so many other utopian ideas for reimagining the private sphere, we once again begin with Plato. In the *Republic*, he openly advocates for group marriage and communal child-rearing among his auxiliaries and philosopher-rulers: "All these women should be shared among all the men, that no individual woman and man should live together, and that the children, too, should be shared, with no parent knowing its own offspring, and no child its parent."[1] Monogamy may have made the ordinary Athenians more cooperative by reducing male-male competition for potential wives, but the private, insular nature of the *oikos* undermined the social cooperation and selflessness that Plato desired for Kallipolis's Guardians.

In his text, Plato takes pains to describe in detail how his arrangement would work in practice. The ruling elites of Kallipolis would have huge mating festivals on a scheduled basis, where men and women would be coupled ostensibly by lottery. All children conceived at a particular mating festival and born around the same time nine months later, would be considered brothers and sisters to each other, and all men and women who participated in the festival would be their collective mothers and fathers (and later their collective grandmothers and grandfathers). To avoid incest, there would be strict prohibitions on sexual relations between all members of the mothers' and fathers' generation with their collective sons and daughters. Behind the scenes, secret matchmakers would also be deciding which men and women should mate to produce the healthiest children possible, and how often which people could mate, since Plato unfortunately shared the eugenicist views of most of his ancient Greek contemporaries.

Plato comes close to suggesting the nationalization of women, although he also nationalizes men, since he clearly states that the reproductive capacities of both sexes must serve the larger goals of the Republic. Plato proposes that women will participate in these "lottery-based" festivals for twenty years, from the age of twenty to forty. A man would take part "from the time he passes his prime in swiftness in running to the age of fifty-five."[2] After they age out of their respective reproductive primes, both women and men are free to enjoy sexual relations with whomever they choose, so long as their liaisons do not result in pregnancy.[3] Interestingly, Plato's suggestion that women should begin bearing children at the age of twenty was much closer to the social norms of the Spartans than to those of the Athenians at the time. The latter married their daughters off in their early teens. Since Plato wrote the *Republic* after the Athenian defeat in the Peloponnesian Wars, his ruminations about the relative advantages of thinking beyond the *oikos* must have taken some inspiration from the victor's model of organizing familial life.

The Spartans called their elite warrior class the *homoioi* (literally: those who are alike). The aristocratic Spartan boys of the *homoioi* left their families at the age of seven and lived in barracks with other Spartan men until the age of thirty. During this period, they were exempted from all manual labor and trained for warfare, and Sparta's many battlefield successes earned them the reputation as the fiercest warriors in ancient Greece. Although still subject to patriarchal control, the wives of the *homoioi* enjoyed a unique level of power, influence, and sexual freedom compared to other Greek women at the time. *Homoioi* men married late and lived with their families only after the age of thirty, giving wives control of their own households.

Because Spartans prized strong and healthy children, an elderly Spartan husband could allow a younger man whom he admired to sleep with his wife in the belief that she might bear a more robust baby.[4] Men who wanted children but did not wish to marry could also ask the permission of another man to gain temporary access to his wife. Spartan brothers sometimes shared one wife and raised their children in common. Fathers who felt they had sired enough children might also share their wives with close friends or allow their wives to choose new sexual partners. It seems that at least some Spartan women also actively sought out younger males who might give them healthier children.

These polyandrous relations increased women's status in Spartan society. Spartan women could inherit, control, and dispose of wealth and resources on their own initiative, giving them power and influence in the households that they ran. The Athenians often portrayed Spartan women as unfeminine, such as Aristophanes's comic portrayal of Lampito in *Lysistrata* as a sort of country bumpkin figure who is so muscular that Lysistrata suggests she could strangle a bull, or disloyal, as in tales of Helen of Sparta's willing betrayal of her husband to follow Paris to Troy. But the Greek philosopher Plutarch also claimed that the unique family relations among Spartans might free them "from jealousy and possessiveness in their sexual relations by making it honorable for all worthy men to share in the production of offspring."[5]

But where Plato advocated group marriage and collective child-rearing, some religious traditions came to reject family life altogether. When we talk about the nuclear family, many people imagine a binary between monogamy and polygamy/polyamory, but celibacy is as much a challenge to monogamy as any form of plural marriage. Celibacy was rare in the ancient world, and citizens in Greece and Rome faced punitive legislation if they remained unmarried. There were a few notable exceptions for religious figures: Vestal Virgins and the eunuch priests of Cybele, a Near Eastern Great Mother fertility goddess whose castrated priests oversaw ritual orgies in her honor.[6] The Christian embrace of celibacy for laypeople was a definitive break with prevailing customs. As with the ancient Greeks and Romans, the Japanese government expected its men to get married and sire children. Eight years before it outlawed polygyny in emulation of the West, the Meiji government also issued the Nikujiku Saitai Law, which allowed monks to eat meat and marry, specifically to undermine the Buddhist practice of celibacy. As a result, many Japanese Buddhist monks still marry and have families to this day.[7] States can accept low levels of celibacy or voluntary childlessness, but if too many citizens make this choice, it stymies the production of new workers, soldiers, and tax-payers, which is seen as especially problematic in societies like Japan that place a high premium on ethnic homogeneity.

Choosing a celibate life has a deep history in Europe, as we discussed back in chapter 2. When Paul the Apostle wrote the First Epistle to the Corinthians in 53–54 CE, he specifically criticized the institution of marriage. In this letter to the members of the Christian community he founded in Greece, Paul explains that "those who marry will face many troubles in this life."[8] Paul's religious rationale for celibacy is not so different than Plato's rationale for group marriage among the Guardians of Kallipolis—the establishment of private households distracts people from the support of higher causes. "I would like you to be free from concern," Paul writes. "An unmarried man is concerned about the Lord's affairs—how he can please the Lord. But a married man is concerned about the affairs of this world—how he can please his wife—and his interests are divided. An unmarried woman or virgin is concerned about the Lord's affairs: Her aim is to be devoted to the Lord in both body and spirit. But a married woman is concerned about the affairs of this world—how she can please her husband."[9]

The First Epistle to the Corinthians suggests a scriptural basis for the celibacy of Catholic priests and nuns. The Bogomil, Cathar, and Shaker practices of celibacy also linked back to Paul's idea that unmarried people prioritized spiritual affairs over worldly ones. Chastity became a prized cultural ideal for centuries thereafter; those who abstained from sexual relations were considered morally superior to those who could not, in Paul's words, "control themselves" and who he thought "should marry, for it is better to marry than to burn with passion."[10] When you consider that cenobitic monks and nuns live collectively in what could be considered chosen families, and that celibate communities often look after orphans and other abandoned children (like the Baptistine nuns who cared for my mother for eight years), celibates also provide a powerful example of a successful history of nonconsanguineous collective living and cooperative child-rearing.

"The Most Odious of All Monopolies"

Henry VIII's ill-fated Lord Chancellor also provided specific details about how the inhabitants of the island of Utopia arranged their private lives. Although More kept the basic structures of patrilocality that most of his sixteenth-century contemporaries would have considered normal, with women marrying out of their natal homes and joining the households of their husbands, he set a higher minimum age for marriage: eighteen for brides and twenty-two for grooms. More also recounts that among the Utopians no husband may abandon his wife against her will no matter what health problems she may have or develop as she ages, including, presumably, infertility. Utopians lived in large multigenerational households under the authority of the oldest male, and each family had no less than ten members and no more than sixteen. If one household grew beyond sixteen people due to excess fertility, More explains that the Utopians removed "some of the children of a more fruitful couple to any other family that does not abound so much in them," meaning that Utopian families gifted their excess babies to their neighbors.[11]

Mothers worked outside the home and wives fought beside their husbands in times of war, and the Utopians, who shared their wealth in common, raised their children confident that they would be provided for. In More's Utopia, husbands and wives were monogamous, but biparental care was unnecessary because there existed no competition between households. A Utopian father, More writes, "is not afraid of the misery of his children, nor is he contriving how to raise a portion [dowry] for his daughters; but is secure in this, that both he and his wife, his children and grandchildren, to as many generations as he can fancy, will all live both plentifully and happily."[12]

A more equitable distribution of wealth also preoccupied the minds of proto-anarchist and utopian socialist thinkers in the late eighteenth century. Unlike Thomas More, who abolished private property but kept the patriarchal structures of the family, men like William Godwin believed that the abolition of marriage proved an essential precondition for true freedom. In his 1793 text, *Enquiry Concerning Political*

Justice, the father of philosophical anarchism called marriage "the most odious of all monopolies" because it locked husbands and wives into indissoluble bonds for the sake of protecting private property and hereditary privilege. Godwin understood that the liberation of sexuality from the confines of matrimony would undermine men's control over women's bodies, and in his vision, fathers would no longer be concerned about the paternity of their children: "It is aristocracy, self love and family pride that teach us to set a value upon it at present," he wrote.[13] Godwin also proposed that a truly democratic society required the eradication of all surnames. If people only had given names (that is, mononyms), the last vestiges of patrilineality could be eradicated at one stroke, since there would be no mechanism to keep track of which child belonged to which father.

Over in France, the utopian socialist visions of Henri de Saint-Simon, a French businessman and political philosopher with a variety of interests, gained widespread influence across Europe in the 1820s and '30s. Following Saint-Simon's death in 1825, a Frenchman named Barthélemy Prosper Enfantin consolidated the Saint-Simonians around him and founded first a school, then a social movement, and ultimately a Christianity-adjacent religious community. Enfantin rejected the individual as the basic unit of society in favor of a sacred male-female dyad, which reflected the Saint-Simonian view of the dual nature of God: a divine masculine combined with a divine feminine. Rather than just one supreme male representative, Enfantin's theology required a divine couple-pope who would represent God's will on earth. He declared himself the "pope-father" of the community and sent his followers out to find the female messiah who would sit by his side as the "pope-mother." The Saint-Simonians lived together communally in *maisons de famille* (family houses), governed by a Saint-Simonian "brother" and "sister" pair. They also set up cooperative workshops that were co-run by a "director" and a "directress."[14]

Enfantin and his followers promoted peaceful cooperation between social strata over class conflict and violent revolution. Although they allowed for private property, they proposed the abolition of all inheritance. If there was no intergenerational transfer of resources from father to son, the legal bonds of monogamous matrimony that served to ensure paternity would become unnecessary. Without heritable property, both men and women would be free to engage in sexual relations without worrying about the legitimacy or illegitimacy of any children born from their unions. Whereas Plato wanted to abolish the traditional family to prevent men from focusing their efforts on the accumulation of heritable wealth, the Saint-Simonians proposed to do away with inheritance to liberate people from what they considered the oppressive constraints of bourgeois marriage.

Saint-Simonian women also demanded a complete overhaul of the laws regulating familial relations in the French Civil Code. After the Revolution in 1789, French women enjoyed the right to divorce, but this provision was abolished as a repugnant remnant of French Republicanism in 1816, once again trapping women in their marriages. Although not all Saint-Simonian women agreed with Enfantin's ideas about sexual freedom, they did establish an all-woman newspaper in 1832, the *Tribune des femmes*, where they pressed for a return of liberalized divorce laws and debated Saint-Simonian doctrine. They signed their articles and letters with only their first names, an explicit rejection of their fathers' or husbands' surnames (and an effort to preserve some anonymity). According to the historian Clare G. Moses, the newspaper was "likely the first female collective venture in history whose purpose was specifically and exclusively feminist."[15]

Some prominent Saint-Simonian women also attempted to forge lives independent of patriarchal authority by having sex and children out of wedlock. The feminist and utopian socialist Pauline Roland had two partners and four biological children, one of whom died in infancy. (She was also the adoptive mother of Flora Tristan's daughter, Aline, after Tristan's early death.) Her first surviving child resulted from a brief affair of less than six months, but she spent almost fourteen years in a free association with the father of her subsequent children. Each of her three surviving children bore Roland's surname instead of their father's, and she attempted to support them all financially without male support. Another independent Saint Simonian advocate of sexual freedom was Claire Démar, who in her 1883 *Appel d'une femme au peuple sur l'affranchissement de la femme* (Appeal of a Woman to the People on the Enfranchisement of Women) scandalously described marriage as a form of legal prostitution.

A utopian socialist named Suzanne Voilquin divorced her husband to embrace the ideal of free womanhood. She worked as a midwife for the unwed, hoping to win them legal recognition as "real" mothers, and thereby prove them worthy of kindness and support. But French society had no interest in legitimating "bastard" children who might clamor to inherit their fathers' property. Both Roland and Voilquin ended their lives in abject poverty because women's wages in 1830s France were simply not sufficient to support single women, let alone single mothers. After selling all her furniture to support herself while she wrote, Claire Démar took her own life. And after Enfantin and his associates went to prison in 1832 for preaching ideas considered an outrage against public morality, many Saint Simonian communities disbanded or relocated to Egypt in hopes of finding the female messiah there. Harsh economic realities forced the remaining Saint-Simonian feminists to abandon the rhetoric of sexual freedom and their hopes of forging lives independent of men. Instead, they concentrated on the more modest goal of marriage reform, particularly French women's right to divorce and to retain custody of their children.

The trace of utopian socialist ideas about liberating sexual relations from marriage besmirched the reputation of almost all the scientific socialists, communists, and anarchists who followed in their footsteps. When Marx and Engels published *The Communist Manifesto* in 1848, they explicitly addressed the accusation that their desire to liberate women was a necessary precursor to the nationalization of wives. "But you Communists would introduce community of women, screams the bourgeoisie in chorus," Marx and Engels wrote. "The bourgeois sees his wife as a mere instrument of production. He hears that the instruments of production are to be exploited in common, and, naturally, can come to no other conclusion that the lot of being common to all will likewise fall to the women. He has not even a suspicion that the real point aimed at is to do away with the status of women as mere instruments of production."[16] Husbands who viewed their wives as privately owned machines for the manufacture of "legitimate" heirs could not imagine a world in which those "machines" might desire independent lives outside of marriage and motherhood.

The King of the Workers

One man who fully embraced women's capacity for both rational thought and revolutionary activity was the German socialist August Bebel, who also viewed the monogamous nuclear family as a prison that trapped women by making them economically dependent on fathers, husbands, or sons. Born in 1840, Bebel grew up in relative poverty, the child of a widow who struggled to support her family after her husband's death. Bebel cofounded the Social Democratic Party and was elected to the Reichstag when he was only twenty-seven years old. Vladimir Lenin would later describe Bebel as "the most gifted parliamentarian in Europe,

Figure 7.1. A street art portrait of August Bebel in Prenzlauer Berg, Berlin, in 2019.

the most talented organiser and tactician, the most influential leader of international Social-Democracy."[17] Germans called him the "king of the workers" and many families hung his framed portrait in their homes.[18]

In 1871, the German government imprisoned Bebel for high treason, and he spent his four-year sentence writing and reading a wide variety of books, including Plato's *Republic*, Thomas More's *Utopia*, and a history of Thomas Müntzer and the German Peasants' War.[19] Inspired by his study of "French socialistic and communistic Utopias,"[20] Bebel wrote a book that would change the course of history. First published in German in 1879, *Woman Under Socialism* went through more than fifty editions, and was translated into over twenty languages by Bebel's death in 1913, despite being initially banned under Otto von Bismarck's anti-socialist laws. Unlike other men in the labor movement, who viewed women workers as potential competitors, Bebel, following the utopian socialists of France, embraced women as natural allies. Women stood the most to gain from a future where workers' common ownership of industry would allow them to support themselves outside of marriage. "The woman of the future society is socially and economically independent," Bebel wrote, "she is no longer subjected to even a vestige of domination or exploitation, she is free and on a par with man and mistress of her destiny."[21]

Like Flora Tristan and the Saint-Simonians, Bebel attacked marriage and the traditional family, hoping to liberate human sexuality from the stranglehold of the church and state. "The gratification of the sexual instinct is as much a private concern as the satisfaction of any other natural instinct," Bebel wrote. "In choosing the object of her love, woman, like man, is free and unhampered. She woos or is wooed and enters into a union from no considerations other than her own inclinations."[22] And his demand for privacy extended beyond heterosexual relations. As a member of parliament, August Bebel is credited with being the first politician in the world to speak out publicly in favor of gay rights by lobbying in 1898 to repeal the paragraph of the German penal code that criminalized sodomy.[23]

So thorough and shocking was Bebel's attack on the monogamous nuclear family that when the New York Labor News Company published the first American edition of *Woman Under Socialism* in 1904, the translator, Daniel De Leon, a prominent American revolutionary socialist and the cofounder of the Industrial Workers of the World, felt compelled to break with Bebel on this specific point: "I hold that the monogamous family—bruised and wounded in the cruel rough-and-tumble of modern society, where, with few favored exceptions of highest type, male creation is held down, physically, mentally and morally, to the brutalizing level of the brute . . . —will have its wounds staunched, its bruises healed, and, ennobled by the slowly acquired moral forces of conjugal, paternal, and filial affection, bloom under Socialism into a lever of mighty power for the moral and physical elevation of the [human] race."[24]

Note that De Leon only seems concerned with staunching the wounds and healing the bruises of "male creation" (that is, men) through the slowly "acquired moral forces of conjugal, paternal, and filial affection" as embedded in the nuclear family. De Leon understood that European family abolitionism would never fly in the more conservative milieu of the USA. But it would briefly find fertile soils in the first workers' state.

Liberating Romance

Just as Bebel found inspiration in the works of the French utopian socialists, Alexandra Kollontai, who we already met in chapter 3, educated herself by reading the works of thinkers like August Bebel and Friedrich Engels. From her own experience as a young wife and mother, she understood that women's oppression had its roots in the institution that shaped domestic life and the legal structures that subsumed married women under the authority of their husbands. In a 1909 pamphlet, Kollontai wrote: "In the family of today, the structure of which is confirmed by custom and law, woman is oppressed not only as a person but as a wife and mother. In most of the countries of the civilised world the civil code places women in a greater or lesser dependence on her husband and awards the husband not only the right to dispose of her property but also the right of moral and physical dominance over her."[25]

Two of the first administrative decrees after the Russian Revolution liberalized divorce and replaced church marriage with civil marriage. In October 1918, the highest legislative body of the Soviet Union incorporated these decrees into a new family law, which unraveled the thick webs of ecclesiastical control of women's lives. While eliminating church authority over marriage and divorce, Kollontai and the Soviets rejected all legislation that rendered women the property and dependents of their fathers or husbands. They made men and women juridical equals. The new Family Code also did away with the distinction between "legitimate" and "illegitimate" children, making all offspring eligible for the support of their fathers as well as the state. In 1920, the Soviet Union also legalized abortion during the first twelve weeks of pregnancy.[26] Kollontai deliberately targeted the laws, customs, and institutions which upheld patriarchal authority in the home.

As if challenging the Russian Orthodox Church and rewriting the Family Code were not enough, Kollontai followed in the footsteps of the earlier Saint-Simonian feminists and attempted to liberate sexuality from the confines of traditional marriage. In her 1923 essay, "Make Way for Winged Eros: A Letter to Working Youth," Kollontai proposed a new framework for romantic relationships whereby both men and women might enjoy simultaneous connections with partners who met their different emotional, intellectual, or sexual needs. Kollontai's vision hinged on the creation of a new society with strong collective bonds and a dramatic increase in opportunities for state-funded alloparenting through the expansion of kindergartens and children's homes as discussed in chapter 3.

Kollontai proposed that both men and women needed to rethink their relations with romantic partners. Rather than treating significant others as the sole source of affection, validation, emotional support, and sexual satisfaction, Kollontai hoped that young Soviets would collectively evolve beyond the need for socially imposed monogamy once they lived in a more equitable and cooperative society. Kollontai recognized the ubiquity of jealousy and possessiveness that people felt when they fell in love. Kollontai also accepted that infidelity, abandonment, and unrequited love caused people great emotional distress, and that passionate romantic love could drive people to do outrageous things. But she believed that people would be less wounded by betrayal or rejection if they received affection and support from a wider network of colleagues and friends. "The stronger the ties of all members of the collective," Kollontai explained in 1921, "the less the need for the creation of strong marital relations."[27] In other words, unlike the Oneidans who attempted to prohibit exclusive sexual relations between couples, she merely wanted to immerse couples into a sea of robust social relations that could assuage some of the inevitable pains that come with the unpredictability of romantic love.

In Kollontai's ideal, the expansion of safety nets and the socialization of domestic labor would also reduce the stresses of everyday life. She believed that the precarity and selfishness of capitalism made partners cling to each other in unhealthy and unnatural ways. Rather than acting as kindred souls working together toward common goals, couples often demanded exclusive rights to each other's sexual and emotional attentions. "The ideal of the bourgeoisie was the married couple, where the partners complemented each other so completely that they had no need of contact with society. Communist morality demands, on the contrary, that the younger generation be educated in such a way that the personality of the individual is developed to the full, and the individual with his or her many interests has contact with a range of persons of both sexes. Communist morality encourages the development of many and varied bonds of love and friendship among people."[28]

Kollontai advocated for something she called "comradely-love," and hoped that all people would one day be free to interact with their romantic partners as they interacted with their friends. In contrast to political leaders who used the state to advocate for marriage, Kollontai wanted the Soviet state to promote a culture of robust platonic relationships. "Friendship is a more sociable emotion than sexual love," Kollontai once said. "You can have many friends at a time, because there are different strings which vibrate in contact with different people."[29] While Kollontai's ideas about a new sexual morality challenged the traditional mores of the conservative Russian peasantry, urban Soviet youth proved receptive. A 1922 survey of students at one Moscow university found that only 21 percent of young men and 14 percent of young women believed that marriage was the best way to organize one's sexual life.[30]

These changes were unprecedented not only in Russia, but also in Europe and North America. In the West, it would take more than six decades for women to achieve the same rights. But Kollontai faced many obstacles. She never had the full support of her prudish male comrades, who worried, like Daniel De Leon in the United States, that any position against monogamy would alienate male workers. And as in 1830s France, Russian women's wages were simply too paltry to allow them to support their families without a husband. Liberalized divorce laws meant that men disappeared when their lovers got pregnant. The indissolubility of the old marriage ties had the advantage of forcing fathers to pay for the care of their children. The more utopian provisions of the 1918 family law were slowly reversed over the next two decades. But Kollontai's critiques of the monogamous nuclear family would echo across the entire twentieth century, inspiring new generations of activists, who continued to challenge state-imposed definitions of the "normal" family.

South Korean Bihon and Japanese Christmas Cake

If you are reading this book in the mid-2020s, you live in a world vastly different from the one Kollontai inhabited in the 1920s. The invention of the birth control pill and the sexual revolutions of the 1960s and '70s swept away many of the old social restrictions governing love, sex, and marriage. Divorce and single motherhood are less stigmatized, and access to education and work outside the home means that many women can support themselves independent of men. Premarital sex and cohabitation have become more common, and the once-feared state of spinsterhood has become a lifestyle choice even in the most traditionally patriarchal cultures. In South Korea, some young women forswear matrimony altogether, a lifestyle referred to as *bihon*. As one twenty-five-year-old student in Seoul told a reporter for *The Guardian* in early 2021, "I didn't pledge not to get married because there are no good men, but because society dictates that women be in a more disadvantageous position when they enter a relationship."[31] In Japan, where unmarried women over the age of twenty-five are often called "Christmas Cake" (referring to unsold holiday baked goods still on the shelves after December 25), marriage and birth rates have plummeted as more young women embrace singledom. An unmarried, professional Japanese forty-nine-year-old explained to the *New York Times*, "One reason to get married for a woman is to have a stable financial life. I don't have any worries about being alone with myself or any financial worries. So I did not have to chase myself into a corner and choose marriage for financial reasons."[32] This is a world that earlier generations of utopian feminists could scarcely have dreamed of.

The changes that occurred over the hundred-year period that the Romanian-American historian Maria Bucur calls the "Century of Women" required a broad coalition of many different social movements that engaged in pitched struggles to transform the status quo.[33] In the United States, the courts have played their part as well. Since the 1965 *Griswold v. Connecticut* decision, American women have had access to safe and effective contraception. In 1967, the Supreme Court overturned legal prohibitions on interracial marriage in *Loving v. Virginia*, and in 1973, *Roe v. Wade* granted American women reproductive control over their own bodies for almost fifty years before it was overturned in 2022. In *Lawrence v. Texas*, the court struck down an anti-sodomy statute in 2003, over a century after August Bebel advocated for a similar decision on the floor of the Reichstag in 1898. Same-sex couples in England, Wales, and Scotland won the right to marry in 2014, in the United States in 2015, and in Northern Ireland in 2020.

I could go on and discuss the many other struggles fought by various utopian thinkers in the last hundred years, including the pointed critiques of feminists like Shulamith Firestone, who carried the torch of family abolitionism in the 1970s, imagining a future of artificial wombs and parenting collectives that both inspired and outraged her contemporaries. The essential point is that although many feminists continued to identify the nuclear family as a necessary place of political intervention, it continued as an ideal. Despite the progress in allowing people to enjoy more freedom in how they want to arrange their private lives, the idea of two people meeting, falling in love, getting married, getting pregnant, and raising a family together in a single-family home filled with their own private property still dominates our social imagination.

Most people intrinsically link mating practices, like serial monogamy, with child-rearing practices, like the idea that children are best raised in a household with their two biological parents. Although it is now more acceptable to have multiple partners before settling down in the West, the expectation that we *should* all eventually "settle down" with our own spouses and kids profoundly shapes our collective idea of what it means to become a grown-up. Our own parents and older relatives, friends, colleagues, and neighbors may implicitly (or explicitly!) put pressure on us to conform to these norms. Heads shake and crests fall if we deviate from the expected path, and even same-sex couples often reproduce the nuclear family structure by getting married and having kids that they raise together in their suburban abodes. Those committed single women in South Korea and Japan face an onslaught of continued cultural pressures to embrace matrimony and make babies.

While we may maintain capacious networks of friends, colleagues, classmates, and neighbors as young singles, our lateral relationships begin to fall off as we age unless we make a concerted effort to maintain them. It's harder to make new friends in a society where everyone else "settles down." This lack of a wider circle of friends begins to isolate the couple and they become more possessive of each other because each partner now provides a greater portion of the other partner's needs. Sometimes this isolation happens naturally as couples gravitate toward other "couple friends." Then, the busyness of our daily lives makes it harder to get together even with our couple friends and we find ourselves flopped with exhaustion on the couch binging Netflix after finally getting the kids to bed. In some pairs, a partner might prevent the other from enjoying a wider range of social relations— either consciously or unconsciously. One partner might hope to make the other more dependent and committed to the relationship by limiting their contacts with others who might provide social, economic, or psychological support. In other cases, one partner just might not share the same interests or connect well with the other partner's preexisting friends, which might lead to a cooling of those friendships in favor of the relationship or other "couple friends."

The increasing isolation of the parental couple prevents the formation of relationships that would make it easier to raise our children more cooperatively in wider networks of alloparents. People recognized the inherent weakness of the biparental model during the COVID-19 lockdowns when they hastily formed "pandemic pods" with other parents to share childcare and homeschooling responsibilities. Outside of these exceptional circumstances, most kids are still raised and provided for by one or two parents. But what if we could somehow separate out our mating practices from our child-rearing practices to think creatively about how we might arrange our private lives to maximize the amount of love, care, and support both we and our children could enjoy?

Chosen Families

As many utopian thinkers over the last two millennia have suggested, the way we arrange our family lives has profound political consequences, and one way to challenge a particular political system is to reimagine the fundamental institutions that underpin it. Across the world today, in pockets of resistance and creativity, a wide range of individuals and groups from all points on the political spectrum are pushing back against the family form that we inherited from the ancient Greeks and that centuries of religious and state authorities have imposed and defended. They struggle not to get rid of the family per se, but to expand the definition of what counts as family and to give us all more freedom to decide how and with whom we want to share our private lives. At the root of these legal challenges and new domestic practices lies a desire to accept multiple ways of organizing the smallest social unit in our societies in a way that better reflects the diversity of our collective past.

To understand these efforts, we must break the nuclear family into two of its constituent parts: sexual monogamy between two individuals and relatively exclusive biparental care for children. These two components are absolutely separable; they are often related, but do not need to be. In terms of our mating practices, we have a wide variety of potential models to choose from, models that all have long histories: including celibacy, serial monogamy, "complex marriage," platonic pair bonding, polygamy, polyamory, and open non-monogamy. Sexualities and romantic proclivities come in a plethora of diverse forms, and just because most people gravitate toward some form of serial monogamy does not mean that this should be the state-approved and socially acceptable model for everyone.

Kollontai believed in a possible future where people might find emotional, intellectual, and physical companionship in wider networks of people bound together by "comradely love," which was simultaneously freed from the demands of child-rearing. She wanted the state to take a more active role in caring for the next generation so that romantic relationships could be unsaddled from the decidedly unromantic burdens of organizing and performing various forms of domestic labor.[34] More recently, Kim TallBear suggests that having more than one partner can be a political act of modeling non-possessiveness. "How does the different sustenance I gain from multiple lovers collectively fortify me and make me more available to contribute in the world?" she asks. "If I am richly fed, what and who am I able to feed? What is possible with a model in which *love* and *relations* are not considered scarce objects to be hoarded and protected, but which proliferate beyond the confines of the socially constituted couple and nuclear family?"[35]

Still others have no interest in forming romantic or sexual attachments and prefer instead to nurture lateral relationships with close friends, a trend that has led to a recent rise in "platonic marriages" or "non-conjugal" marriages.[36] Although the legal definition of marriage in many countries still requires some form of conjugal relationship to apply for particular benefits, such as attaining citizenship through marriage, the idea of sharing a life and raising children with a platonic friend provides an alternative to the traditional nuclear family model. One twenty-five-year-old Texan told Danielle Braff of the *New York Times*: "Meeting people is hard, getting a bond and romantic feelings is hard, and more and more young people are starting to realize that there are other benefits to marriage other than romantic love: I mean, isn't the point to marry your best friend? So why can't it be your literal best friend?"[37]

And if you don't want to marry your best friend, there are other ways to enjoy the love, care, and support associated with the concept of family. Among the LGBTQIA+ community, the concept of "chosen family" proposes that nonconsanguineous ties should be legally recognized and validated as much as consanguineous ones. As far back as the Vietnam War, the United States federal government allowed its employees to take bereavement leaves for the combat deaths of close friends. The 1994 Federal Employees Family Friendly Leave Act, which allows full-time employees to use their sick days to care for a relative or to make arrangements for or to attend a funeral, also gave a capacious definition of family. This included "any individual related by blood or affinity whose close association with the employee is the equivalent of a family relationship."[38] In recent years, many US states have also extended their family leave policies to include chosen family, and the 2020 Families First Coronavirus Response Act mandated that employers with paid sick leave policies should allow their employees to take up to two weeks of leave to support individuals for whom there was an expectation of care, whether that person was considered a traditional member of the family or not.[39] In late 2021, the UK government also confirmed a new provision for employees to be able to take a "caregiver's leave" of up to one week for a family member or "a person who reasonably relies on the employee for care."[40]

On the other end of the spectrum are those living in intentional communities that practice both polyamory and collective child-rearing. Like the Oneida Community in the nineteenth century, the permanent residents of the ecovillage of Tamera in southern Portugal do not believe in the nuclear family. They live in individual dwellings or in single-sex dorms, and although most residents nurture a primary emotional or romantic pair-bond, they are encouraged to pursue sexual liaisons with other members of the community to overcome or invert negative feelings like jealousy (a process sometimes called "compersion"). "There can't be peace on Earth as long as there's war in love. Humanity has wrongly organized love, locked it into narrow cages of possession and fear, which is why it so often turns into anger and hatred. The global epidemics of violence ravaging this planet result from a culture that has inhibited love," explains Sabine Lichtenfels, one of the cofounders of Tamera.[41]

She proposes eleven explicit ethical guidelines for their practice of free love, including the idea that "Partnership and free sexuality are complementary not contradictory" and "There are no legal claims in love and sexuality."[42] If children are born, they stay with their mothers until the age of four, and then join the nearby "Children's Place," which doubles as a school. Residents of Tamera educate their children within the community following the curriculum of Portuguese public schools. As in other intentional communities, all adults take responsibility for the care and provisioning of the younger generation, and the older children enjoy nurturing relationships with multiple alloparents.

The way we organize our romantic lives does not need to determine the way we choose to experience and organize parenthood. Even if you are part of a monogamous couple, you can still decide to raise your children in a loving network of both consanguine and nonconsanguineous adults. If the biological or adoptive parents reside near their kinship networks, it is common for grandparents, aunts, and uncles, as well as older cousins to help with the raising of children. Maternal and paternal grandmothers often provide important support to the new parents, and in some countries and cultures, this grandmotherly care is expected and relied upon. But nonrelatives have always had a large role in more cooperative models of child-rearing.

In a variety of different religious and cultural traditions, the parents of a newborn infant can choose a set of "godparents" who will be symbolically or practically involved in the raising of the child. In Catholic and Christian Orthodox traditions, becoming a godparent is a special honor and responsibility. In many Spanish-speaking cultures, the children have *padrinos*, and after the baptism, the parents and the godparents become *compadres* (co-parents) to each other. The child's parents will call the godmother their *comadre* (co-mother) and the godfather their *compadre* (co-father). Depending on the culture, this is a relatively formal relationship and the godparents pledge to raise and care for the child should anything happen to the parents. Other Christian denominations also allow for godparents, and these alloparents develop a special relationship with the child as they grow up. In some Chinese traditions, couples can designate a childless relative or friend to become a godparent, allowing that person to nurture a close alloparental bond with their child.[43] In Judaism, the role of *sandek* is similar to that of a godfather, and in certain traditions the *Kvatter* and *Kvatterin* (or the parents' messengers), usually a married couple, participate in the circumcision ceremony. This honor is often given to a childless pair and is analogous to that of godparents.

Despite the ubiquity of godparenting, in the United States they have no legal rights, and in most countries, laws prohibit a single child from having more than two legal parents. Birth certificates only have two spaces, and little accommodation is made for other adults in committed-care relationships with a minor. High divorce and remarriage rates have led to an increase in blended families with stepparents (or "bonus parents," as they are sometimes called) becoming an important source of alloparental care. In the United Kingdom, when a stepparent decides to adopt their partner's child from a previous relationship, this terminates the legal relationship between the other parent, meaning that the first parent is no longer responsible for maintenance or support, and the child is no longer eligible to inherit that parent's wealth. The child instead becomes a legal heir to the new stepparent's estate, and the new stepparent will remain legally responsible for the child even if the relationship with the child's parent ends in a divorce.[44] Similarly, in the United States, when a stepparent adopts a child, it requires the consent of both "natural" parents, and all legal obligations of the biological parent will be forfeited in favor of the stepparent. Many fathers agree to give up their legal right to their children because it usually means they can stop paying child support.

Parenting for the Future

In same-sex couples, the sperm donor, egg donor, or gestational parent may all want to share caregiving roles, and laws that insist on only two parents per child ignore the complex reality of these new family forms and the advances of reproductive technologies. In 2016, the first child was born using the new technique of mitochondrial replacement therapy (MRT) that allows for child to have the DNA of three parents: two mothers and one father.[45] Developed to fight infertility and prevent the inheritance of certain genetic diseases passed down from the mother's mitochondrial DNA, MRT allows two women to have a baby biologically related to them both. MRT is currently legal in the UK to prevent genetic disorders, but remains prohibited in the United States because of ethical concerns about so-called designer babies. For those wealthy enough and willing to travel to Ukraine (at least before the war started), a fertility clinic in Kyiv used the procedure for anyone able to pay the $15,000 fee.[46] The reality of three-parent children makes our current laws mandating only two parents little more than a quaint anachronism.

An increasing number of single parents are also co-parenting with non-romantic partners, a trend often referred to as "platonic parenting." Like platonic marriages, platonic parenting can involve two or more adults who agree to legally commit to raise a child together. Co-parents can include two heterosexual friends, best friends with different sexualities, or two strangers ready to start families who might connect through a website like Modamily.[47] In a 2011 article on "tri-parenting" in the *Journal of Medical Ethics*, the scholar Daniela Cutas argues that platonic co-parenting or multi-parenting might actually be better for children because adults will tend to choose their potential co-parents more rationally than they choose their romantic partners. Platonic friendships are also less likely to dissolve once the romance and attraction fade, thus providing more long-term stability.[48]

In response to increasing demand, three parent adoption (three adults adopting a child together or adding a nonbiological parent to a family with two biological parents) is legal in some states such as California, Rhode Island, Vermont, Maine, Massachusetts, and Washington, which means that all three parents share status as full legal guardians and have the right to make all decisions regarding the child's welfare, to gain custody should the other parents die, or to win visitation rights with the child should the family break up. A September 2020 article in the *Atlantic*, "The Rise of the Three-Parent Family," profiled a heterosexual married couple that were legally triparenting with David Jay, the founder of the Asexual Visibility and Education Network (AVEN): "If you're someone like me," Jay explained, "who really wants kids in my life and doesn't want a primary romantic and sexual partner, then there are ways to do that."[49] As of early 2022, although the UK only allows children to have two legal parents, a stepparent can petition for "parental responsibility" for a partner's child. This includes the financial responsibility to shelter, care for, and educate the minor.[50]

Children born into polygamous or polyamorous families are also disadvantaged by legal structures that limit guardians to two. In 2017, a New York judge made a historic ruling that granted "tri-custody" to a polyamorous trio after it broke up.[51] A married couple began a consensual relationship with their downstairs neighbor. Because the wife was infertile, they all agreed that the husband and the neighbor should have a child together, which the three would raise in common. When the two women decided to leave the relationship together and the legal wife filed for divorce, the court initially granted custody only to the two biological parents. Because the child recognized both women as his mothers, Suffolk County Supreme Court Judge H. Patrick Leis III made the landmark decision to award full parental rights to all three parties. In a 2021 book, *Three Dads and a Baby*, Ian Jenkins, a medical doctor living in Southern California, also detailed his legal battles to win parental recognition for all three fathers of his polyamorous triad. He and his two partners fought for the right to all be listed on the birth certificates of their two children, brought into the world with the help of one egg donor and two surrogate mothers.

Triparenting is not without its potential downsides. In the first place, by having three parents in a family, the possibility for disagreements between them is greater than if there were only two, and children might face a higher likelihood of abandonment if three-parent families are somehow less stable than two-parent families. Three parents might also have more instances of discord when it comes to parental decision-making. "We knew that if there were three of us," Ian Jenkins explained, "the usual issue where a kid can play parents off each other becomes multiplied."[52] But in reviewing the case for three-parent families, ethicist Daniela Cutas sees no reason why three-parent families should be any more or less harmonious than two-parent households.[53] Because those who choose to form untraditional families do so in the face of most social expectations, Cutas suggests that triparents actually might be more deliberate and cooperative in their relationships and decision-making.

The other potential downside lies in the stigma from a child's peers for having a nontraditional family form. Although Cutas recognizes that stigma is a serious, often psychologically damaging issue for children, she emphasizes the fluidity of social norms around the family and suggests that what is stigmatized today may be accepted in a few years. Having two moms or two dads used to be much less common than it has become, and there is no reason to believe that having three parents of any gender will be less acceptable in the future. Finally, while having a third parent might increase the number of potential abusers in a household, and there is some contested evidence that stepfathers are more likely to abuse stepchildren (the so-called Cinderella effect), having other committed adults in the home might offer more protection for vulnerable kids.[54] If one parent becomes depressed, unstable, or violent, there are two other adults around to intervene. In my own case, the lucky coincidence of having my grandmother in the house probably saved my mother's life.

The philosophers Anca Gheaus and Kalle Grill have also weighed the pros and cons of multiparenting, with Grill asking in a 2020 article, "How many parents should there be in a family?"[55] Surveying the arguments and evidence, Grill opines that while two parents are better than one, three or four are probably better than two, especially in families with multiple children, and that we should "jettison the two-parent presumption and make different numbers of parents more socially accepted as well as legally possible."[56] Anca Gheaus further argues that another benefit of multiparenting is that it can undermine "the existing monopoly of power that parents have over their children." Since children cannot choose their parents and remain fully dependent on their resources, they are in a uniquely vulnerable position. If a parent has a limited income and decides to spend it on beer instead of food, there isn't much a child can do. If a parent moves to another city, children must follow; if a single parent starts dating again or moves in with a new partner, children have little say in the matter. Few legal relationships formalize such an asymmetry in power relations as that between parents and children. To the extent that parents can abuse this power, Gheaus proposes that "children's dependency on their caregivers can be eliminated by multiplying the sources of care for children."[57]

Family Expansionism

And it's not only the children who stand to gain from multiparenting arrangements. The persistence of cultural ideals about the nuclear family, and particularly the traditional, isolated, male breadwinner and female homemaker version of it, hurts men, too. In a society that emphasizes the importance of biparental care of children to the exclusion of other forms of alloparental care, the expected division of labor within the household pressures fathers in the role of financial provider, a role that our economies make it harder for men to fulfill, even if they want to. In a provocative 2019 paper in the *American Economic Review*, "When Work Disappears: Manufacturing Decline and the Falling Marriage Market Value of Young Men," economists David Autor, David Dorn, and Gordon Hanson showed that, controlling for other factors, marriage and fertility rates fell in areas that experienced a decline in blue-collar employment due to international trade pressures that precipitated the dismantling of local coal and steel industries. Obviously, the loss of good and often unionized jobs reduces men's earnings, but these circumstances also "curtail the availability and desirability of potentially marriageable young men," increase the prevalence of male idleness (the percentage of those neither employed nor going to school), and "induce a differential and economically large rise in male mortality from drug and alcohol poisoning, HIV/AIDS, and homicide."[58]

Rather than encouraging couples to form nuclear households through marriage initiatives, such as public advertising campaigns or attempts to reduce "the disincentives to marriage in means-tested aid programs" by cutting benefits to single mothers, expanding the definition of family can move us away from thinking of our potential partners as people whose worth we determine on a "marriage market."[59] Challenging the persistence of the traditional nuclear family also means challenging the underlying expectation that fathers' only value lies in providing financial support for their children. Distributing the care of children among three or more parents reduces the pressure on any one member of the group to be the primary provider. Men will be freed to bring other types of nonmaterial assets into their relationships and families.

In other words, potential partners—of both the romantic and platonic variety—will value men for more than their ability to earn a living in increasingly unstable and unpredictable labor markets. Reimagining the role of men will also help us deal with the widespread male mental health crises, which have led to countless unnecessary excess deaths among those who find themselves excluded from an economy that continues to outsource or automate once-good-paying jobs. The solution is not to bring back the economic and family forms of the past so that men can be "real men" again. We need to redefine what it means to be a "real man" by realizing that our current definitions of masculinity exist to uphold a particular set of social relations that don't benefit most of us, regardless of our gender.

Finally, given the worries that many youth have about the carbon footprint of having babies, multiparenting might allow for more people to experience parenthood while still limiting future population growth to protect the environment. Anca Gheaus, who believes that "it is imperative to limit population growth worldwide in order to prevent or mitigate the harmful effects of excessive consumption," also sees potential long-term benefits of multiparenting for the planet.[60] I often find it curious that some of my younger colleagues and students will embrace veganism, give up all air travel, or swear to remain childless, but are unwilling or unable to imagine a world where more than two parents can cooperate in raising a child.

In the future, pairs of couples might be happy to share their children in common. It might become normal to have cooperatives of single mothers who commit to being co-mothers to their kids, or even to have a whole community of adults, like the residents of Tamera or Twin Oaks, who raise children together without worries about legal parenthood or guardianship. Reflecting on her parenting experience at Twin Oaks, Kristen "Kelpie" Henderson explained to me that "I had many adults to help me and my boys become educated. I had dependable childcare and good friends. If I reached out, I got help, sometimes more help than needed. . . . Specifically: as a mother of young children, I often had no idea what I was doing. I had many adults around who'd raised kids, and I could ask advice. Twin Oaks provided educational opportunities so I could learn how to parent before I became a parent." Rather than defining one natural family state for everyone, family expansionism allows us to live closer to our long history of cooperative breeding. We can embrace a diversity of ways to forge lateral platonic relationships, to nurture romantic and sexual ties, and to bear and care for the next generation. Although these can be linked together, there is no reason they have to be.

Building our own visions of everyday utopia requires us to think outside the box of the traditional nuclear family. Once upon a time, a high school English teacher and her husband did just this. Tom and

Betty Olson were not my parents or my relatives or in any way responsible for my care, but they shared their resources and cared for me, nonetheless. Around the world today, there are stepparents, godparents, and alloparents of all kinds joining in the adventure of raising the next generation. Nourishing our lateral relationships and expanding our chosen families will allow us all to live in wider communities of affection and care, something perhaps now more necessary than ever before.

CHAPTER 8

The *Star Trek* Game Plan

How Radical Hope Defeats Dystopian Despair

On May 16, 1988, while I was still living with the Olsons, *Star Trek: The Next Generation* aired its season one finale. Starring Patrick Stewart, a former member of the Royal Shakespeare Company, as Captain Jean-Luc Picard, *The Next Generation* attempted to reboot the relentlessly optimistic 1960s *Star Trek* franchise in an era characterized by cynicism and late Cold War angst. Only about a month before our graduation, most of my high school classmates and I believed that we faced a doomed future, not so different from that imagined by the high school students of today. But instead of a catastrophic climate crisis, a violent coup d'état, or another pandemic, we feared nuclear war. At the tail end of the Reagan and Thatcher eras, the United States and the Union of Soviet Socialist Republics maintained weapons arsenals sufficient to destroy the earth and all life upon it multiple times over. Back then, hawkish Americans championed the idea of tactical first strikes, but those of us clearheaded enough to understand the science of nuclear winter accepted the nihilistic truth: humanity was toast if the superpowers started World War III.

The last episode of the first season of *The Next Generation*, "The Neutral Zone," finds the USS *Enterprise-D* on the edge of Federation space. They encounter a satellite with three cryogenically frozen humans from the twentieth century: Americans from the late 1980s. One is a musician, and one is a woman who is identified as a "homemaker," which the android, Data, assumes to be a profession related to "construction work." The third is a financier, Mr. Ralph Offenhouse, who believes that he has woken up three centuries after his death to enjoy the accumulated interest on his now ancient bank accounts. Played by the actor Peter Mark Richman, Offenhouse demands to see his lawyer so he can access his wealth. Picard impatiently tells Offenhouse: "A lot has changed in the last three hundred years. People are no longer obsessed with the accumulation of things. We've eliminated hunger, want, the need for possessions. We've grown out of our infancy."

Coming only one year after Gordon Gekko's era-defining "greed is good" speech in the 1987 movie *Wall Street*, "The Neutral Zone" thumbed its nose at the materialism and selfishness characterized by then popular television shows like *Dallas*, *Dynasty*, *Falcon Crest*, and *Lifestyles of the Rich and Famous*. In an era saturated with extreme-wealth porn, *Star Trek* projected one of these so-called "masters of the universe" into a dollar-free future. At the end of the episode, Picard decides to return the three twentieth-century humans to their home planet of Earth. Ralph Offenhouse whines in dismay: "Then what will happen to us? There's no trace of my money. My office is gone. What will I do? How will I live?"

"This is the twenty-fourth century," Picard says. "Material needs no longer exist."

Offenhouse sighs. "Then what's the challenge?"

Picard looks annoyed. "The challenge, Mr. Offenhouse, is to improve yourself, to enrich yourself. Enjoy it."

This final bit of dialogue landed on me like an anvil. There I was, just turned eighteen, living in my English teacher's spare room, a confused refugee from a violent and now "broken" home, terrified of mutually assured destruction. Like the young Whoopi Goldberg seeing Uhura on the bridge of the original *Enterprise* and realizing that Black people would exist in the future, I remember considering for the first time that if there was a future, it could be profoundly different from the present. Unlike *Star Wars* in its galaxy far, far, away, or the *Wonder Woman* parallel universe filled with Greek gods and magic lassos of truth, *Star Trek* was *my world*, a world I believed to be stuck and impossible to change. Lost in my daydreams about Amazon islands and Jedi training planets, it never occurred to me that the status and glamour of being rich and successful in 1988 might not mean anything by the twenty-fourth century, just as things that mattered in 1688 no longer mattered in the late eighties. And if things could be completely different in the next three hundred years, then why not the next fifty? Or the next ten?

I marveled at the thought that we might one day live in a world where "hunger, want, [and] the need for possessions" had been overcome; that what would matter most was who we were as people and how we could improve ourselves. Rather than worrying too much about how we got there, *Star Trek*'s creators just presented the future as if it had already been accomplished, like the racially integrated crew of the original series. The denizens of the *Enterprise-D* used machines called replicators to synthesize food, drink, clothes, musical instruments, or whatever else they wanted. Scarcity faded into the past—a pesky old problem solved by the advent of a new technology. For men like Offenhouse, the accumulation of wealth was the point of life. But without scarcity, no one cared if one person had more than everyone else, because anybody could accumulate as much stuff as they wanted.

And with this abundance came freedom and relative sexual equality. No one worried about provisioning their kids, if they chose to have them at all. Although people fell in love, formed pairs, and raised children on the ship, the family was no longer the basic economic unit of society. It was a utopian vision in the extreme. It broke my brain. I realized that the most important elsewhere was the temporal one; if I could allow myself the freedom to believe in a different future, maybe I could reach out into the world that I wanted to live in and pull it a little bit closer to me.

This positive vision of the future has inspired fans across the globe for almost sixty years since the first episode aired in 1966, making *Star Trek* one of the most successful media franchises of all time, with a massive cultural impact. This is all the more remarkable given its inauspicious beginnings: the television network NBC decided to cancel the show after only two seasons. In an unprecedented, coordinated act of fandom activism, over one hundred and fifty thousand people wrote pleading letters and two hundred Caltech students marched to NBC's Burbank studios to demand the show's renewal. Shocked by the fans' commitment, NBC relented, and the original series continued for one more full season.[1] The popularity of the original seventy-nine episodes grew the *Star Trek* fan base for two decades, and by 1986, it earned the distinction as American television's most syndicated show.[2] In that year, Gene Roddenberry launched *The Next Generation*, which became an instant ratings success and was nominated for a prime-time Emmy Award for "Outstanding Drama Series" in its seventh and final season in 1994.

Star Trek's enduring appeal in part arises from its positive vision of the future, a vision increasingly rare in the landscape of popular culture. As of May 2022, the *Star Trek* canon consists of eight live-action television series, three animated series, and one series called *Short Treks*, as well as thirteen feature films. It would take approximately a month of nonstop, twenty-four-hour viewing to work your way through all seven-hundred-plus episodes in addition to the movies. Five of the current series are ongoing, with more series and films still in production.[3] American fans organized the first major *Star Trek* convention in 1972, and FedCon (Federation Convention), the largest annual *Star Trek* convention in Europe, began in 1992.[4] The longevity, diversity, and multigenerational dedication of *Star Trek* fans is unparalleled and continues to grow each year. In 2019, *The Guardian* reported on how *Star Trek* fans saved people's lives, including the story of one woman who escaped a violent boyfriend because her fellow aficionados crowdfunded a security deposit so she could get her own apartment. "More than 150 Trekkies rushed to my aid, many of them total strangers. I felt like I'd sent out a distress call and an armada of Starships had come to my rescue," she explained.[5]

Militant Optimism

The whole *Star Trek* franchise embodies the German philosopher Ernst Bloch's idea of "militant optimism," a social and psychological commitment to imagining a better world and striving to make it real. Rather than thinking that historical processes lie beyond our control—that history happens *to us*—Bloch's three-volume rumination on the politics of hope proposes that people actively produce history every day through the collective actions of those living through it as an ever-contingent present. Although there will always be those who seek to convince us that there is no alternative to the current state of things, Bloch wants us to recognize that if we are all participating in the making of the world in which we live, then that world is malleable. We have the power to contest, challenge, and change history because all histories begin first in the current moment. You are reading these words in a temporal frame that we call the present, but by tomorrow this sentence will be in your past and on its way into the realm of what we call "history." As David Graeber and David Wengrow assert in their wonderfully contrarian tome, *The Dawn of Everything*, "We are all projects of collective self-creation," so how is it that we came "to be trapped in such tight conceptual shackles that we can no longer even imagine the possibility of reinventing ourselves?"[6]

The stability of the world around us is a fiction we all accept so we can go about our daily lives. Let me give you an example. If I take a twenty-dollar bill out of my wallet right now, I can go to the store and buy a decent bottle of wine. But the bill is just a piece of paper, and my ability to buy that wine rests on a shared belief that this particular piece of paper stores value. If I tear a sheet out of my notebook and write the words "twenty dollars" on it, the shopkeeper will not accept it. If I go to the store with a twenty-euro bill or a twenty-dollar Canadian bill, the shopkeeper will also not accept it because I live in the United States. If inflation is rampant, the bottle of wine that costs twenty dollars today might cost sixty dollars tomorrow or even two hundred dollars by next week. Anyone who has lived in a country with runaway inflation will know exactly how useless paper money can become almost overnight. Germans in the 1930s paid for groceries with wheelbarrows full of currency, and my ex-in-laws in Bulgaria lost much of their life's savings in the hyperinflation that followed the sudden and unexpected collapse of communism in 1989. I know this and yet I still use paper money, and keep dollars in my bank account, because it is convenient and because that's what everyone expects of me. Even at my local farmers market, barter is more or less off the table, as it is in most complex societies, until paper money becomes worthless, and people start burning it to keep warm.

In a similar way to how we collectively believe in paper money, many of us also embrace the fiction that the way we organize our private lives is the only way available to us. Even if we understand in the abstract about the pressures parents face, the strain that child-rearing places on romantic relationships, the high divorce rate, the prevalence of child abuse and intimate partner violence, and the very real possibilities of our own or our partner's long-term unemployment, disability, or death, we replicate the domestic form that makes us the most vulnerable to these problems because it is convenient and because that's what everyone expects of us. Just as our entire economy rests on the fiction of what economists call a fiat currency, it also rests on a particular notion of the family, one that is often viewed as either natural or divinely mandated, but which acts to uphold a specific set of social and economic relations. If you look, for instance, at the mission statement of the conservative Institute for Family Studies, it openly admits the potential economic repercussions of challenges to the nuclear family: "The fact that roughly one in two children in America grow up outside of an intact, married family constitutes one of the most significant threats to *America's future stability and prosperity*" (my emphasis).[7] And in early 2022, one of the institute's top research issues was precisely "the connection between strong marriages and a thriving economy."[8]

American conservatives recognize a fundamental threat to their way of life when they look around and see the declining marriage rate, the plummeting birth rate, the millennials refusing to saddle themselves with huge mortgages, as well as growing demands for what the cultural theorist Kate Soper has called "alternative hedonism," a new post-consumerist definition of pleasure that no longer rests on the acquisition of material goods. Worrying about the breakdown of the "intact, married family" may also reveal underlying fears about the potential end of American economic hegemony in the world. If the next generation refuses to embrace the values and aspirations required to maintain the social and economic system that underpins this hegemony, the whole edifice can crack, which might actually improve the lives of many ordinary people. "It is not simply about the creation of worlds or ways of living that will better meet people's interests *as they currently are*," writes the political theorist Davina Cooper. "Utopia is also centrally concerned with those changing interests, desires, identifications, and forms of embodiment that happen as people . . . experience other ways of living."[9] If people stop believing in the rewards of finding partners, making babies, buying homes, and hoarding stuff, it is potentially as destabilizing as when people stop believing in the value of twenty-dollar bills.

In the chapters you've read in this book so far, I've explored a wide variety of utopian experiments about rearranging the private sphere, some of them deep in the past and some very much active in this thing we call the present. I know that many of you still have doubts, and that some of these ideas seem far-fetched and possibly unworkable given the state of the world today. Most of us can imagine universal childcare or dormitory living for grown-ups because in some sense they already exist. We grasp how they might work. It's harder to wrap our heads around sharing property in common or raising our children in non-nuclear families because these ways of being in the world feel unfamiliar and challenge some of our most basic assumptions about the correct way, or the "healthy" way, to organize our domestic lives. Sharing a washing machine in common with our neighbors might trigger thoughts of inconvenience before it inspires pride that one less appliance will end up in a landfill after its planned obsolescence. Raising our kids with more than one other parent might fuel fears that they won't need us as much before it fills us with confidence that our children will ultimately benefit from growing up basked in the affections of multiple caring adults.

Utopias by their definition are either a "good place" or a "no place," and what matters most is taking the journey and considering the kinds of changes that might make our domestic lives less isolated, more flexible, and more ecologically sustainable: things like universal childcare, cooperative living, ethical education for self-reliance and critical thinking, shared property, and family expansionism. I'm not saying it's easy to change these things, but the path to change lies in the continued struggle. As the Uruguayan writer Eduardo Galeano once explained: "Utopia is on the horizon. I move two steps closer; it moves two steps further away. I walk another ten steps and the horizon runs ten steps further away. As much as I may walk, I'll never reach it. So what's the point of utopia? The point is this: to keep walking."[10]

If you've made it this far in the book, and you still disagree with everything I've explored in these pages, that's okay. You don't have to be convinced of anything, but I do hope you will take a moment to reflect on the sources of your resistance.

Hope as a Cognitive Capacity

According to Ernst Bloch, the value of utopian thinking lies in its ability to inspire hope in both of its related but distinct forms: hope as a cognitive capacity and hope as an emotional state. In terms of the architecture of our minds, hope is to the future what memory is to the past. If you have a good memory, you have the ability to remember specific details of events that occurred long ago. You may never forget a face; or you can recall the full melody of a song after hearing just the first few notes. Memory is also the ability to root your sense of self and identity in past events, to create a narrative about who you are based on what you have experienced. Memory as a cognitive capacity can be useful when it helps you to study for an important exam or allows you to savor a cherished experience.

Hope, on the other hand, is the mental ability to imagine the future; to project forward a perception of what might come to pass and to orient yourself to those contingent possibilities. From a psychological perspective, C. R. Snyder, one of the leading psychologists who did research in this area, proposed that "hope is defined as the perceived capability to derive pathways to desired goals, and motivate oneself via agency thinking to use those pathways."[11] Put more simply, people who are good at hoping are those who can set clear goals, can ponder multiple ways of attaining those goals, and muster the willpower to pursue them in the face of obstacles or the specter of disappointment. We all know people who refuse to try something new because they fear failure.

Psychologists believe that this type of hope as a cognitive capacity can be learned over time, and studies reveal that "hope training" can combat depression, anxiety, and stress.[12] Most hope therapy originates from C. R. Snyder's work and includes a variety of mental exercises such as hope mapping, guided daydreaming, hope journaling, and other techniques that allow people to clearly visualize specific goals (both great and small), to consider potential obstacles (both internal and external), and then unleash their imaginations to conjure up multiple pathways to how those obstacles might be overcome, not so different from the blue sky thinking that scientists do when faced with an intractable problem.

One specific technique, which goes by the fancy name "mental contrasting with implementation intentions" (MCII) strengthens our cognitive capacity to pursue goals by forcing us to make specific plans about how we will deal with roadblocks. While these techniques are often used in clinical settings at the individual level, there is no reason they cannot be adapted to deal with larger social problems, or even challenge entire social and economic systems.[13] Hope differs from optimism because the latter is just a belief that everything will work out well, whereas hope is an active thought process that affirms our ability to influence the future course our lives or societies will take. You might think of it as chess strategy for life: having multiple countermoves already planned for each of your opponent's potential moves.

I am hoping right now that I will finish this book, and that people will read it when I'm done. I can imagine this book being published over a year from now, partially because I have published books before, and partially because I understand how the book publishing process works. Still, this book is not writing itself. I must haul my butt out of bed every day and sit in front of my computer for hours on end to write these words. I could be watching the first season of *Star Trek: Strange New Worlds* or going for a walk or sitting outside drinking Pinot Gris. I could call a friend or take a nap or read a novel. But I write knowing full well that after all this work my editor might hate it, or that readers will hate it, or that even I might hate it at some later point. Hope is not just about me writing because I can clearly imagine a day when this book will be done, it is also about writing against the gnawing doubts that I am wasting my time and making a clear plan to resist the things I know that will distract me from writing.

This brings us to hope as an emotional state that exists on a spectrum from hopefulness to hopelessness. For Ernst Bloch, the opposites of hope are fear and anxiety. Hope as a cognitive capacity relies on my ability to limit the influence of these two powerful negative emotions. How many people in unhappy relationships stay because they are afraid of being alone? The fear of not meeting someone else overrides the possibility of meeting someone who might make them happier. Similarly, hopes for changing the world for the better get clobbered by fears of potentially making it worse.

If utopian visions exist to inspire this more emotional sense of hope, then dystopian worlds prey on our fears and anxieties, forcing us to stay in our unhappy relationship with the present. Similarly, if utopianism stimulates our cognitive capacities to imagine living in a different and better future and helps us find the will to effect the social changes necessary to realize that future, then dystopianism constantly reminds us of the failed social experiments of the past, especially those that have gone tragically and horribly wrong. By forcing us to look back rather than forward, by privileging memory over hope, the ubiquity of dystopian thinking browbeats us into accepting the status quo.

In this final chapter, I want to think through the value of utopianism as a project of "militant optimism," and to challenge the "capitalist realism," to borrow a term from the late cultural theorist Mark Fisher, that has permeated mainstream Western culture for much of the last century. Capitalist realism refers to a particular cultural mindset that convinces us that there are no workable alternatives to the way things are today. It finds its most powerful expression in the ubiquity of dystopian films, books, and television shows that bombard us with the message that any deviation from our current way of doing things will inevitably make us worse off. Davina Cooper has also reflected on this tension: "Utopia conventionally depends on stimulating desire and hope in order to inspire and motivate change. Dystopias, by contrast, aim to stimulate action in order to resist or halt what is feared to be emerging. Dystopic narratives assume change, that the world is not a static or stable place but moving toward, indeed in some cases already enacting, its own ruin."[14] But dystopian thinking can also weaponize the general zeitgeist of despair to immobilize us. It nips our nascent social dreams in the bud by convincing us that working toward a better future will destroy the imperfect but familiar present. And the most effective visions of dystopia prey on our deepest fears of being alone and unloved.

The Political Bludgeons of Dystopia

The most popular and enduring dystopian novels of the twentieth century often describe worlds where a desire for more equality and social harmony has eradicated romantic love and the nuclear family. Consider the influence of Aldous Huxley's 1932 novel, *Brave New World*. This famous work regularly appears on curated lists of the "100 Greatest Novels of All Time," and in 1999, the readers of the American publishing house Modern Library ranked it fifth of the "100 Best English-Language Novels of the 20th Century."[15] In the United States, a HarperCollins teacher's guide suggests that *Brave New World* is appropriate for students in grades nine and ten (for fourteen- to fifteen-year-olds) and advises that teachers should use the novel as an "anchor text" for units that explore the theme of "the individual vs. society."[16] The internet overflows with high school lesson plans and discussion questions that highlight the book's portrayal of a utopia gone wrong and the many negative outcomes "that stem from an attempt to cultivate a perfect society."[17] Originally written to poke fun at the utopian fiction of the British author H. G. Wells, the influence of Huxley's novel has far exceeded that of the original books it parodied.

Long before the feminist Shulamith Firestone called on women to seize the "means of reproduction" and produce babies via ectogenesis, Huxley imagined a world where human beings are manufactured in test tubes and bottle-conditioned to accept their designated roles in society. The novel begins with the director of the Central London Hatchery and Conditioning Centre giving a tour of the facility to a group of newly arrived students. Huxley accomplishes his initial dystopian world-building by describing the processes through which his future society has finally abolished the traditional family. New technologies have decoupled sexuality from reproduction. Seventy percent of females are decanted from their bottles as "freemartins," or infertile women, to uphold the lauded ideal that "civilization is sterilization."[18] For the 30 percent of non-freemartin females, natural reproduction is considered backward and disgusting. Fertile women are paid the equivalent of six months' salary to have their ovaries surgically removed and handed over to the hatchery.

The industrial manufacture of people is purported to bring Huxley's imagined society "out of the realm of mere slavish imitation of nature into the much more interesting world of human invention."[19] In the year 2540, no one has a family, since they are all raised collectively in dormitories, and the words "mother" and "father" are reduced to obscenities, with the latter being a "comically smutty word" that was "merely gross, a scatological rather than a pornographic impropriety."[20] In perhaps a nod to William Godwin, Huxley tells us that in a World State of two billion people, there are only ten thousand last names. Sharing a surname means nothing.

Promiscuous sex and easy pleasures characterize Huxley's dystopia, and although the mind-controlling uses of "soma" often dominate discussions of the novel, the author doesn't introduce the drug until he has thoroughly described the full eradication of romantic and familial attachments that underpins this supposedly perfect society. At one point in the novel, Mustapha Mond, Resident World Controller for Western Europe, explains that: "The world's stable now. People are happy; they get what they want, and they never want what they can't get. They're well off; they're safe; they're never ill; they're not afraid of death; they're blissfully ignorant of passion and old age; they're plagued with no mothers or fathers; they've got no wives, or children, or lovers they feel strongly about; they're so conditioned that they practically can't help behaving as they ought to behave."[21] Huxley's *Brave New World* portrays a society where the full socialization of reproduction has liberated women's sexuality—"everyone belongs to everyone else"—but created a shallow, meaningless world where people drug themselves into submissive compliance with their place in life, and even the highest-ranking "Alpha-Plus" men like Bernard Marx and Helmholtz Watson feel frustrated and dissatisfied.

When Eric Blair (George Orwell)—briefly a student of Aldous Huxley—set out to write his own dystopian vision of a failed utopia, he also highlighted the breakdown in traditional family relations. By almost any measure, *1984* is one of the most influential novels in the English language. "*Nineteen Eighty-Four* has not just sold tens of millions of copies—it has infiltrated the consciousness of countless people who have never read it," wrote Dorian Lynskey, Orwell's biographer, on the seventieth anniversary of the book in 2019. "No work of literary fiction from the past century approaches its cultural ubiquity while retaining its weight."[22] Even more so than *Brave New World*, children in secondary schools in both the United States and Great Britain must read *1984* as teenagers. Taught on its own or together with *Animal Farm*, Orwell's last novel is a dystopian tale designed to warn readers specifically against the dangers of totalitarianism. Although Orwell himself embraced socialism, he hated Stalinism, and most American high school curricula specifically use *1984* to teach about the dangers of socialist ideologies.

In the superstate of Oceania, Big Brother has severed the links between love, sex, and child-rearing. In *1984*, members of the Party do not cultivate romantic or familial attachments. Where Huxley diminishes the importance of sexuality by making it freely available, Orwell conjures the Junior Anti-Sex League, which promotes political celibacy. "The aim of the Party was not merely to prevent men and women from forming loyalties which it might not be able to control. Its real, undeclared purpose was to remove all pleasure from the sexual act."[23] Although people are encouraged to marry and have children in the "prole" district, they are considered no better than animals. For the poorest classes, "Promiscuity went unpunished, divorce was permitted" and the Party tacitly allowed prostitution: "Mere debauchery did not matter very much, so long as it was furtive and joyless and only involved women of a submerged and despised class."[24]

The ultimate link between dystopia and the destruction of the family comes when O'Brien explains to Winston that: "We have cut the links between child and parent, and between man and man, and between man and woman. No one dares trust a wife or a child or a friend any longer. But in the future there will be no wives and no friends. Children will be taken from their mothers at birth, as one takes eggs from a hen. The sex instinct will be eradicated. Procreation will be an annual formality like the renewal of a ration card. We shall abolish the orgasm. Our neurologists are at work upon it now."[25] As with Huxley before him, Orwell's dystopian vision stokes fears that the state will interfere in our most intimate lives, breaking down the attachments that people hold most dear.

Because *Brave New World* and *1984* both explicitly discuss sexuality and reproduction, a third text has become an increasingly popular choice to teach to American preadolescents.[26] Lois Lowry's 1993 book, *The Giver*, won the 1994 Newbery Medal of the Association for Library Service to Children, one of the two most prestigious literary awards for children's literature, although it has also often been banned for its discussion of suicide and euthanasia. The book has sold millions of copies around the globe, and a 2012 poll conducted by the *School Library Journal* listed *The Giver* as the fourth most popular "chapter book" for children.[27] In one review of the 2014 film adaptation starring Meryl Streep and Jeff Bridges, Sheila O'Malley noted that the book had become "a staple in middle-school literature curriculum, . . . introducing young students to sophisticated ethical and moral concepts that will help them recognize its precedents when they come to read the works of George Orwell or Aldous Huxley."[28] Taught as a sort of tween prequel to the more serious dystopias on the horizon, American youth are sometimes taught all three books in quick succession—a veritable smorgasbord of anti-utopianism.

The Giver also creates a world where the traditional family has been replaced by artificial "family units" for the sake of "Sameness."

In this future community, children are born to designated "Birthmothers," but never allowed to meet or interact with them. Instead, babies spend their first year in a collectively run "Nurturing Center" with all of the other "newchildren." If they thrive, one-year-olds get placed with family units for the remainder of their upbringing. At the age of twelve, all children are assigned to a job that suits their unique talents and interests (including that of Birthmother). As they age, individuals can apply for a compatible person who will become their spouse, and each couple will be assigned exactly two babies. When the children reach the age of maturity, the family unit dissolves and the adults go to live in large childless communities until they are transferred to the "House of the Old," where they await their euphemistic "release" from life. Because it is a children's book, Lowry avoids sex by creating a world where the community intentionally suppresses emotions, passions, desires, or memories of what those things felt like. The carnal urges of *Brave New World* and *1984* are reduced to the twelve-year-old protagonist's growing desire to kiss his female best friend, and to experience this strange thing called "love."

In all three of these influential dystopian novels, and in many more contemporary books, films, and TV series that have followed in their footsteps, authors portray the eradication of eroticism and romantic love as well as the breakdown of the traditional family as the inevitable collateral damage of attempts to build a different world, no matter how well-intentioned those attempts may be. The community in *The Giver* gives up love, beauty, passion, and connection so as to rid themselves of hatred, prejudice, hunger, cruelty, and war. But the promised better world always turns out to be worse than the world it replaced; brutally worse in *1984*, existentially worse in *Brave New World*, and sentimentally worse in *The Giver*, but always and inevitably worse. The message of these books is loud and clear: you may be unhappy with the way things are, but forget about trying to change them. Any challenge to the "natural" order of things will end with an irretrievable loss of individualism and a slow slide into totalitarian hell.

This tactic has worked for a long time. As we saw with Marx and Engels's attempts to defend their critique of the family in *The Commu-*

nist Manifesto or Daniel De Leon's monogamy-upholding translator's note to August Bebel's book *Woman Under Socialism*, even the most committed revolutionaries get squeamish when faced with the idea that a revolution in the streets might entail a revolution in the bedroom. And Vladimir Lenin, who overhauled the entire political and economic foundations of imperial Russia in a few short years, quickly soured on Kollontai's ideas for replacing the traditional family with more collective forms of affinity. This is partially why people are so resistant to ideas about reorganizing the private sphere. The most persuasive dystopias will always make us fearful of losing the only reliable source of unconditional love and domestic coziness that we crave. Especially for the poor, for immigrants, and for racial and ethnic minorities struggling against hostile dominant cultures, the traditional family can provide comfort and protection against the frigid world of free market economies. As the cultural theorist Mark Fisher writes:

> The values that family life depends upon—obligation, trustworthiness, commitment—are precisely those which are held to be obsolete in the new capitalism. Yet, with the public sphere under attack and the safety nets that a "Nanny State" used to provide being dismantled, the family becomes an increasingly important place of respite from the pressures of a world in which instability is a constant. . . . Capitalism requires the family (as an essential means of reproducing and caring for labor power; as a salve for the psychic wounds inflicted by anarchic social-economic conditions), even as it undermines it (denying parents time with children, putting intolerable stress on couples as they become the exclusive source of affective consolation for each other).[29]

Given that modern life is already tearing our traditional families to shreds, shouldn't we resist by protecting them? If we further erode sexual monogamy and nuclear family ties, won't we accelerate the forces of hyper individualism and social atomization? If blood is thicker than water, why should we be diluting the strength of our consanguineous bonds at precisely the historical moment when those bonds provide the only form of safety and stability upon which we can rely? These are good questions. Any plan to rearrange our domestic lives must address the fears and anxieties that people feel when faced with the further erosion of an institution that, despite its weaknesses, many still hold in high esteem.

But now let me tell you why it's worth it.

"The Miseries of Traditional Life Are Familiar"

Where I live in the United States, representatives of organized religious denominations stand on the front lines of fearmongering about the breakdown of the family and traditional forms of heterosexual monogamy. But while some of the fiercest resistance to changes in the way we organize domesticity originates from people like the late professor of literature Mitchell Kalpakgian, who asserted the "self-evident truth of the natural law that man and woman are created for each other in love and marriage and for the procreation and education of children,"[30] it is complemented by the ideological warfare waged in defense of the nuclear family by market fundamentalists. These strident defenders of capitalism consider all challenges to the status quo as potentially destabilizing factors to the social systems that underpin the free market. Some things, like girl boss liberal feminist demands to break the glass ceiling or expanding the legal institution of marriage to same-sex couples, pose no real threat to conservative interests as long as the work of bringing up the next generation remains in the private sphere. But other sorts of demands prove more difficult to commodify or co-opt, especially those that change people's expectations about how society should be organized.

The paradigmatic example of this secular defense of tradition comes from Jeane J. Kirkpatrick in her infamous 1979 essay, "Dictatorships & Double Standards."[31] Kirkpatrick was an influential neoconservative who served as the first American woman ambassador to the United Nations and on President Ronald Reagan's National Security Council and Foreign Intelligence Advisory Board. She shaped

Reagan's rabidly anti-communist foreign policy in the wake of the Iranian Revolution and the rise of the Sandinistas in Nicaragua. In what would later become known as the "Kirkpatrick doctrine," the Reagan administration justified its support of what she called "'right-wing' dictators or white oligarchies" in the Global South because they helped check the spread of communism. Throughout the 1980s, the United States supported military leaders and capricious monarchs—including those who "sometimes invoked martial law to arrest, imprison, exile, and occasionally, it was alleged, torture their opponents"—precisely because they defended the status quo. Kirkpatrick writes (and I swear these are her actual words):

> Traditional autocrats leave in place existing allocations of wealth, power, status, and other resources which in most traditional societies favor an affluent few and maintain masses in poverty. But they worship traditional gods and observe traditional taboos. They do not disturb the habitual rhythms of work and leisure, habitual places of residence, habitual patterns of family and personal relations. Because the miseries of traditional life are familiar, they are bearable to ordinary people who, growing up in the society, learn to cope, as children born to untouchables in India acquire the skills and attitudes necessary for survival in the miserable roles they are destined to fill.[32]

If test-tube babies were bottle-conditioned to accept their lot in life in *Brave New World*, Kirkpatrick views "the habitual rhythms of work and leisure, habitual places of residence, [and] habitual patterns of family and personal relations" as a similar technology to make people content with "the miserable roles they are destined to fill." In this passage, Reagan's foreign policy guru basically admits that challenging the ordinary structures of everyday life—reimagining the way we raise and educate our children, the homes we dwell in, the property we hoard or share, and the form of the families we choose—can have profound, long-term effects on people's desire to live in a more just and equitable world, one in which they collectively resist the familiar "miseries of traditional life." Kirkpatrick saw left-wing governments as a mortal threat to the American aspiration of eventually bringing "freedom" to the countries of Latin America, Africa, and Asia, because they instituted changes at the level of everyday life. Even the most dramatic changes in the public sphere, such as suspending free speech, free assembly, and basic due process of law, could apparently be reversed in her view so long as the familiar rhythms of the private sphere remained intact. Utopian ideals and political movements are dangerous precisely because they give people hope: the cognitive capacity to imagine that a better world is possible and seek to make it real.

Kirkpatrick's reflections on the role of ordinary domestic life in upholding the status quo builds on a much longer political theoretical tradition of viewing the family as a basic training ground where future subjects learn to respect the absolute authority of monarchs. In his famous 1651 work, *Leviathan*, Thomas Hobbes proposes that people will trade obedience for the protection of an absolute sovereign since the state of nature is violent and unpredictable.[33] Without a strong, undivided state to control and direct them, human lives will be "nasty, brutish, and short." Hobbes predicated his theory upon the republican Roman ideal of *patria potestas*, where the father had unquestioned power over the life and death of his children.[34] Teaching children to accept the ultimate authority of the father in the home produced adults who would, in Hobbes's view, subordinate themselves to strong leaders in the public sphere. As a result, the patriarchal nuclear family played an essential role in producing docile political subjects. Conservatives like Kirkpatrick understood that disrupting the habitual rhythms of family life might ignite challenges to the authority of states as well as the unequal distribution of property that those states protect. It's not a coincidence that right-wing dictators and "white oligarchies" promote conservative family values and strive to keep women and children in the home under patriarchal authority.

Rather Than Paradise, What If It's Hell?

But the pejorative connotations of the word "utopian" thrive well beyond conservative circles. Centrists and leftists both nurture their own

critiques of those wild-eyed dreamers who want to reshape our domestic spheres and propel us into uncertain (but better) futures. In the
first case, self-styled reformers prefer to eschew revolutionary projects
and visions in favor of more limited and achievable short-term policy
goals. Rather than making a clean break with the present, pragma-
tists can point to dystopian novels like *Brave New World*, *1984*, and
The Giver as justifications for their cautious approach to political and
economic change. When the Saint-Simonian feminists gave up their
fight for free love and focused instead on reinstating women's right to
divorce, the realists won out over those dreamers still waiting for the
female messiah to come and build a new world where women gave
their children their own names and earned enough to support them
without a husband or father. Closer to our own time, advocates of
same-sex marriage chose to reinforce rather than challenge the ideal
of the loving monogamous nuclear family. Given the wide array of
legal and financial benefits afforded to married people, it was easier to
ask to expand them to include all couples than to question why those
benefits exist to encourage monogamous marriage in the first place.

Believers in incremental reform fear abrupt change, and not necessarily for bad reasons. Dystopian fearmongering aside, utopian impulses to remake the world anew might change things so fast that they
spin out of control. When the world is turned upside down, no one
knows what will come next. Rather than paradise, what if it's hell?
The unsettling thing about the future is its almost total unknowabil-
ity. Today, many fear that a political upheaval is more likely to usher
in some form of white supremacist fascism or a Gilead-like theoc-
racy than it will a system that promotes justice, sustainability, and
direct democratic control of the economy. Given the risks involved in
"dreaming dangerously," to borrow a phrase from the Slovenian philosopher Slavoj Žižek, some people prefer to focus on small improve-
ments, or what the linguist Noam Chomsky once called "expanding
the floor of the cage."[35]

But if necessity is the mother of invention, do we preclude utopian
solutions when we give in to the tyranny of our immediate needs?
Does the proliferation of co-living and cohousing arrangements act

as a gateway to more communal dwellings? Or are these things half measures that prevent the growth of the kinds of intentional communities that will better serve to shrink our collective carbon footprints and break down patriarchal relations in the private sphere? When we let the good be the enemy of the perfect, are we not shackling our political imaginations to the choices already laid out before us? In their sweeping review of the diversity of the ways our evolutionary ancestors organized their political and economic lives, Davids Graeber and Wengrow suggest that, "If something did go terribly wrong in human history, then perhaps it began to go wrong precisely when people started losing that freedom to imagine and enact other forms of social existence."[36] Continuing to emphasize the pragmatism of incremental reform can also produce a strong disciplining function on our cognitive capacities to hope.

For advocates of full revolution or rebellion, utopianism is a different kind of half measure, but also one to be avoided. Marx and Engels drew their inspiration from the utopian socialists, but they criticized Fourier, the Saint-Simonians, and people like Flora Tristan for proposing that the new world could be built within the decaying carcass of the old one. Those who believe that a total rupture with the past is necessary reject the transformative value of a group of people joining together to build a phalanstery or live in an intentional community. Utopians are derided as clueless dreamers at best; as wealthy, self-indulgent, virtue-signalers at worst.

This disdainful attitude rears its ugly head in the comments on the niche TikTok hashtag #communelife, where disenchanted Generation Zers who have decamped to sustainable farms post about their experiences.[37] Marxist TikTok, or LeftTok as it is sometimes called, is peopled with a fair number of utopia bashers. One representative video posted by @namastehannah on December 4, 2021, racked up more than three thousand comments in its first month on the platform. In response to the idyllic footage showing an attempt to live more simply and sustainably, some commenters expressed admiration or envy, while others called out the perceived privilege of those who dare to retreat from society in this way. One user, Rustybucketkam, commented, "I don't know where these people live, but they are obviously wealthy . . . almost no one can afford to live like this." Others wrote: "I just know y'all have rich parents." "Rich ppl vibes." "It's giving extreme privilege from parents." "We get it you're rich." "I wish I was rich enough to do this." "Where is my trust fund?!" "Oh honey it's funny how money makes everything sunny." But @namastehannah also had her defenders. A user named roxi_sixx responded, "it's literally way more expensive to live in an apartment in a big city and get mcdonalds and star bucks everyday [*sic*]. Why is everyone hating." Another user, Violit420, tried to educate her peers on the whole point of ecovillages: "Why are people saying only rich can do this? The point of a commune is ppl pooling assets to serve a greater community."

But the TikTok haters highlight a real fear about the potentially escapist politics of utopianism. Those who decide to forge new lives in ecovillages or other intentional communities may contribute little to wider movements for social change. If too many people begin to isolate themselves away from mainstream society, walling themselves off into little pockets of resistance, the rest of us may be left alone to deal with the decaying system that remains without the support and resources of those intent on building a better world. On some level, this is not an unfair charge. At least in the United States, the majority of those living in what we might consider utopian communities or forging plural chosen family relations or moving into co-living or cohousing developments, are relatively more educated, middle- or upper-middle-class white people.

As a professor who has taught at elite American institutions, I know that it is often the most privileged young adults who can drop out and join a protest camp or live in an urban collective. If things go south or they change their minds, parental safety nets will support their reentry into the so-called real world. And the kids of the top 1 percent of the income distribution are sometimes the most honestly and ideologically committed to living a different kind of life. On the one hand, they have benefited from a more expansive education about alternative ways of being in the world, but on the other, they also have the economic security to take the kinds of risks most people are too precarious to even consider.

But while I understand the derision and skepticism people feel toward them, I think it is misplaced. Some of the most important utopian thinkers, thinkers whose ideas have reverberated across the centuries, hailed from the most privileged classes. Sir Thomas More was High Lord Chancellor. Peter Kropotkin was a prince. Henri de Saint-Simon was a count. Plato and Alexandra Kollontai were born into influential, aristocratic families. Friedrich Engels was the wealthy son of a successful German industrialist with a taste for fine wine and caviar. Julius Nyerere was the son of an African tribal chief. Many others benefited from solid middle-class educations and never spent a significant portion of their lives laboring in the fields or toiling in factories. And while it is true that men like Charles Fourier and Jean-Baptiste André Godin had private fortunes to build their pocket utopias, their efforts set valuable precedents and showed the world that alternative ways of living were possible.

If hope is a cognitive capacity that can be learned and strengthened with use, it is not surprising that those with the most leisure time to read and think and daydream have the mental bandwidth to imagine alternative futures. And while we might prefer to live in a world shaped by the ideas of what the Italian social theorist Antonio Gramsci called "organic intellectuals" from the less privileged classes, we shouldn't ignore potentially transformative social dreams because they arise in the minds of those who were born to wealthy parents.[38] Utopian ideas that turn the world upside down have often originated from the minds of those who have the most to gain from keeping it right side up.

As to the claim that utopians are ineffective idealists trying to build little model paradises that persuade by example rather than by revolution, the histories presented in this book have conflicting stories to tell. While Godin's Familistery did manage to survive for over a hundred years, other industrialists in Europe did not rush to replicate his experiment. But other "harmless" little communities had to be forcibly eradicated. The Romans wiped out the communal, slave-abhorring Essenes; the Bulgarians exiled the vegan, anarchistic Bogomils; and the Inquisition hunted down and murdered every last proto-feminist, celibate Cathar who dared question the Church's hunger for material wealth. Thomas More and Thomas Müntzer were both executed, and the Anabaptists were forced to flee across oceans. The Beguines were declared heretics and disbanded. Prosper Enfantin and other prominent Saint-Simonians were sent to prison for their outrages against public morality. Members of the Oneida Community faced charges of adultery and threats that their children would be taken away from them. Today, ecovillages and intentional communities like Tamera are derided as "cults." Tax lawyers admit that our economy *could be* destabilized if too many groups decide to live together out of community treasuries. If utopian ideas and the communities they inspire are so harmless, why are those in power always so eager to crush them? Creating viable examples of alternative ways of living threaten the status quo because they may trigger our cognitive capacities for hope. This is a good thing.

Practice Radical Hope

We live today in a world where the preexisting pathways to instigating change are increasingly foreclosed to most ordinary citizens. An erosion in democratic institutions, the rise of illiberal populist leaders, or an overall disgust with the corrupt machinations of the political system have weakened the belief that social change can be pursued by influencing the shape of our elected governments. Given the chaos and precarity of daily life, many people feel too overwhelmed to sustain the level of political engagement or activist commitment required in a system increasingly designed to distract us or grind us down. In a world of alternative facts and awash in conspiracy theories, public trust has collapsed, and it is harder than ever to sustain broad-based social movements. One only has to spend a few moments witnessing the tribalism and divisiveness on social media to realize that any strategic political coalition that becomes too powerful will be almost immediately undermined by internal infighting.[39]

Aside from the practical difficulties of influencing the shape of our governments, many have long been suspicious of states with their legitimate monopolies on violence. Both revolutionaries and reformers set their sights on the state, hoping to use its authority and resources to instantiate change. As someone who has spent her entire adult life studying the ideals and realities of twentieth-century state socialism in Eastern Europe, I understand how bold social visions can devolve into horrendous nightmares. But the lessons of the twentieth century must not frighten us into submissively accepting the status quo. The failure of past dreams should not mean an end to social dreaming. Without recognizing the possibility of failure and disappointments, hope is little more than wishful thinking.

We must learn from the past and make plans to avoid previous mistakes. One of the strengths of utopian ideas and movements is that they don't necessarily require state intervention. Utopian dreams can grow into revolutionary upheavals or concrete policies for reform, but just as often they stay far out beyond the margins of what seems achievable in the present day, existing as "utopian demands" in the words of feminist theorist Kathi Weeks.[40] That's part of their value— to push the limits of what seems politically, scientifically, or psychologically feasible, to boldly go where no one has gone before. That's what makes them utopias.

If, for whatever reason, our ability to influence state power and authority are foreclosed to us, this doesn't mean that we should just give up. Changing how we live our daily lives is a form of politics. Transformations in the private sphere can be more powerful and enduring than grand sweeping gestures of public activism. As Jeane Kirkpatrick so astutely observed in 1979, only by disrupting the habitual rhythms of how we eat, sleep, love, educate, and raise our children can we shake ourselves and others out of our acquiescence to the miseries of the world in which we live. The growing levels of inequality and the atomizing individualism that pervade our societies have their roots in the way we choose our partners and raise our children, in where we live and with whom we share our possessions. Our governments have a vested interest in upholding the monogamous nuclear family, encouraging the ownership of single-family homes, and making us all worry about the care and education of our own children to the exclusion of the children of others. People with big mortgages are not free to quit their jobs and run off to a communal farm. Houses, kids, and consumer debt trap us in a certain way of life. This is why governments write tax codes to encourage marriage and homeownership.

In a world of real or imagined scarcity, we arrange our domestic lives to protect ourselves against an uncertain future, hoarding as many resources and privileges as possible. In a society with less precarity and with resources more equitably distributed, we will worry less about hustling to make sure we have a bigger slice of the pie than those around us. But it works the other way, too. If we lived in wider networks of people who shared their resources, we would become less precarious. Both processes are interdependent. It may be that we will geoengineer our way out of the climate crisis, and that one day we will all share unlimited, free solar power; enjoy universal basic incomes funded by our collective ownership of the robots and algorithms that will do most necessary labor; and live in real democratic societies where "material needs no longer exist," but none of that is possible without fundamentally rethinking the basis upon which we organize our intimate lives to free us from selfish individualism.[41]

Domestic transformation is therefore a key node—if not *the key node*—of resistance and reinvention. On a purely practical level, living with more people means buying fewer things. In the United States, consumer spending accounts for about two-thirds of the gross domestic product, which means that individual decisions about how we arrange our private lives and define who counts as family can undermine the internal logics of a growth-obsessed economy. Fewer babies means fewer future consumers. If more people share their homes and stuff, there are fewer demands for new things. If people have wider social networks within which they find love, support, and companionship, people may begin to care less about chasing the external accoutrements of material success. Status markers matter less in more equitable societies.

This doesn't mean that we will lose our individualism. It does mean that the ways we mark ourselves as different and interesting will be decoupled from how much those markers increase our value on competitive labor or marriage markets. Personal branding will be a thing of the past. Our tastes and passions will be shaped by what we truly love and not by what we think will look good on a college application, résumé, or LinkedIn page. By undermining the wasteful planned obsolescence that underpins competitive acquisitiveness, we can reduce the environmental impacts of our materialistic lifestyles. This doesn't necessarily mean that we will enjoy access to less stuff, it just means that stuff will be useful to a wider network of people rather than sitting unused in our closets, basements, attics, and garages. Why buy a new wheelbarrow when you can borrow one? Public libraries, free stores, and websites like Rent the Runway model how sharing our stuff might work in practice. We might even have access to *more* stuff if building local networks allows us to pool monies to buy things we might not be able to afford on our own.

When I speak and write about transforming the way we imagine our private lives, the most frequent comments I hear concern the politics of bringing children into this world at this particular historical moment. In the last five years, I have met an increasing number of younger adults who believe that a BirthStrike is the only way to responsibly deal with the reality of the climate crisis. Others fear they will never enjoy the financial stability necessary to start their own families or worry that their career prospects will be limited by the very real burdens of caregiving. Everyone suffered during the pandemic, but mothers and fathers of young children faced many extra challenges as they struggled to care for their kids when kindergartens and schools closed, setting a daunting precedent for those considering parenthood in the future. While I respect those who feel confident in their decision to forgo children, I know there are BirthStrikers out there who want to start families but feel overwhelmed by the many compelling reasons not to, not least of which are the cynical government diktats encouraging young people to get busy and reproduce for the sake of the nation-state. I fully sympathize with the big middle finger to society that childlessness represents.

And there is a long tradition of childlessness among utopian communities. Often, prohibitions on reproduction grew from the recognition that children tied parents too closely to the material world. Bogomils, Cathars, Shakers, and Catholic monastics focused their collective efforts on creating the conditions to achieve spiritual salvation. In the Buddhist tradition, worldly attachments hinder the quest for enlightenment. Family means attachment. Those who seek peace must break the cycle of birth, death, and rebirth. But for those utopian movements that sought to create a better future in the here and now, children were always part of the plan.

Instead of not bringing children into this world at all, utopians have often committed to bringing them in differently: challenging parents' unique investments in their own biological offspring to return to a form of cooperative breeding that would ensure a better future for the community. Having babies is political. Raising children is political. And even if you don't want to have your own children, you can participate in the utopian project of raising the next generation by helping others who do decide to have them. Instead of ceding the task of making new people to those who would uphold the status quo, raising a militantly optimistic next generation— nurturing, nourishing, and protecting their cognitive and emotional capacities for hope—is one of the most radical things we can do.

In this book, I have tried to review various utopian ideas that have come down to us through the ages, with examples of the individuals and communities still experimenting with these ideas today. Many failed or faded away. And no doubt they each had their problematic aspects. But similar visions have persisted over millennia, in many different cultural contexts, and we dismiss them at our peril. Part of developing our own cognitive capacities for hope involves a remembrance of the sometimes humble, sometimes astounding victories of the many social dreamers who came before us, victories that those who would uphold the status quo want us to forget. As the historian Howard Zinn reminds us:

> To be hopeful in bad times is not just foolishly romantic. It is based on the fact that human history is a history not only of cru-

elty, but also of compassion, sacrifice, courage, kindness. What we choose to emphasize in this complex history will determine our lives. If we see only the worst, it destroys our capacity to do something. If we remember those times and places—and there are so many—where people have behaved magnificently, this gives us the energy to act, and at least the possibility of sending this spinning top of a world in a different direction. And if we do act, in however small a way, we don't have to wait for some grand utopian future. The future is an infinite succession of presents, and to live now as we think human beings should live, in defiance of all that is bad around us, is itself a marvelous victory.[42]

Each one of us, right now, has the power to start building a different world, beginning with our own families and communities. There are countless things you can do to cultivate change in your daily life as it is. If you are in a monogamous pair, try to spend more time with your non-couple friends and make sure your partner does the same. Nurture all sorts of lateral relationships by finding novel ways to share with your neighbors and colleagues. Get back in touch with old friends. Chat with people at the grocery store. Daydream.

If you have kids, let them spend more time with their grandparents, godparents, aunts, uncles, and family friends. Try to swap more childcare with other parents and create long-term parenting pods. Consider different housing arrangements or join a book club or some form of continuing adult education. And if you have the freedom and opportunity to do so, why not shake things up entirely? Start a free store or join an upcycling collective. Uproot and resettle in an intentional community or ecovillage. Explore different forms of cooperative living and working. Adopt a mononym. Try to meet new people way outside of your established circle of acquaintances. Make strangers into kin.[43] There are many creative ways to resist the lingering effects of patrilineality and patrilocality in our daily lives. As the historian Gerda Lerner reminds us, "The system of patriarchy is a historic construct; it has a beginning; it will have an end."[44]

Perhaps even more pressing is the need to flex our cognitive capacities for hope. We must imagine the future that we want, to think of it as a concrete goal, and consider the different pathways available to realize that future, no matter how outlandish or impossible this future might seem to us now. Sometimes the sheer imagination of something helps to make it real. We can all cultivate the ability to project ourselves into the future if we resist the fear and anxiety that immobilizes our inherent abilities to dream. The more we hope, the better we get at hoping, and the more we inspire those around us to flex their own cognitive capacities for hope. This is not just fluffy positive thinking; it is learning to "remember" the future using a similar set of mental acuities as those we use to remember the past.

For those of us afraid of regret, fearful of risk, and frozen by the thought that things could get worse, the hardest step will be to give in to hope. As the Dutch historian Rutger Bregman observes, embracing a positive vision for the future usually means "weathering a storm of ridicule. You'll be called naive. Obtuse. Any weakness in your reasoning will be mercilessly exposed. Basically, it's easier to be a cynic."[45] That is why we need to hope together: out loud, with each other, every day. Believing that the future cannot be changed by our actions is just a convenient way of absolving ourselves of the need to take those actions. "Pessimism (or rather what is called such) is, in brief, playing the sure game. You cannot lose at it; you may gain. It is the only view of life in which you can never be disappointed," wrote the English novelist Thomas Hardy in 1902.[46]

Visions of a bleak future saturate our cultural world and conspire to breed fear and anxiety at the prospect of organizing our lives differently. Those in power benefit from our despair. It's hard to fight the urge to retreat. We often consider our homes as refuges from the world, hiding behind locked doors, and envying the rich, beautiful people living rich, beautiful lives on our social media feeds. Books and films like *The Hunger Games*, *Divergent*, and *Uglies*, as well as streaming series like *Black Mirror*, *Squid Game*, and *The Handmaid's Tale* exacerbate our despondency, filling us with specters of a cruel, brutal future. Dystopian stories are edgy and filled with plot-propelling existential struggles. Action, conflict, and violence titillate audiences and capti-vate attention. But these cultural products also work to diffuse our dissatisfaction with our present societies, since after all, things could become much worse if we try to change things too drastically. But we must reject the ubiquity of cynicism and dejection. Which brings me back to *Star Trek*.

Anything Is Possible

In 2017, after a twelve-year hiatus, a new show joined the fran-chise. Launched as a prequel to the original series, *Star Trek: Discov-ery* introduced a new generation of viewers to Gene Roddenberry's post-scarcity world of the United Federation of Planets, the interga-lactic union of semi-independent civilizations.[47] Starfleet is the Federa-tion's research, defense, and diplomatic arm, operating as a uniformed force of multispecies space Samaritans who must follow a strict code of conduct.[48] The *Discovery* is a special Starfleet science vessel con-ducting research in the mid-twenty-third century.

After two seasons of adventures, the beginning of the third season finds *Discovery* and her crew catapulted nine centuries into the future to a time when the Federation no longer exists. The former member worlds have descended into poverty, violence, and isolationism with scarce resources controlled by a brutal criminal syndicate of avari-cious green and blue humanoids called the Emerald Chain. When the ship gets spit out of a wormhole into the year 3189, only a few "true believers" still have faith that one day a renewed Federation can re-store peace and prosperity to the galaxy. The plot of the next two seasons follows the efforts of the captains and the crew of *Discovery* as they try to rebuild the Federation world by world, faced with the suspicion and hostility of embittered and deeply divided populations.

The fourth episode of the fourth season is called "All Is Possible." In it, an official of the newly reopened Starfleet Academy, Dr. Kovich, tells Lieutenant Tilly of the *Discovery*, "When *Discovery* first arrived, no one here trusted you. It wasn't just that you were in a nine-hundred-

and-thirty-year-old starship. . . . It was the way you carried yourself, like you grew up in a world that believes anything is possible. Quite frankly, it stung."[49]

More than fifty years since the original series began on network television, *Star Trek: Discovery* carries on the militant optimism of Gene Roddenberry's vision by showing how the people of the future find their way back to hope.[50] The presence of *Discovery* and its crew, people who "grew up in a world that believes anything is possible," rekindles faith that things can be different again. If the recovery of a certain past can make a different future possible, then, now more than ever before, it is essential for us to mine past utopian ideas and experiments, to reject the stuff that didn't work out so well, and rescue and repurpose the things that did. If our schools insist on assigning dystopian novels to our children, and our media environment feeds us nothing but a steady diet of doom, gloom, and the impending apocalypse, we must fight against them by allowing ourselves to dream.

Although progress is made in fits and starts, social change does happen; utopian proposals for the private sphere that once seemed impossible—childcare, divorce, and same-sex marriage—are now relatively commonplace. Change is always fueled by the perseverance of those who believe that we can do better. Hope is a muscle we must use. Some people train their memories; why not get into the habit of routinely flexing our emotional and cognitive capacities for hope by imagining a better tomorrow together? This is not to merely engage in naive optimism or self-help-style positive psychology, but rather to remember that, as Zinn pointed out, the stories we tell ourselves about the past determine the possibilities for our future.

Radical hope is the most powerful weapon we have. It's time we use it.

Acknowledgments

Writing a book that surveys over two millennia of utopian history and its contemporary resonances is no easy feat in normal times, but it proved especially challenging during a global pandemic when libraries and archives were closed, travel was often difficult, and many communities understandably closed their doors to outsiders. Given the limitations, I relied heavily on many colleagues and friends around the world to help me do the research necessary for this book. While I have been teaching about utopian socialists, communists, and anarchists for over twenty years, I really pushed myself out of my comfort zone to explore a diversity of utopian visions for rearranging our private lives, inspired initially by the history of the Bogomils, the Oneida Community, and the religion that grew out of the Saint-Simonian movement. In many ways, all utopians must take a huge leap of faith to imagine a different world than the one they are living in. People with different backgrounds draw their strength and inspiration from different sources, both secular or spiritual, and this is how it should be. Although all mistakes and oversights are most definitely my own, this book is truly the collective project of many wonderful minds who shared their time and knowledge with me in person, on the phone, over Zoom, or in email exchanges between April 2020 and August 2022.

As I grappled with Plato's *Republic*, Professor Emerita Sarah Conly was about as patient as they come. As someone who learned her ancient philosophy from T. H. Irwin, Sarah pushed me to really dig in to Book V of the *Republic* to try to make sense of Plato's various proposals for organizing the family life of the Guardians. Professor

Emerita Joan Roelofs gave me feedback on my passages about Charles Fourier and the Oneida Community, and Professor Barry Logan graciously reviewed and commented on the sections of chapter 6 that deal with primatology and evolutionary biology. For my discussion of the evolutionary anthropology of the nuclear family, I shared several valuable conversations with Professor Karen L. Kramer during our "monogamy happy hours" on Zoom. Her work and her generosity with her time have been a great inspiration to me. On the economics of the family, childcare, and the history of the kibbutz, my former colleague and coauthor, Professor Rachel Connelly, provided essential insights. Our long walks in Maine gave me an opportunity to air different arguments and ideas, and she gave me detailed feedback on an early draft of the entire childcare chapter.

My PhD student at the University of Pennsylvania, Elisheva Levy, inspired me to think about the utopian implications of the *kommunalka* and the idea of thinking "beyond monogamous architecture." She also assisted me in finding current statistics on the kibbutzim in Hebrew. In Bulgaria, Dr. Maria Stoilkova generously shared her knowledge and experience of the Bulgarian Educational-Professional Complexes of the 1980s, and in Serbia, Professor Radina Vučetić gave me an insider's perspective on what it was like to grow up in New Belgrade under Yugoslav socialism. In Modena, Professor Paola Rinaldi hosted me during the Festival of Philosophy and let me bounce ideas off her as I struggled with the education chapter. Kristen "Kelpie" Henderson of Twin Oaks was exceedingly thorough with her email replies to my tedious and detailed questions about communal living and owning property in common.

This whole project would never have seen the light of day without the amazing efforts of Mel Flashman. Although this is my twelfth published book, it is my first with a literary agent. During the chaos of the pandemic, Mel took me under her wing and labored tirelessly to help me write a strong proposal and find the right home for the project. Her professional knowledge of the publishing world is truly awe-inspiring, but she is also a talented author whisperer. When I was dejected or overwhelmed by the enormity of the project, Mel provided essential moral support, while never compromising her high standards. I am profoundly grateful for all of her efforts on my behalf, and I sincerely hope that one day we will actually meet in real life and go thrifting together at the Junior League.

I also benefited from the incredible editorial direction of Megan Hogan at Simon & Schuster. Megan was basically my dream editor, always willing to push back with hard questions and suggesting the deep cuts necessary to prevent me from descending into too many pedantic scholarly rabbit holes. As I worked through multiple versions of different chapters, there were long weeks when my only form of social interaction was with Megan's comment bubbles in my Microsoft Word documents. In so many ways, this book is a dialogue between Megan and me, a meeting of two minds over a primordial mass of initial drafts. Megan encouraged me to think far beyond academic or activist audiences, and the book was much enriched by her suggestions to include examples of contemporary communities experimenting with utopian ideas for rearranging their domestic lives.

But if the author-editor relationship is usually a monogamous one, Megan generously opened it up, and we had a sort of consensual poly-editorial relationship that included two British men. At Bodley Head, Will Hammond and Con Brown both gave comments on early drafts of the chapters and made essential suggestions for how to increase its legibility to international audiences. Will, in particular, gave me the courage to share some of my own personal family history after he read the first outline of chapter 6. I was profoundly uncomfortable writing about something that I have spent my entire life avoiding, but Will convinced me of the power of sharing these kinds of experiences in print, if only to help destigmatize them for readers in other countries where the personal discussion of childhood trauma is not as encouraged or accepted as it is in the United States. In fact, writing that chapter brought me much closer to my mother, with whom I had scarcely discussed this past. My mom generously agreed to allow me to tell her story, which meant she had to relive a lot of those painful memories, and for her courage in this regard, I am extremely grateful.

In many ways, if I am the mother of this book, it was well provisioned by a wide variety of alloparents. At Penn, my wonderful colleagues—Mitchell Orenstein, Kevin M. F. Platt, Julia Verkholanstev, Brian Kim, Maria Alley, Maria Bourlatskaya, Molly Peeney, Mila Nazyrova, and the rest of our lecturers and affiliated faculty—held things together in Russian and East European studies while I was on leave for three different semesters between fall 2020 and spring 2022. Much gratitude to Vita Raskevičiūte for final proofreading. Heartfelt thanks as well to Bernd Kortmann, Nik Binder, Sandra Geller, and Marina Jones at the Freiburg Institute for Advanced Studies (FRIAS) in Germany, where I spent two months during the copyediting phase of this book in the summer of 2022. The intellectual climate and camaraderie of the international group of scholars from diverse disciplines enriched my thinking and provided a real social life for the first time since the beginning of the pandemic. At Simon & Schuster, Elizabeth Venere and Shannon Hennessey also gave their time and energy to getting this book out into the world. Finally, on my many long days of solo research and writing, the ambient music of Jean-Michel Jarre always kept me in the appropriate utopian state of mind.

My dear friend Annie Finch read and offered comments on early drafts of the introduction, and Pope Brock and Sarah Braunstein both provided valuable advice about navigating the commercial publishing industry. The many conversations I shared with Page Herrlinger, both in person and on Zoom, as I was writing the manuscript kept me grounded and sane. The refreshingly contrarian Hayden and Jo never resisted opportunities to remind me of the existential threat of the climate crisis, which forced me to consider the environmental necessity of building everyday utopias. Finally, my former student and sometimes coauthor, Julia Mead, swept in at the last minute to help with one final round of copyedits and a sensitivity read to help fix my often outdated or too academic prose. Although I take full responsibility for all remaining mistakes and clunky word choices, her assistance was absolutely invaluable.

I simply cannot thank my daughter enough for the many small acts of love and affection she gave me as I struggled to do the research for this book and often found myself insecure and nervous about writing something that might make her question her importance in my life. It's quite intimidating to write a book about family expansionism when you know your own biological child will read it. She's been an incredibly good sport, and I hope she knows how very much I love her and respect the amazing young woman she's become. Her father, my ex-husband in Bulgaria, and I have also remained close friends for almost eighteen years after our divorce. He has been an attentive co-parent to our daughter, and I am grateful to him for remaining in her life despite the distance and logistical difficulties. His family in Sofia, my ex-in-laws and ex-brother- and sister-in-law, have continued to welcome me at their family table for Christmas, Easter, and name days when I am in the country. They never excluded me from the warmth of their hearth even when I traveled without my daughter. Their continued kindness reinforces the idea that we can all choose our own kin no matter what the legal or consanguineous ties.

Perhaps the person most uncomfortable with my discussions of non-monogamy, and who always provided the harshest and unforgiving criticisms of my early drafts, is my partner of the last fifteen years. Although we remain unmarried and do not live together in any traditional sense, we share an incredibly rich life of laughter, adventure, and endless intellectual debate about everything from the intricacies of German domestic politics to the epistemology of truth. A grammar absolutist and a fierce proponent of logical soundness, he catches the slightest hint of argumentative laziness and always demands clearly articulated premises and equally transparent prose. He read almost every word of my drafts and provided detailed, numbered-step synopses to help me hone and clarify my assertions. He fact-checked and proofread and encouraged me when I was despairing. A one-of-a-kind man who challenged patrilineal traditions in his own life by giving his first-born child his ex-wife's surname, he respects my independence and never balks at my need for long stints of fieldwork in Europe without him. Whether we are watching the World Cup, drinking half liters of beer at Christopher Street Days, doing marathon *Battlestar Galactica* or *TNG* rewatches, playing card games with our grown kids, or silently strolling the grounds at Chanticleer, we share a special "comradely-love" that would have made Alexandra Kollontai proud. My gratitude to him is boundless.

Although I have already thanked my mom above, I want her to know how much I love her despite our differences in the past. Learning about the abuses she suffered at my father's hands and the many threats he made against her helped me better understand her situation, something incomprehensible to me as a child and young adult. I am proud of her for surviving and for everything she did for me despite the many hardships. My grandmother passed away while I was writing this book, and I miss her. For saving my mother's life and for being there when times got hard, she deserves to be beatified. And finally, to Tom and Betty Olson, without whom I would never be writing these words. Although they have also both passed on from this life, their light continues to shine upon it.

The 1987 Wim Wenders film, *Der Himmel über Berlin* (*The Sky over Berlin* or *Wings of Desire*), follows the story of two angels who listen in on the thoughts and secret desires of the residents of the divided city. One of the angels, Daniel, falls in love with a human woman, and longs to give up his immortality to join the mortal world. When the actor Peter Falk arrives in Berlin to make a film about the Nazi past, we learn that he, too, was once an angel, but now lives in corporeal form as a man. It is a glorious film that continues to haunt me even decades later. If Wenders's imagination is true, and we share this mortal world with ex-angels who walk among us, I've absolutely no doubt that Tom and Betty were two of them.

Notes

Author's Note

1 See chapter 30 in Iamblichus, *Life of Pythagoras*, trans. Thomas Taylor, available at Project Gutenberg, https://www.gutenberg.org/files/63300/63300-h/63300-h.htm.

2 Alisha Haridasani Gupta, "Why Some Women Call This Recession a 'Shecession.'" *New York Times*, May 9, 2020, https://www.nytimes.com/2020/05/09/us/unemployment-coronavirus-women.html.

3 Alexandra Topping, "UK Working Mothers Are 'Sacrificial Lambs' in Coronavirus Childcare Crisis," *The Guardian*, July 24, 2020, https://www.theguardian.com/money/2020/jul/24/uk-working-mothers-are-sacrifical-lambs-in-coronavirus-childcare-crisis.

4 "Parenting in Lockdown: Coronavirus and the Effects on Work-Life Balance," Office for National Statistics, July 22, 2020, https://www.ons.gov.uk/people populationandcommunity/healthandsocialcare/conditionsanddiseases/articles/parentinginlockdowncoronavirusandtheeffectsonworklifebalance/latest.

Chapter 1: To Boldly Know Where No One Has Known Before

1 Jill Lepore, *The Secret History of Wonder Woman* (London: Vintage, 2015).

2 Thucydides, *The History of the Peloponnesian War*, Project Gutenberg, https://www.gutenberg.org/ebooks/7142.

3 Nikolai Chernyshevsky, *What Is to Be Done?*, trans. Michael Katz (Ithaca, NY: Cornell University Press, 1989).

4 Peter Kropotkin, "Anarchist Morality," Anarchist Library, https://theanarchistlibrary.org/library/petr-kropotkin-anarchist-morality.

5 Christopher Klien, "The Real History That Inspired 'Star Wars,'" *History*, August 22, 2018, https://www.history.com/news/the-real-history-that-inspired-star-wars.

6 Aristophanes, *A Parliament of Women*, in *Four Plays by Aristophanes*, trans. Paul Roche (New York: Signet Classics, 2004), 203.

7 Emma Goldman, "Socialism Caught in the Political Trap," in *Red Emma Speaks: An Emma Goldman Reader*, ed. Alix Kates Shulman, freely available at the Anarchist Library, https://theanarchistlibrary.org/library/emma-goldman -socialism-caught-in-the-political-trap.

8 Karl Mannheim, *Ideology and Utopia: An Introduction to the Sociology of Knowledge* (1936; New York: Martin, 2015): 341–43.

9 William Samuelson and Richard Zeckhauser, "Status Quo Bias in Decision-Making," *Journal of Risk and Uncertainty* 1, no. 1 (February 1988): 7–59.

10 Daniel Kahneman and Amos Tversky, "The Psychology of Preferences," *Scientific American* 246, no. 1 (January 1982): 160–73.

11 Scott Timberg, "The Novel That Predicted Portland," *New York Times*, December 12, 2008, https://www.nytimes.com/2008/12/14/fashion/14ecotopia .html.

12 Mannheim, *Ideology and Utopia*, 232–33.

13 Thomas Piketty, *Capital in the 21st Century* (Cambridge, MA: Harvard University Press, 2013).

14 Rutger Bregman, *Utopia for Realists: How We can Build the Ideal World* (New York: Little, Brown, 2017).

15 Wade Davis, "Keynote Speech: The Ethnosphere and the Academy," 2014, https://www.wheretherebedragons.com/wp-content/uploads/2014/09/Davis EthnosphereAcademy.pdf.

16 For the full text and a video of the 1997 Apple "Think Different" ad, see: http://www.thecrazyones.it/spot-en.html.

17 See the website of the Center for Climate Repair at Cambridge University: https://www.climaterepair.cam.ac.uk.

18 Fred Pearce, "Geoengineer the Planet? More Scientists Now Say It Must Be an Option," YaleEnviroment360, May 29, 2019, https://e360.yale.edu/features /geoengineer-the-planet-more-scientists-now-say-it-must-be-an-option; Pallab Ghosh, "Climate Change: Scientists Test Radical Ways to Fix Earth's Climate," *BBC News*, May 10, 2018, https://www.bbc.com/news/science-environment -48069663.

19 See the website for the Coalition for the Radical Life Extension: https://www .rlecoalition.com/about.

20 See the website for the International Society for Artificial Life: https://alife.org.

21 Maddy Savage, "Why Do Women Still Change Their Names?" *BBC*, September 23, 2020, https://www.bbc.com/worklife/article/20200921-why-do-women -still-change-their-names.

22 Lucy Robinson, "Whose Last Name Should You Give Your Baby?" BabyCenter,

November 26, 2018, https://www.babycenter.com/0_whose-last-name-should
-you-give-your-baby_10327041.bc.

23 "Giving a Name," Kingdom of Belgium Foreign Affairs, Foreign Trade and
Development Cooperation, May 4, 2022, https://diplomatie.belgium.be/en/services
/services_abroad/registry/giving_a_name.

24 Sandra Dijkstra, *Flora Tristan: Feminism in the Age of George Sand* (New
York: Verso, 2019).

25 Jayne Orenstein, "How My Great-Grandmother Lost Her U.S. Citizenship
the Year Women Got the Right to Vote," *Washington Post*, August 13, 2020,
https://www.washingtonpost.com/history/2020/08/13/expatriation-act
-citizenship-women-suffrage/; Meg Hacker, "When Saying 'I Do' Meant Giving
Up Your U.S. Citizenship," *Prologue*, spring 2014, https://www.archives.gov
/files/publications/prologue/2014/spring/citizenship.pdf.

26 Helen Fink, *Women After Communism: The East German Experience*
(Lanham, MD: University Press of America, 2001).

27 *Dunn v. Palermo*, 522 S.W.2d 679, 1975, Supreme Court of Tennessee, https://
law.justia.com/cases/tennessee/supreme-court/1975/522-s-w-2d-679-2.html.

28 Thisanla Siripala, "Japan's Same Surname Law for Married Couples Is in the
Hands of the Diet," *The Diplomat*, July 08, 2021, https://thediplomat.com
/2021/07/japans-same-surname-law-for-married-couples-is-in-the-hands-of
-the-diet/.

29 Heather Long, "Should Women Change Their Names After Marriage? Consider
the Greek Way," *The Guardian*, October 6, 2013, https://www.theguardian
.com/commentisfree/2013/oct/06/women-change-name-after-marriage-greece;
"Charter of Human Rights and Freedoms," *Légis Québec*, November 21, 2021,
http://legisquebec.gouv.qc.ca/en/ShowDoc/cs/C-12.

30 Chelsea Vowel, "Giving My Children Cree Names Is a Powerful Act of Recla-
mation," *CBC News*, November 4, 2018, https://www.cbc.ca/amp/1.4887604.

31 Kim Parker and Renee Stepler, "Americans See Men as the Financial Providers,
Even as Women's Contributions Grow," Pew Research Center, September
20, 2017, https://www.pewresearch.org/fact-tank/2017/09/20/americans-see
-men-as-the-financial-providers-even-as-womens-contributions-grow/.

32 Claire Cain Miller and Quoctrong Bui, "Equality in Marriages Grows, and So
Does Class Divide," *New York Times*, February 23, 2016, https://www.nytimes
.com/2016/02/23/upshot/rise-in-marriages-of-equals-and-in-division-by-class
.html.

33 Londa Schiebinger, Andrea Davies Henderson, and Shannon K. Gilmartin,
Dual-Career Academic Couples: What Universities Need to Know, Michelle
R. Clayman Institute for Gender Research, Stanford University, 2008, https://
stanford.app.box.com/s/y5bicy7o3cxwtmgy22iu.

34 Gretchen Livingston, "Stay-at-Home Moms and Dads Account for About One-in-Five U.S. Parents," Pew Research Center, September 24, 2018, https://www.pewresearch.org/fact-tank/2018/09/24/stay-at-home-moms-and-dads-account-for-about-one-in-five-u-s-parents/.

35 Aliya Hamid Rao, "Even Breadwinning Wives Don't Get Equality at Home," Atlantic, May 12, 2019, https://www.theatlantic.com/family/archive/2019/05/breadwinning-wives-gender-inequality/589237/.

36 For all citations to Plato's Republic, I use the C. D. C. Reeve translation, but the full text of the Benjamin Jowett translation is available at Project Gutenberg: https://www.gutenberg.org/ebooks/55201; Plato, The Republic, trans. C. D. C. Reeve (Indianapolis: Hackett, 2004), 465c.

37 Plato, The Republic, Book V, 464c-d.

38 Dwight E. Neuenschwander, ed., Dear Professor Dyson: Twenty Years of Correspondence Between Freeman Dyson and Undergraduate Students on Science, Technology, Society and Life (Hackensack, NJ: World Scientific, 2012), 17–18. Online at: https://www.worldscientific.com/worldscibooks/10.1142/9592.

39 Mark Matousek, "The Eros of Friendship: What to Do with Platonic Passion?" Psychology Today, May 12, 2013, https://www.psychologytoday.com/us/blog/ethical-wisdom/201305/the-eros-friendship-what-do-platonic-passion.

40 Elle Hunt, "BirthStrikers: Meet the Women Who Refuse to Have Children Until Climate Change Ends." The Guardian, March 12, 2019, https://www.theguardian.com/lifeandstyle/2019/mar/12/birthstrikers-meet-the-women-who-refuse-to-have-children-until-climate-change-ends.

41 Eli Finkel, The All-or-Nothing Marriage: How the Best Marriages Work (New York: Dutton: 2017).

42 Kayleen Devlin, "The World's First Artificial Womb for Humans," BBC News. October 16, 2019. https://www.bbc.com/news/av/health-50056405.

43 Rebecca Solnit, Hope in the Dark: Untold Histories, Wild Possibilities (Chicago: Haymarket Books, 2016), 4.

44 Spoken by the hologram of Captain Kathryn Janeway in "Starstruck," Star Trek: Prodigy, season 1, episode 3, https://memory-alpha.fandom.com/wiki/Starstruck_(episode).

45 Richard Duff, "'Star Trek' actress Nichelle Nichols: Martin Luther King Jr. Impacted Decision to stay on Enterprise." Daily News. January 17, 2011, https://www.nydailynews.com/entertainment/tv-movies/star-trek-actress-nichelle-nichols-martin-luther-king-jr-impacted-decision-stay-enterprise-article-1.154674.

46 Dave Nemetz, "Whoopi Goldberg Explains Why She Wanted to Be on 'Star Trek.'" Yahoo! Entertainment, June 24, 2014: https://www.yahoo.com/entertainment/blogs/tv-news/exclusive-video-whoopi-goldberg-star-trek-213710247.html.

47 Albert Einstein, *Einstein: On Cosmic Religion and Other Opinions and Aphorisms* (London: Dover, 2009), 97.

Chapter 2: Home Is Where the Walls Are

1 "Combatting Loneliness One Conversation at a Time: A Call to Action," Jo Cox Commission on Loneliness, April 2018, https://www.ageuk.org .uk/globalassets/age-uk/documents/reports-and-publications/reports-and -briefings/active-communities/rb_dec17_jocox_commission_finalreport.pdf.

2 "Loneliness at Epidemic Levels in America," Cigna, https://newsroom.cigna .com/loneliness-in-america.

3 Elisheva Levy, "Beyond Monogamous Architecture; Rebellious Homes for Communism," *From the Margins* podcast, May 24, 2020, https://anchor.fm/from -the-margins-arch/episodes/Elisheva-Levy—-Beyond-Monogamous-architecture -Rebellious-homes-for-communism-eee948.

4 "Neolithic Site of Çatalhöyük," World Heritage List, UNESCO, https://whc .unesco.org/en/list/1405/.

5 Marin A. Pilloud and Clark Spencer Larsen, "'Official' and 'Practical' Kin: Inferring Social and Community Structure from Dental Phenotype at Neolithic Çatalhöyük, Turkey," *Physical Anthropology* 145, no. 4 (August 2011): 519–30.

6 Pilloud and Larsen, "'Official' and 'Practical' Kin," 527–28.

7 Plato, *Republic*, Book III, 417a.

8 James 1: 27 (New International Version).

9 George W. Bernard, "The Dissolution of the Monasteries," *History* 96, no. 324 (September 2011): 390.

10 "Heaven on Earth: The Plan of St. Gall," *The Wilson Quarterly* 4, no. 1 (Winter 1980): 171–79.

11 Campus Galli's website: https://www.campus-galli.de.

12 "Introduction and History," University of Oxford, https://www.ox.ac.uk/about /organisation/history.

13 Thomas More, *Utopia*, Project Gutenberg [1516], https://www.gutenberg.org /ebooks/2130.

14 Walter Simons, *Cities of Ladies: Beguine Communities in the Medieval Low Countries, 1200-1565* (Philadelphia: University of Pennsylvania Press, 2003).

15 Carol Neel, "The Origins of the Beguines," *Signs* 14, no. 2 (Winter 1989): 321–41.

16 Hadewijch of Antwerp, "Letter 6: Live in Christ," in *Hadewijch: The Complete Works*, trans. Mother Columba Hart, O.S.B. (Mahwah, NJ: Paulist Press, 1980), 59.

17 "Flemish Béguinages," World Heritage List, UNESCO, http://whc.unesco.org/en
    /list/855.

18 Manon Legrand, "Des béguines aux Babayagas, quelles alternatives de
    logement pour les femmes?" Alter Échos, April 2019, https://www.alterechos
    .be/wp-content/uploads/2019/04/AE472_web-25-30_focale.pdf; "Beguinal
    Movement Today," Beguinal Movement, https://beguines.info/?p=319&lang=en.

19 Frank E. Manuel and Fritzie P. Manuel, Utopian Thought in the Western World
    (Cambridge, MA: Harvard University Press, 1979), 584.

20 Leslie F. Goldstein, "Early Feminist Themes in French Utopian Socialism: The
    St.-Simonians and Fourier," Journal of the History of Ideas 43, no. 1 (January–
    March 1982): 91–108.

21 Charles Fourier, Theory of the Four Movements, eds. Gareth Stefan Jones
    and Ian Patterson, Cambridge Texts in the History of Political Thought
    (Cambridge, UK: Cambridge University Press, 1996), 132.

22 Fourier, Theory of the Four Movements, 137.

23 Fourier, Theory of the Four Movements, 148.

24 Gregory Claeys, Searching for Utopia: The History of an Idea (London:
    Thames & Hudson, 2011), 134; Fourier, Theory of the Four Movements, 4.

25 Fourier, Theory of the Four Movements, 50nd.

26 Jonathan Beecher and Richard Bienvenu, eds., The Utopian Vision of Charles
    Fourier: Selected Texts on Work, Love, and Passionate Attraction (Cambridge,
    MA: Beacon Press, 1971).

27 André Godin quoted in Michel Lallement, "An Experiment Inspired by Fourier:
    J. B. Godin's Familistere in Guise," Journal of Historical Sociology 25, no. 1
    (March 2012): 37.

28 André Godin quoted in Edward Howland, "The Social Palace at Guise,"
    Harper's New Monthly Magazine (New York: Harper and Bros, 1872),
    701–16: 712.

29 "Original Miscellany: Le Familistére de Guise. Description and Character of
    the Industry Upon Which the Working People of the Social Palace Depend,"
    American Artisan, October 1, 1875, 271.

30 Howland, "The Social Palace at Guise," 716.

31 "Familistery of Guise," The American Socialist: Devoted to the Enlargement
    and Perfection of Home 1, no. 15 (July 6, 1876): 114.

32 "Original Miscellany: Le Familistére de Guise," 271.

33 Friedrich Engels, "Part Two: How the Bourgeoisie Solves the Housing
    Question," in The Housing Question, 1872. Free online at: Marxists Internet
    Archive, https://www.marxists.org/archive/marx/works/1872/housing-question
    /ch02.htm.

34 Website of Le Familistère de Guise: https://www.familistere.com/fr/decouvrir

/collections-ressources/references-documentaires-sur-le-familistere; François
Bernardot, *Le Familistère de Guise, Association du Capital et du Travail et son
fondateur, Jean-Baptiste André Godin. Étude faite au nom de la Société du
Familistère de Guise Dequenne & Cie*, deuxième édition (Guise: Imprimerie de
E. Barré, 1889).

35 Faith Hillis, *Utopia's Discontents: Russian Émigrés and the Quest for Freedom,
1830s–1930s* (London and New York: Oxford University Press, 2021).

36 *Stilgayi (Hipsters)*, dir. Valeriy Todorovskiy, Kino Lorber, 2008, https://www
.imdb.com/title/tt1239426/.

37 Ilya Utekhin, Alice Nakhimovsky, Slava Paperno, and Nancy Ries,
"Communal Living in Russia: A Virtual Museum of Soviet Everyday Life,"
Colgate University, https://kommunalka.colgate.edu/cfm/essays.cfm?ClipID=
361&TourID=910.

38 Svetlana Boym, *Common Places: Mythologies of Everyday Life in Russia*
(Cambridge, MA: Harvard University Press, 1994), 123.

39 Eli Rubin, *Amnesiopolis: Modernity, Space, and Memory in East Germany*
(London and New York: Oxford University Press, 2016).

40 See the website of the 15-Minute City Project: https://www.15minutecity.com.

41 Łukasz Stanek, "Gift, Credit, Barter: Architectural Mobilities in Global
Socialism," e-flux Architecture, July 2020, https://www.e-flux.com/architecture
/housing/337850/gift-credit-barter-architectural-mobilities-in-global-socialism/;
Łukasz Stanek, *Architecture in Global Socialism: Eastern Europe, West Africa,
and the Middle East in the Cold War* (Princeton, NJ: Princeton University
Press, 2020).

42 Starcity was acquired by Common in 2021 and no longer has an independent
website. These quotes come from the website in May 2021.

43 "About Us," Collective, https://www.thecollective.com/about-us.

44 Zoë Bernard, "Take a Look Inside the Stylish, Modern-Day Communes That
Are Taking Over US Cities," *Business Insider*, February 28, 2018, https://www
.businessinsider.com/common-co-living-spaces-is-spreading-into-more-us-
cities-2018-2.

45 "Welcome to the New Frontier of Shared Housing," Common brochure,
https://www.common.com/common-in-metropolitan-home.pdf.

46 "Why Common," Common, https://www.common.com/why-common/.

47 Nellie Bowles, "Dorm Living for Professionals Comes to San Francisco," *New
York Times*, March 4, 2018, https://www.nytimes.com/2018/03/04/technology
/dorm-living-grown-ups-san-francisco.html.

48 Patrick Sisson, "Can Coliving Help Solve the Urban Housing Crunch?" *Curbed*,
March 10, 2016, https://archive.curbed.com/2016/3/8/11178598/cooperative
-housing-city-living-coliving.

49 Will Coldwell, "'Co-Living': The End of Urban Loneliness—Or Cynical Corporate Dormitories?" *The Guardian*, September 3, 2019, https://www.theguardian.com/cities/2019/sep/03/co-living-the-end-of-urban-loneliness-or-cynical-corporate-dormitories.

50 "Coliving Spaces: The Ultimate Guide to Coliving," Outsite, https://www.outsite.co/coliving-spaces.

51 Rob Warnock, "Apartment List's 2021 Millennial Homeownership Report," Apartment List, February 9, 2021, https://www.apartmentlist.com/research/millennial-homeownership-2021.

52 Bérénice Magistretti, "Starcity Raises $30 Million in a Post–WeWork, COVID Crisis to Scale Its Affordable Co-Living Spaces," *Forbes*, April 27, 2020, https://www.forbes.com/sites/berenicemagistretti/2020/04/27/starcity-raises-30-million-in-a-post-wework-covid-crisis-to-scale-its-affordable-co-living-spaces/?sh=557e14ff48f7.

53 "Habyt Acquires Quarters and Becomes the Leading Co-Living Player in Europe," Quarters press release, https://global.quarters.com/habyt-acquires-quarters/.

54 Kynala Phillips, "Did Shawnee really ban roommates? Here's what the new 'co-living' restrictions mean." *Kansas City Star*, May 6, 2022, https://www.kansascity.com/news/politics-government/article260995857.html.

55 City of Shawnee, Ordinance to amend Shawnee Municipal Code Title 17 - Zoning, related to room rental in residential zoning district, April 25, 2022. https://cityofshawnee.civicweb.net/document/88149/Consider%20an%20ordinance%20to%20amend%20Shawnee%20Municipa.pdf.

56 Miles Brignall, "Communal Living: Grand Designs on Living in Perfect Harmony," *The Guardian*, October 23, 2009, https://www.theguardian.com/money/2009/oct/24/communal-living-grand-designs.

57 Bodil Graae, "Børn skal have hundrede forældre," *Politiken*, April 9, 1987, 49–50.

58 J. Gudmand-Høyer, "Det manglende led mellem utopi og det forældede enfamiliehus," *Dagbladet Information*, June 26, 1968, 3.

59 Quoted in Saskia de Melker and Melanie Saltzman, "Cohousing Communities Help Prevent Social Isolation," *PBS NewsHour Weekend*, February 12, 2017, https://www.pbs.org/newshour/show/cohousing-communities-help-prevent-social-isolation.

60 Lucy Sargisson, "Second-Wave Cohousing: A Modern Utopia?" *Utopian Studies* 23, no. 1 (January 2012): 28–56.

61 Website of the Ibsgården intentional community: http://www.ibsgaarden.dk.

62 de Melker and Saltzman, "Cohousing Communities Help Prevent Social Isolation."

63 Sargisson, "Second-Wave Cohousing."

64 Dansk Bygningsarv, *Fremtidens bofællesskaber* (*Co-housing Communities of the Future*) (Copenhagen: Udlaendinge-, Integrations- og Boligministeriet, 2016), quoted in Henrik Gutzon Larsen, "Three Phases of Danish Cohousing: Tenure and the Development of an Alternative Housing Form," *Housing Studies* 34, no. 8 (2019): 1349–71.

65 Larsen, "Three Phases of Danish Cohousing," 1363.

66 Tong-Jin Smith, "Rich and Sexy: Booming Berlin Is Driving Up Real Estate Prices," *German Times*, October 2018, https://www.german-times.com/rich-and-sexy-booming-berlin-is-driving-up-real-estate-prices/.

67 Kristien Ring, "Reinventing Density: How Baugruppen Are Pioneering the Self-Made City," *The Conversation*, November 21, 2016, https://theconversation.com/reinventing-density-how-baugruppen-are-pioneering-the-self-made-city-66488.

68 Jessica Bridger, "Don't Call It a Commune: Inside Berlin's Radical Cohousing Project," *Metropolis*, June 10, 2015, https://www.metropolismag.com/architecture/residential-architecture/dont-call-it-a-commune-inside-berlin-radical-cohousing-project/.

69 Max Pedersen, "Senior Co-Housing Communities in Denmark," *Journal of Housing for the Elderly* 29, nos. 1–2 (January 2015): 126–45.

70 V. Quinio and G. Burgess, "Is Co-Living a Housing Solution for Vulnerable Older People?" Cambridge Center for Housing & Planning Research Technical Report, University of Cambridge, 2018.

71 Legrand, "Des béguines aux Babayagas."

72 "Finalist 2015: Nashira, a Song of Love, a Women-Led Project," World Habitat Awards, https://world-habitat.org/world-habitat-awards/winner-and-finalists/nashira-a-song-of-love-a-women-led-project/.

73 "Nashira Eco-Village in Colombia a Matriarchal Example of Women Empowerment," ACEI-Global blog, April 26, 2019, https://acei-global.blog/2019/04/26/nashira-eco-village-in-colombia-a-matriarchal-example-of-women-empowerment/.

74 Brian J. Burke and Beatriz Arjona, "Creating Alternative Political Ecologies Through the Construction of Ecovillages and Ecovillagers in Colombia," in eds., Joshua Lockyer and James R. Veteto, *Environmental Anthropology Engaging Ecotopia: Bioregionalism, Permaculture, and Ecovillages* (New York: Berghahn Books, 2013), 235–50.

75 See the Nashira website, http://www.nashira-ecoaldea.org.

76 Kathryn McCamant, Charles Durrett, and Ellen Herzman, *Cohousing: A Contemporary Approach to Housing Ourselves*, 2nd ed. (Berkeley: Ten Speed Press, 1994).

77 de Melker and Saltzman, "Cohousing Communities Help Prevent Social Isolation."

78 Zeynep Toker, "New Housing for New Households: Comparing Cohousing and New Urbanist Developments with Women in Mind," *Journal of Architectural and Planning Research* 27, no. 4 (December 2010): 325–39: 334.

79 Toker, "New Housing for New Households," 334.

80 Toker, "New Housing for New Households," 334.

81 Cathrin Wassede, "Doing Family in Cohousing Communities," in *Contemporary Co-Housing in Europe: Toward Sustainable Cities?* ed. Pernilla Hagbert, Henrik Gutzon Larsen, Hakan Thörn, and Cathrin Wasshede (New York: Routledge, 2020).

82 Courtney Martin, "Coming of Age in Cohousing," *Curbed*, February 13, 2019, https://archive.curbed.com/2019/2/13/18194960/cohousing-families-communities -united-states-muir-commons.

83 Quoted in Martin, "Coming of Age in Cohousing."

84 Quoted in Martin, "Coming of Age in Cohousing."

85 Martin, "Coming of Age in Cohousing."

86 Jacob Ausubel, "Older People Are More Likely to Live Alone in the U.S. Than Elsewhere in the World," Pew Research Center, March 10, 2020, https://www .pewresearch.org/fact-tank/2020/03/10/older-people-are-more-likely-to-live -alone-in-the-u-s-than-elsewhere-in-the-world/.

87 Jacob Ausubel. "Globally, Women Are Younger Than Their Male Partners, More Likely to Age Alone," Pew Research Center, January 23, 2020, https:// www.pewresearch.org/fact-tank/2020/01/03/globally-women-are-younger -than-their-male-partners-more-likely-to-age-alone/.

88 A. P. Glass and N. Frederick, "Elder Cohousing as a Choice for Introverted Older Adults: Obvious or Surprising?" 69th Annual Scientific Meeting of the Gerontological Society of America, New Orleans, LA, *The Gerontologist 56*, suppl. 3 (November 2016): 172.

89 Anne P. Glass, "Sense of Community, Loneliness, and Satisfaction in Five Elder Cohousing Neighborhoods," *Journal of Women & Aging* 32, no. 3 (October 2019): 1–25.

90 Vivian Puplampu, Elise Matthews, Gideon Puplampu, Murray Gross, Sushila Pathak, Sarah Peters, "The Impact of Cohousing on Older Adults' Quality of Life," *Canadian Journal on Aging / La Revue canadienne du vieillissement 39*, no. 3 (September 2020): 406–20.

91 J. Carrere, A. Reyes, L. Oliveras, et al., "The Effects of Cohousing Model on People's Health and Wellbeing: A Scoping Review," *Public Health Reviews* 41, no. 1 (October 2020): https://doi.org/10.1186/s40985-020-00138-1.

92 Graham Meltzer, "Cohousing: Verifying the Importance of Community in

the Application of Environmentalism," *Journal of Architectural and Planning Research* 17, no. 2 (Summer 2000): 110–32; Jason R. Brown, *Comparative Analysis of Energy Consumption Trends in Cohousing and Alternate Housing Arrangement*, MIT MSc thesis, 2004.

93 Lee Wallender, "The Life Expectancy of Major Household Appliances," *The Spruce*, January 2, 2022, https://www.thespruce.com/lifespan-of-household -appliances-4158782.

94 Sabrina Helm, Joyce Serido, Sun Young Ahn, Victoria Ligon, and Soyeon Shim, "Materialist Values, Financial and Pro-Environmental Behaviors, and Well-Being," *Young Consumers* 20, no. 4 (July 2019): 264–84.

95 Krisztina Fehérváry, *Politics in Color and Concrete: Socialist Materialities and the Middle Class in Hungary* (Bloomington: Indiana University Press, 2013).

96 Maria L. Ruiu, "Differences Between Cohousing and Gated Communities. A Literature Review," *Sociological Inquiry* 84, no. 2 (May 2014): 316–35.

97 Holly Harper, "I'm a Single Mom Who Shares a House with Other Single Moms. Cohousing Saved Me $30,000 Last Year," *Business Insider*, January 31, 2022, https://www.insider.com/cohousing-single-mom-saved-over-30000-per -year-living-together-2022-1.

98 L. Tummers and S. MacGregor, "Beyond Wishful Thinking: A FPE Perspective on Commoning, Care, and the Promise of Co-Housing," *International Journal of the Commons* 13, no. 1 (May 2019): 62–83.

99 Peter Kropotkin, *The Conquest of Bread*, ed. Paul Avrich (1892; New York: New York University Press, 1972), 110–11.

100 Kathy McLaughlin, "Jeff Bezos Buys David Geffen's Los Angeles Mansion for a Record $165 Million," *Wall Street Journal*, February 12, 2020, https://www.wsj .com/articles/jeff-bezos-buys-david-geffens-los-angeles-mansion-for-a-record -165-million-11581542020?mod=e2tw;, "2020 Greater Los Angeles Homeless Count Results," Los Angeles Homeless Services Authority, June 12, 2020, https://www.lahsa.org/news?article=726-2020-greater-los-angeles-homeless -count-results.

Chapter 3: Kids as Public Goods

1 Sylvia Ann Hewlett, "Executive Women and the Myth of Having It All," *Harvard Business Review*, April 2020, https://hbr.org/2002/04/executive -women-and-the-myth-of-having-it-all.

2 Mark Lino, "The Cost of Raising a Child," US Department of Agriculture, February 18, 2020, https://www.usda.gov/media/blog/2017/01/13/cost-raising-child.

3 Anne Crittendon, *The Price of Motherhood: Why the Most Important Job in the World Is Still the Least Valued* (New York: Picador, 2010).

4 Andrew E. Clark, Ed Diener, Yannis Georgellis, and Richard E. Lucas, "Lags and Leads in Life Satisfaction: A Test of the Baseline Hypothesis," IZA Discussion Paper No. 2526, December 2006, http://ftp.iza.org/dp2526.pdf.

5 Jean M. Twenge, W. Keith Campbell, and Craig A. Foster, "Parenthood and Marital Satisfaction: A Meta-Analytic Review," *Journal of Marriage and Family* 65, no. 3 (February 2004): 574–83.

6 Jennifer Glass, R. W. Simon, and M. A. Andersson, "Parenthood and Happiness: Effects of Work-Family Reconciliation Policies in 22 OECD Countries," *American Journal of Sociology* 122, no. 3 (November 2016): 886–929.

7 Antti O. Tanskanen, Mirrka Danielsbacka, David A. Coall, and Markus Jokela, "Transition to Grandparenthood and Subjective Well-Being in Older Europeans: A Within-Person Investigation Using Longitudinal Data," *Evolutionary Psychology* 17, no. 3 (July–September 2019): 1–12.

8 Glass, Simon, and Andersson, "Parenthood and Happiness."

9 David VanOpdorp, "Germany with Massive Shortage in Day Care Spots, Study Finds." *Deutsche Welle*, October 11, 2020, https://www.dw.com/en/germany -with-massive-shortage-in-day-care-spots-study-finds/a-55232526.

10 "3 in 4 German Daycare Children Not Getting Proper Care: Study." *Deutsche Welle*, August 25. 2020, https://www.dw.com/en/3-in-4-german-daycare -children-not-getting-proper-care-study/a-54693175.

11 "20 Hours ECE for ECE Services," New Zealand Ministry of Education, https://www.education.govt.nz/early-childhood/funding-and-data/20-hours -ece-for-ece-services/; "Help Paying For Early Childhood Education," New Zealand Government, https://www.govt.nz/browse/education/help -paying-for-early-childhood-education/.

12 "Births and Deaths: Year Ended June 2021," Stats NZ, August 16, 2021, https://www.stats.govt.nz/information-releases/births-and-deaths-year -ended-june-2021.

13 "Young Children Develop in an Environment of Relationships," Working Paper 1, National Scientific Council on the Developing Child, 2004, https:// developingchild.harvard.edu/wp-content/uploads/2004/04/Young-Children -Develop-in-an-Environment-of-Relationships.pdf.

14 Brenda L. Bauman et. al, "Vital Signs: Postpartum Depressive Symptoms and Provider Discussions About Perinatal Depression—United States, 2018," *CDC Weekly* 69, no. 19 (May 2020): 575–81.

15 Anne Kingston, "I Regret Having Children," *Macleans*, January 2018, https:// www.macleans.ca/regretful-mothers/.

16 Diana Karklin, "The Women Who Wish They Weren't Mothers: 'An Unwanted Pregnancy Lasts a Lifetime.'" *The Guardian*, July 16, 2022, https://www

.theguardian.com/lifeandstyle/2022/jul/16/women-who-wish-they-werent
-mothers-roe-v-wade-abortion.

17 Nancy Folbre, "Children as Public Goods," *American Economic Review* 84,
no. 2 (May 1994): 86–90.

18 "Death Gratuity Fact Sheet," Military OneSource, https://www.militaryonesource
.mil/products/death-gratuity-fact-sheet-263/; "Military Compensation," Department
of Defense, https://militarypay.defense.gov/benefits/death-gratuity/.

19 Plato, *Republic*, Book V, 457d.

20 Plato, *Republic*, Book V, 460b.

21 Plato, *Republic*, Book V, 460b.

22 Friedrich Engels. *The Condition of the Working Class in England*, Project
Gutenberg [1844], https://www.gutenberg.org/ebooks/17306.

23 Friedrich Engels, "Draft of a Communist Confession of Faith," June 9, 1847, in
Birth of the Communist Manifesto, ed. Dirk Struik (New York: International
Publishers, 1971).

24 Friedrich Engels, "The Principles of Communism," in Struik, *Birth of the
Communist Manifesto*.

25 Friedrich Engels and Karl Marx, *The Communist Manifesto*, Project Gutenberg
[1848], https://www.gutenberg.org/ebooks/61.

26 Geraldine Youcha, *Minding the Children: Child Care in America from Colonial
Times to the Present* (New York: Scribner, 1995), 108.

27 Susan M. Matarese and Paul G. Salmon, "Heirs to the Promised Land: The
Children of Oneida," *International Journal of Sociology of the Family* 13, no. 2
(Autumn 1983): 35–43.

28 Quoted in Youcha, *Minding the Children*, 99.

29 Harriet Worden, "Old Mansion House Memories," *Circular*, January 30, 1871,
quoted in Constance Noyes Robertson, "History of the Oneida Community,"
https://library.syracuse.edu/digital/guides/o/OneidaCommunityCollection
/umifilm.htm.

30 Quoted in Youcha, *Minding the Children*, 110.

31 *Hand-Book of the Oneida Community*, Syracuse University Library, https://
library.syr.edu/digital/collections/h/Hand-bookOfTheOneidaCommunity/.

32 *Hand-Book of the Oneida Community*.

33 "Oneida Community (1848–1880)," Oneida Community Mansion House,
https://www.oneidacommunity.org/our-history.

34 Nellie Munin, "Collectivism v. Individualism: Can the EU Learn from the
History of the Israeli Kibbutz?" *Bratislava Law Review* 1 (January 2017):
29–47.

35 Henry Near, *The Kibbutz Movement: A History; Volume 1: Origins and
Growth, 1909–1939* (Oxford, UK: Oxford University Press, 1992); Henry

Near, *The Kibbutz Movement: A History; Volume 2: Crisis and Achievement, 1939–1995* (Oxford, UK: Oxford University Press, 2007).

36 Near, *The Kibbutz Movement*, vol. 2.

37 Noam Shpancer, "Child of the Collective," *The Guardian*, February 18, 2011, https://www.theguardian.com/lifeandstyle/2011/feb/19/kibbutz-child-noam -shpancer.

38 Miriam K. Rosenthal, "Daily Experiences of Toddlers in Three Child Care Settings in Israel," *Child and Youth Care Forum* 20 (February 1991): 37–58.

39 Ora Aviezer, Marimus H. van IJzendoorn, Abraham Sagi, and Carlo Schuengel, "'Children of the Dream' Revisited: 70 Years of Collective Early Child Care in Israeli Kibbutzim," *Psychological Bullentin* 116, no. 1 (July 1994): 99–116.

40 Marc H. Bornstein, Sharone L. Maital, and Joseph Tal, "Contexts of Collaboration in Caregiving: Infant Interactions with Israeli Kibbutz Mothers and Caregivers," *Early Child Development and Care* 135, no. 1 (May 1997): 145–71.

41 Karen L. Kramer, "The Human Family—Its Evolutionary Context and Diversity," *Social Sciences* 10, no. 191 (May 2021): https://doi.org/10.3390/ socsci10060191.

42 Alfred Meyer, *The Feminism and Socialism of Lily Braun* (Bloomington: Indiana University Press, 1986), 66.

43 Second International Conference of Socialist Women. Full text report available online at: https://archive.org/details/InternationalSocialistCongress1910Second InternationalConferenceOf, 22.

44 Alexandra Kollontai, "Working Woman and Mother," in Alexandra Kollontai, *Selected Writings*, ed. Alix Holt (New York: W. W. Norton, 1980), 127–39.

45 Kollontai, "Working Woman and Mother."

46 Kollontai, "Working Woman and Mother."

47 Wendy Goldman, *Women State and Revolution: Soviet Family Policy and Social Life, 1917–1936* (Cambridge, UK: Cambridge University Press, 1993), 93.

48 Josie McClellan, *Love in the Time of Communism: Intimacy and Sexuality in the GDR* (Cambridge, UK: Cambridge University Press, 2011), 65.

49 J. Schmude, "Contrasting Developments in Female Labor Force Participation in East and West Germany Since 1945," in *Women of the European Union: The Politics of Work and Daily Life*, ed. M. D. Garcia-Ramon and J. Monk (New York: Routledge, 1996).

50 Susan L. Erikson, "'Now It Is Completely the Other Way Around': Political Economies of Fertility in Re-unified Germany," in *Barren States: The Population 'Implosion' in Europe*, ed. Carrie B. Douglas (Berlin: Berg, 2005).

51 Kristen Ghodsee, *Second World, Second Sex: Socialist Women's Activism and Global Solidarity During the Cold War* (Durham, NC: Duke University Press, 2019).

52 Amanda E. Devercelli and Frances Beaton-Day, "Better Jobs and Brighter Futures: Investing in Childcare to Build Human Capital," World Bank, December 2020, https://openknowledge.worldbank.org/bitstream/handle /10986/35062/Better-Jobs-and-Brighter-Futures-Investing-in-Childcare-to -Build-Human-Capital.pdf.

53 Devercelli and Beaton-Day, "Better Jobs and Brighter Futures."

54 "Early Childhood Education and Care Policy in Sweden," OECD, December 1999, https://www.oecd.org/education/school/2479039.pdf; Miho Taguma, Ineke Litjens, and Kelly Makowieki, "Quality Matters in Early Childhood Education and Care: Sweden," OECD, 2013, https://www.oecd.org/education /school/SWEDENpercent20policypercent20profilepercent20-percent 20publishedpercent2005-02-2013.pdf.

55 Anita Nyberg, "Lessons from the Swedish Experience," in *Kids Count: Better Early Child Education and Care in Australia,* ed. Elizabeth Hill and Barbara Pocock (Sydney: Sydney University Press, 2007), 38–56.

56 Leslie Boreen, "Study: Preschools Top Home-Based Care in Preparing Children for School," *UVA Today,* June 1, 2016, https://news.virginia.edu/content/study -preschools-top-home-based-care-preparing-children-school.

57 Sylvana M Côté et al., "Short- and Long-Term Risk of Infections as a Function of Group Child Care Attendance: An 8-Year Population-Based Study," *Archive of Pediatrics and Adolescent Medicine* 164, no. 12 (December 2010): 1132–37.

58 "Centre-Based Child Care: Long Hours Do Not Cause Aggression and Disobedience," Norwegian Institute of Public Health, January 28, 2013, https://www .fhi.no/en/news/2013/centre-based-child-care-long-hours-/.

59 "Centre-Based Child Care."

60 Kate Schweitzer, "New Study Finds Some BIG Behavioral Benefits to Kids Who Attend Daycare," *Popsugar,* October 3, 2018, Https://Www.Popsugar .Com/Family/Kids-Daycare-Better-Behaved-45342276; Ramchandar Gomajee, Fabienne El-Khoury, Sylvana Côté, Judith van der Waerden, Laura Pryor, and Maria Melchior, "Early Childcare Type Predicts Children's Emotional and Behavioural Trajectories into Middle Childhood. Data from the EDEN Mother–Child Cohort Study," *Journal of Epidemiological and Community Health* 72, no. 11 (November 2018): 1033–43.

61 Jean Kimmel and Rachell Connelly, "US Child Care Policy and Economic Impacts," in *The Oxford Handbook of Women and the Economy,* ed. Susan L. Averett, Laura M. Argys, and Saul D. Hoffman (Oxford, UK: Oxford University Press, 2018), 303–22; Deborah A. Phillips and Amy E. Lowenstein, "Early Care, Education, and Child Development," *Annual Review of Psychology* 62, no. 1 (January 2011): 483–500.

Chapter 4: The Good School

1 Fabius Wittmer and Christian Waldhoff, "Religious Education in Germany in Light of Religious Diversity: Constitutional Requirements for Religious Education," *German Law Journal* 20, no. 7 (October 2019): 1047–65.

2 "Ethik" on the website of the Geschwister Scholl Gymnasium: https://www.gsg-waldkirch.de/unterricht/geisteswissenschaften/ethik.html.

3 "Learn More, Earn More: Education Leads to Higher Wages, Lower Unemployment," Career Outlook, US Bureau of Labor Statistics, May 2020, https://www.bls.gov/careeroutlook/2020/data-on-display/education-pays.htm.

4 Melanie Hanson, "Student Loan Debt Statistics," Education Data Initiative, April 10, 2022, https://educationdata.org/student-loan-debt-statistics.

5 Malcolm Harris, *Kids These Days: Human Capital and the Making of Millennials* (New York: Little, Brown, 2017).

6 Milton and Rose Friedman, *Free to Choose: A Personal Statement* (New York: Harcourt, 1980).

7 Zack Friedman, "Student Loan Debt Statistics in 2021: A Record $1.7 Trillion," *Forbes*, February 20, 2021, https://www.forbes.com/sites/zackfriedman/2021/02/20/student-loan-debt-statistics-in-2021-a-record-17-trillion/.

8 Jean-Jacques Rousseau, *Emile* (1763), trans. Barbara Foxley, Project Gutenberg, https://www.gutenberg.org/files/5427/5427-h/5427-h.htm.

9 Rousseau, *Emile*.

10 Stephen Jay Gould, *The Panda's Thumb: More Reflections in Natural History* (New York: W. W. Norton, 1992), 151.

11 Plato, *Republic*, Book V, 451e5; 456c10.

12 Plato, *Republic*, Book V, 451d5.

13 Plato, *Republic*, Book V, 455d5.

14 Thomas More, *Utopia* (1516), Project Gutenberg, https://www.gutenberg.org/ebooks/2130.

15 More, *Utopia*.

16 Tommaso Campanella, *City of the Sun* (1602), Project Gutenberg, https://gutenberg.org/files/2816/2816-h/2816-h.htm.

17 Campanella, *City of the Sun*.

18 G. N. Filonov, "Anton Makarenko," *Prospects: The Quarterly Review of Comparative Education* 24, no. 1–2 (1994): 77–91.

19 Orlando Figes, *A People's Tragedy: The Russian Revolution 1891–1924* (New York: Penguin, 1996), 780.

20 Y. M. Medinsky, "The Dzerzhinsky Commune," in Anton Makarenko, *Makarenko, His Life and Work: Articles, Talks and Reminiscences* (Honolulu: University Press of the Pacific, 2004), 37.

21 Maxim Gorky, "Across the Soviet Union," citied in Makarenko, *Makarenko, His Life and Work*, 50.

22 Anton Makarenko, "From My Own Practice," in Makarenko, *Makarenko, His Life and Work*, 272.

23 Makarenko, "From My Own Practice," 270.

24 "Българското образование между две стратегии" (Bulgarian education between two strategies), Frontalno, November 9, 2018, https://frontalno.com /българското-образование-между-две-ст/.

25 Neal Conan and Sue Shellenbarger, "The Burden of Being 'Most Likely to Succeed,'" *National Public Radio*, May 31, 2011, https://www.npr.org/2011/05 /31/136824390/the-burden-of-being-most-likely-to-succeed.

26 Derek C. Mulenga, "Mwalimu Julius Nyerere: A Critical Review of His Contributions to Adult Education and Postcolonialism," *International Journal of Lifelong Education* 20, no. 6 (November 2001): 446–70.

27 Mulenga, "Mwalimu Julius Nyerere."

28 Yusuf Kassam, "Julius Kambarage Nyerere," *Prospects: The Quarterly Review of Comparative Education* 24, no. 1–2 (1994): 247–59.

29 Julius K. Nyerere, "Education for Self-Reliance," *Ecumenical Review* 19, no. 4 (1967): 382–403: 387, https://onlinelibrary.wiley.com/doi/10.1111/j.1758 -6623.1967.tb02171.x.

30 Nyerere, "Education for Self-Reliance," 396.

31 Nyerere, "Education for Self-Reliance," 396.

32 Wim Hoppers and Donatus Komba, eds., *Productive Work in Education and Training: A State-of-the-Art in Eastern Africa* (The Hague: Center for the Study of Education in Developing Countries, 1993).

33 Candy Gunther Brown, "Conservative Legal Groups Are Suing Public School Yoga and Mindfulness Programs. This Explains Why," *Washington Post*, July 10, 2019, https://www.washingtonpost.com/politics/2019/07/10/conservative -legal-groups-are-suing-public-school-yoga-mindfulness-programs-this-explains -why/.

34 Sydney Bauer, "US School Books—The Latest LGBTQ+ Rights Battleground," Openly, February 4, 2022, https://www.openlynews.com/i/?id=9b222e47-1dd8 -4e81-bbdc-e87823fc9361.

35 Susan Neiman, *Learning from the Germans: Race and the Memory of Evil* (London: Picador, 2020).

36 Kurt Vonnegut, "Harrison Bergeron," in *Welcome to the Monkey House: A Collection of Short Works* (New York: Dial Press, 1998).

37 "Honoring Kurt Vonnegut for Harrison Bergeron: Hall of Fame Acceptance Speeches," *Prometheus Blog*, http://lfs.org/blog/honoring-kurt-vonnegut-for -harrison-bergeron-hall-of-fame-acceptance-speeches/.

38 Mary Ann Lieser, "The High School Where Learning to Farm Is a Graduation Requirement." *Yes!*, May 9, 2018, https://www.yesmagazine.org/democracy/2018 /05/09/the-high-school-where-learning-to-farm-is-a-graduation-requirement ?fbclid=IwAR1z8GuQais7MDG4szTYtMxZmaC_aNtEUqgCn_uOGMfkP WVSCZxq8BRBwCQ.

39 Anya Kamenetz, "Most Teachers Don't Teach Climate Change; 4 in 5 Parents Wish They Did," *National Public Radio*, April 22, 2019, https://www.npr.org /2019/04/22/714262267/most-teachers-dont-teach-climate-change-4-in-5 -parents-wish-they-did.

40 Thomas Friedman, "Justice Goes Global," *New York Times*, June 15, 2011, https://www.nytimes.com/2011/06/15/opinion/15friedman.html.

41 Ed Stannard, "Yale 'Happiness' Professor Taking Leave as Burnout Looms," *New Haven Register*, February, 19, 2022, https://www.nhregister.com/news/article /Yale-professor-taking-leave-because-burnout-16930909.php.

42 Eric Merkely, "Many Americans Deeply Distrust Experts. So Will They Ignore the Warnings About Coronavirus?" *Washington Post*, March 19, 2020, https:// www.washingtonpost.com/politics/2020/03/19/even-with√-coronavirus -some-americans-deeply-distrust-experts-will-they-take-precautions/.

43 "Alle Muurgedichten," Muur Gedichten Leiden, https://muurgedichten.nl/en /muurgedichten.

44 Ivan Dikov, "Wall-to-Wall Poetry: How the Dutch Bring European 'Unity in Diversity' to Sofia," *Novinite*, January 27, 2010, http://www.novinite.com/view _news.php?id=112440.

45 'Poetry in Motion," Poetry Society of America, https://poetrysociety.org/poetry -in-motion.

46 "Poems on the Underground," Transport for London, https://tfl.gov.uk/cor porate/about-tfl/culture-and-heritage/poems-on-the-underground.

47 Jonathan Watts, "Wordsworth Wanders on to the Shanghai Metro," *The Guardian*, March 17, 2006, https://www.theguardian.com/world/2006/mar/17/books.china.

48 "These New York Billboards Got Tons of Attention," *Times Square Chronicle*, June 28, 2021, https://t2conline.com/these-new-york-billboards-got-tons-of -attention/.

49 "Yoko Ono's Imagine Peace—15 Giant Billboards at Times Square, New York," *Public Delivery*, October 30, 2021, https://publicdelivery.org/yoko-ono -times-square-nyc-imagine-peace/.

Chapter 5: Imagine No Possessions, I Wonder Why We Can't

1 David Graeber and David Wengrow, *The Dawn of Everything: A New History of Humanity* (New York: Farrar, Straus and Giroux, 2021), especially ch. 4.

2 Thomas Piketty. *Capital and Ideology* (Cambridge, MA: Belknap Press, 2020), 1.

3 Pierre-Joseph Proudhon, "What Is Property? An Inquiry into the Principle of Right and of Government" (1840), Project Gutenberg, https://www.gutenberg .org/ebooks/360.

4 John Locke, Second Treatise of Government, ch. V, para. 27 (1689), Project Gutenberg, https://www.gutenberg.org/ebooks/7370.

5 John Thorley, *Athenian Democracy*, 2nd ed. (New York: Routledge, 2004).

6 Edwin L. Minar Jr., "Pythagorean Communism," *Transactions and Proceedings of the American Philological Association* 75 (1944): 34–46.

7 C. J. de Vogel, *Pythagoras and Early Pythagoreanism: An Interpretation of Neglected Evidence on the Philosopher Pythagoras* (Netherlands: Royal Van Gorcum, 1966); Christoph Riedweg, *Pythagoras: His Life, Teaching, and Influence* (Ithaca, NY: Cornell University Press, 2005).

8 Plato, *Republic*, Book III, 416d-e.

9 His Holiness the Dalai Lama, *Beyond Dogma: Dialogues & Discourses* (Berkeley: North Atlantic Books, 1996), 109–10.

10 See the Leon Levy Dead Sea Scrolls Digital Library: https://www.deadseascrolls .org.il.

11 Joshua Ezra Burns, "Essene Sectarianism and Social Differentiation in Judaea After 70 C.E.," *Harvard Theological Review* 99, no. 3 (July 2006): 247–74.

12 Acts 2: 44–47 (New International Version).

13 Acts 2: 32–35 (New International Version).

14 Janko Lavrin, "Bogomils and Bogomilism," *Slavonic and East European Review* 8, no. 23 (1929): 269–83.

15 "The Discourse of the Priest Cosmas Against Bogomils," in *Christian Dualist Heresies in the Byzantine World, c. 650–c. 1450: Selected Sources*, ed. Janet Hamilton, Bernard Hamilton, and Yuri Stoyanov (Manchester, UK: Manchester University Press, 1998), 116.

16 Thomas More, *Utopia* (1516), Project Gutenberg, https://www.gutenberg.org /ebooks/2130.

17 "Alcohol and Drug Misuse and Suicide and the Millennial Generation—a Devastating Impact," Wellbeing Trust and the Trust for America's Health, June 2019, https://wellbeingtrust.org/wp-content/uploads/2019/06/TFAH-2019 -YoundAdult-Pain-Brief-FnlRv.pdf.

18 John Stuart Mill, "Of the Stationary State," book IV, ch. VI, para. 2, in *Principles of Political Economy with Some of Their Applications to Social Philosophy* (1848), https://www.econlib.org/library/Mill/mlP.html?chapter _num=64#book-reader.

19 Ben Steverman, "Trillions Will Be Inherited Over the Coming Decades, Further Widening the Wealth Gap," *Los Angeles Times*, November 29, 2019, https://

www.latimes.com/business/story/2019-11-29/boomers-are-thriving-on-an
-unprecedented-9-trillion-inheritance.

20 "Almost One Third of All Wealth in the UK Is Inherited, Rather Than Earned,"
Inequality Briefing, http://inequalitybriefing.org/graphics/inequality_briefing
_26.pdf.

21 Robert Nozick, *Anarchy, State, and Utopia* (New York: Basic Books, 2013), 152.

22 Christine Kearney, "Encyclopaedia Britannica: After 244 Years in Print, Only
Digital Copies Sold," *Christian Science Monitor*, March 14, 2012, https://
www.csmonitor.com/Business/Latest-News-Wires/2012/0314/Encyclopaedia
-Britannica-After-244-years-in-print-only-digital-copies-sold.

23 *Encyclopaedia Britannica* subscription page: https://subscription.britannica
.com/subscribe.

24 Monica Anderson, Paul Hitlin, and Michelle Atkinson, "Wikipedia at 15:
Millions of Readers in Scores of Languages," Pew Research Center, January 14,
2016, https://www.pewresearch.org/fact-tank/2016/01/14/wikipedia-at-15/.

25 Friedrich Engels, *The Origin of the Family, Private Property, and the State*,
Project Gutenberg, https://www.gutenberg.org/ebooks/33111.

26 Graeber and Wengrow, *The Dawn of Everything*.

27 "Frequently Asked Questions," Hutterites, http://www.hutterites.org/day-to
-day/faqs/.

28 "An interview with Manitoba Hutterite Linda Maendel," Amish America,
October 12, 2011, https://amishamerica.com/manitoba-hutterite-linda
-maendel/.

29 "Community of Goods," Maine Shakers, https://www.maineshakers.com/about
/#ourbeliefs.

30 Peggy Grodinsky, "Maine Voices Live: Brother Arnold Talks About the Shaker
Life, Spiritual and Otherwise," *Portland Press Herald*, December 11, 2019,
https://www.pressherald.com/2019/12/11/maine-voices-live-brother-arnold
-talks-about-the-shaker-life-spiritual-and-otherwise/.

31 Website of the Bruderhof: https://www.bruderhof.com/en.

32 Sam Wollaston, "'Just Don't Call It a Cult': The Strangely Alluring World of
the Bruderhof," *The Guardian*, July 23, 2019, https://www.theguardian.com/tv
-and-radio/2019/jul/23/just-dont-call-it-a-cult-the-strangely-alluring-world-of
-the-bruderhof.

33 "Audit Technique Guide—Apostolic Associations—IRC Section 501(d)," IRS,
https://www.irs.gov/pub/irs-tege/atg_apostolic_associations.pdf.

34 "Audit Technique Guide—Apostolic Associations—IRC Section 501(d)."

35 Samuel Brunson, "Taxing Utopia," LAW eCommons, Loyola University
Chicago, 2016, https://lawecommons.luc.edu/cgi/viewcontent.cgi?article=
1572&context=facpubs.

36 Edward SanFilippo, "A Legal Alternative to Modern Living in a Changing America," *JURIST*, January 31, 2012, https://www.jurist.org/commentary/2012 /01/edward-sanfilippo-intentional-community/.

37 Website of the Global Ecovillage Network: https://ecovillage.org.

38 "Ecovillages," Foundation for Intentional Community, https://www.ic.org /directory/ecovillages/; Website of the Federation of Egalitarian Communities: https://www.thefec.org/about/.

39 "About," Tamera, https://www.tamera.org/about/.

40 "How We're Funded," Tamera, https://www.tamera.org/how-were-funded/.

41 "Terra Nova," Tamera, https://www.tamera.org/terra-nova/.

42 Dave Darby, "The Yamagishi Association: Successful, Moneyless, Leaderless Network of Communes in Japan and Elsewhere," Lowimpact, November 17, 2015, https://www.lowimpact.org/the-yamagishi-association-successful -moneyless-leaderless-network-of-communes-in-japan-and-elsewhere/.

43 Website of the Konohana Family: https://konohana-family.org/en/.

44 Wang Xuandi, "In China's New Age Communes, Burned-Out Millennials Go Back to Nature," Sixthtone.com, January 15, 2021, https://www.sixthtone.com /news/1006694/in-chinas-new-age-communespercent2C-burned-out-millennials -go-back-to-nature.

45 Huizhong Wu, "City Dwellers Find Simpler Life in Rural China Commune," *Reuters*, December 30, 2019, https://www.reuters.com/article/us-china -commune-widerimage/city-dwellers-find-simpler-life-in-rural-china-commune -idUSKBN1YY00V.

46 Isabel Kershner, "The Kibbutz Sheds Socialism and Gains Popularity," *New York Times*, August 27, 2007, https://www.nytimes.com/2007/08/27/world/middleeast /27kibbutz.html.

47 Dafna Shermer, "Kibbutz Life: Love It but Leave It?" *Jerusalem Institute*, January 27, 2015, https://jerusaleminstitute.org.il/en/blog/kibbutz-life-love-it -but-leave-it/.

48 Shlomo Getz, "Report on Cooperative Kibbutzim—2018," Kibbutz Research Institute, University of Haifa, 2018, 1–2 (in Hebrew).

49 Noa Shpigel, "Kibbutzim Are Becoming a Magnet for the Younger Gener-ation," *Haaretz*, June 1, 2017, https://www.haaretz.com/israel-news/.premium .MAGAZINE-kibbutzim-a-magnet-for-young-adults-1.5478900.

50 Dina Kraft, "Kibbutz in the City? The Healing Mission of Israel's New Communes," *Christian Science Monitor*, August 2, 2019, https://www .csmonitor.com/World/Middle-East/2019/0802/Kibbutz-in-the-city-The -healing-mission-of-Israel-s-new-communes.

51 Aaron Torop, "What I Learned at an Urban Kibbutz," *Reform Judaism*, September 19, 2017, https://reformjudaism.org/blog/what-i-learned-urban-kibbutz.

52 Twin Oaks Labor Policy: https://www.twinoaks.org/policies/labor-policy
?showall=1.

53 Jessica Ravitz, "Utopia: It's Complicated Inside New-Age and Vintage
Communes," Great American Stories, CNN, September 2015, https://www.cnn
.com/interactive/2015/09/us/communes-american-story/.

54 Twin Oaks Property Code: https://www.twinoaks.org/policies/property
-code#pre-existing-assets.

55 Kenneth Mulder, Robert Costanza, and Jon Erikson, "The Contribution of
Built, Human, Social and Natural Capital to Quality of Life in Intentional and
Unintentional Communities," Ecological Economics 59, no. 1 (February 2006):
13–23.

56 Bjørn Grinde, Ragnhild Bang Nes, Ian F. MacDonald, and David Sloan Wilson,
"Quality of Life in Intentional Communities," Social Indicators Research 137,
no. 2 (June 2018): 625–40.

57 Grinde et al., "Quality of Life in Intentional Communities."

58 Jenny Odell, How to Do Nothing: Resisting the Attention Economy (New
York: Melville House, 2019).

59 Website of Little Free Library: https://littlefreelibrary.org.

Chapter 6: Shall I Compare Thee to a Violent Ape?

1 Kate Sproul, "California's Response to Domestic Violence," California Senate
Office of Research, June 2003, https://sor.senate.ca.gov/sites/sor.senate.ca.gov
/files/Californiaspercent20Responsepercent20topercent20Domesticpercent
20Violence.pdf.

2 Brad Boserup, Mark McKenney, and Edel Elkbuli, "Alarming Trends in US
Domestic Violence During the COVID-19 Pandemic," American Journal of
Emergency Medicine 38, no. 12 (December 2020): 2753–55; "UN Women
Raises Awareness of the Shadow Pandemic of Violence Against Women During
COVID-19," press release, UN Women, May 27, 2020, https://www.unwomen
.org/en/news/stories/2020/5/press-release-the-shadow-pandemic-of-violence
-against-women-during-covid-19; B. Gosangi et al., "Exacerbation of Physical
Intimate Partner Violence During COVID-19 Pandemic," Radiology 298, no. 1
(January 2021): E38–E45.

3 S. G. Smith, X. Zhang, K. C. Basile, M. T. Merrick, J. Wang , M-j Kresnow,
and J. Chen, The National Intimate Partner and Sexual Violence Survey:
2015 Data Brief—Updated Release 2018, Centers for Disease Control and
Prevention, November 2018, https://www.cdc.gov/violenceprevention/pdf
/2015data-brief508.pdf.

4 "How a Law Meant to Curb Infanticide Was Used to Abandon Teens," CBC

News, December 1, 2017, https://www.cbc.ca/radio/outintheopen/unintended
-consequences-1.4415756/how-a-law-meant-to-curb-infanticide-was-used-to-
abandon-teens-1.4415784.

5 Associated Press, "Nebraska Law Allows Abandonment of Teens," *NBC News*,
August 22, 2008, https://www.nbcnews.com/health/health-news/nebraska-law
-allows-abandonment-teens-flna1c9460299.

6 "Nebraska Approves 30-Day Age Limit on 'Safe Haven' Law," *CBC News*,
November 21, 2008, https://www.cbc.ca/news/world/nebraska-approves-30
-day-age-limit-on-safe-haven-law-1.765410.

7 David Brooks, "The Nuclear Family Was a Mistake," *The Atlantic*, March
2020, https://www.theatlantic.com/magazine/archive/2020/03/the-nuclear
-family-was-a-mistake/605536/.

8 1965 Moynihan report: "The Negro Family: A Case for National Action," US
Department of Labor, https://www.dol.gov/general/aboutdol/history/webid
-moynihan.

9 Wendy D. Manning, Susan L. Brown, Krista K. Payne, and Hsueh-Sheng Wu,
"Healthy Marriage Initiative Spending and U.S. Marriage & Divorce Rates,
A State-Level Analysis," FP-14-02, National Center for Family & Marriage
Research, 2014, http://www.bgsu.edu/content/dam/BGSU/college-of-arts
-and-sciences/NCFMR/documents/FP/FP-14-02_HMIInitiative.pdf; Katherine
Boo, "The Marriage Cure." *The New Yorker*, August 10, 2003, https://www
.newyorker.com/magazine/2003/08/18/the-marriage-cure.

10 Susan L. Brown, "Marriage and Child Well-Being: Research and Policy Perspectives," *Journal of Marriage and Family* 72, no. 5 (October 2010): 1059–77.

11 W. Bradford Wilcox and Hal Boyd, "The Nuclear Family Is Still Indispensable,"
The Atlantic, February 21, 2020, https://www.theatlantic.com/ideas/archive
/2020/02/nuclear-family-still-indispensable/606841/.

12 Jessica Fern, *Polysecure: Attachment, Trauma and Consensual Nonmonogamy*
(Portland, OR: Thorntree Press, 2020).

13 J. M. Burkart, S. B. Hrdy, and C. P. Van Schaik, "Cooperative Breeding and
Human Cognitive Evolution," *Evolutionary Anthropology* 18 (October 2009):
175–186: 176.

14 Karen L. Kramer, "Children's Help and the Pace of Reproduction: Cooperative Breeding in Humans," *Evolutionary Anthropology* 14, no. 6 (November
2005): 224–37; Karen L. Kramer, "Variation in Juvenile Dependence: Helping
Behavior Among Maya Children," *Human Nature* 13, no. 2 (June 2002):
299–325; Karen L. Kramer, "Does It Take a Family to Raise a Child?," in
*Substitute Parents: Biological and Social Perspectives on Alloparenting in
Human Societies*, ed. G. Bentley and R. Mace (New York: Berghahn Books,
2009), 77–99.

15 Sarah Blaffer Hrdy, *Mothers and Others: The Evolutionary Origins of Mutual Understanding* (Cambridge, MA: Belknap Press, 2009).

16 Margaret L. Walker and James G. Herndon, "Menopause in Nonhuman Primates?" *Biology of Reproduction* 79, no. 3 (September 2008): 398–406.

17 Burkart, Hrdy, and Van Schaik, "Cooperative Breeding and Human Cognitive Evolution," 177.

18 Burkart, Hrdy, and Van Schaik, "Cooperative Breeding and Human Cognitive Evolution"; Hrdy, *Mothers and Others.*

19 Christopher Opie, Quentin D. Atkinson, and Susanne Shultz, "The Evolutionary History of Primate Mating Systems," *Communicative & Integrative Biology* 5, no. 5 (September 2012): 458–61.

20 Adriana E. Lowe, Catherine Hobaiter, Caroline Asiimwe, Klaus Zuberbühler, Nicholas E. Newton-Fisher. "Intra-community Infanticide in Wild, Eastern Chimpanzees: A 24-year Review" *Primates* 61 (2020): 69–82.

21 Christopher Opie, Quentin D. Atkinson, Robin I. M. Dunbar, and Susanne Shultz, "Male Infanticide Leads to Social Monogamy in Primates," *Proceedings of the National Academy of Sciences* 110, no. 33 (July 2013): 13328–32.

22 D. Lukas and T. Clutton-Brock, "Evolution of Social Monogamy in Primates Is Not Consistently Associated with Male Infanticide," *Proceedings of the National Academy of Sciences* 111, no. 17 (March 2014): E1674; A. F. Dixson, "Male Infanticide and Primate Monogamy," *Proceedings of the National Academy of Sciences* 110, no. 51 (December 2013): E4937.

23 C. Opie, Q. D. Atkinson, R. I. Dunbar, and S. Shultz, "Reply to Lukas and Clutton-Brock: Infanticide Still Drives Primate Monogamy," *Proceedings of the National Academy of Sciences* 111, no. 17 (April 2014): E1675.

24 Opie et al., "Reply to Lukas and Clutton-Brock."

25 Karen L. Kramer and A. F. Russell, "Was Monogamy a Key Step on the Hominin Road? Reevaluation of the Monogamy Hypothesis in the Evolution of Cooperative Breeding," *Evolutionary Anthropology* 24, no. 2 (March–April 2015): 73–83; Ryan Schacht and Karen L. Kramer, "Are We Monogamous? A Review of the Evolution of Pair-Bonding in Humans and Its Contemporary Variation Cross-Culturally," *Frontiers in Ecology and Evolution* 7, no. 230 (July 2019): 1–10.

26 Karen Kramer and Andrew Russell, "Was Monogamy a Key Step on the Hominin Road? Reevaluating the Monogamy Hypothesis in the Evolution of Cooperative Breeding," *Evolutionary Anthropology*, 24 (2015): 73–83.

27 Karen L. Kramer, "The Human Family—Its Evolutionary Context and Diversity," *Social Sciences* 10, no. 6 (May 2021): 191.

28 Gerald D. Berreman, "Himalayan Polyandry and the Domestic Cycle," *American Ethnologist* 2, no. 1 (1975): 127–38.

29 R. S. Walker, M. V. Flinn, K. R. Hill. "Evolutionary History of Partible Paternity in Lowland South America." Proceedings of the National Academy of Sciences 107, no. 45 (2010): 19195–200.

30 Karen L. Kramer, "The Human Family—Its Evolutionary Context and Diversity," Social Sciences 10, no. 6 (May 2021): 191.

31 Exodus 21:10 (New International Version).

32 I Kings 11:3 (New International Version).

33 Tatiana Zerjal, Yali Xue, et al., "The Genetic Legacy of the Mongols," American Journal of Human Genetics 72, no. 3 (March 2003): 717–21.

34 George Smith, Nauvoo Polygamy: ". . . But We Called It Celestial Marriage" (Salt Lake City: Signature Books, 2011).

35 Alasdair Pal and Adnan Abidi, "Man with 39 Wives, Head of 'World's Largest Family,' Dies In India," Reuters, June 16, 2021, https://www.reuters.com/world/india/man-with-39-wives-head-worlds-largest-family-dies-india-2021-06-14/.

36 Amy Barrett, "Alongside Widow and Sons, Mistress and Daughter Attend Funeral," Associated Press, January 11, 1996, https://apnews.com/article/09cefda353f5e98bd47d922abdb30874.

37 Gary S. Becker, "A Theory of Marriage," in Theodore W. Schultz, Economics of the Family: Marriage, Children, and Human Capital (Chicago: University of Chicago Press, 1974), 299–351.

38 Kevin MacDonald, "The Establishment and Maintenance of Socially Imposed Monogamy in Western Europe," Politics and the Life Sciences 14, no. 1 (February 1995): 3–23.

39 Walter Scheidel, "Monogamy and Polygyny in Greece, Rome, and World History," Princeton/Stanford Working Papers in Classics, Version 1.0, June 2008, https://www.princeton.edu/~pswpc/pdfs/scheidel/060807.pdf.

40 MacDonald, "The Establishment and Maintenance of Socially Imposed Monogamy."

41 Laura Fortunato and M. Archetti, "Evolution of Monogamous Marriage by Maximization of Inclusive Fitness," Journal of Evolutionary Biology 23, no. 1 (January 2010): 149–56.

42 Laura Betzig, "Medieval Monogamy," Journal of Family History 20, no. 2 (June 1995): 181–216.

43 William Graham Cole, Sex in Christianity and Psychoanalysis (New York: Routledge, 2015).

44 George P. Murdock and Douglas R. White, "Standard Cross-Cultural Sample," Ethnology 8, no. 4 (October 1969): 329–69.

45 Graeber and Wengrow, The Dawn of Everything, 107.

46 Kim TallBear, "Making Love and Relations Beyond Settler Sex and Family," in Adele Clark and Donna J. Harraway, Making Kin Not Population: Recon-

ceiving Generations (Chicago: Prickly Paradigm Press, 2018), 145–209: 147–48.

47 *Reynolds v. United States*, 98 U.S. 145, October 1878, https://www.law.cornell .edu/supremecourt/text/98/145.

48 *Reynolds v. United States.*

49 Richard S. Van Wagoner, *Mormon Polygamy: A History*, 2nd ed. (Salt Lake City: Signature Books, 1989); Richard A. Vazquez, "The Practice of Polygamy: Legitimate Free Exercise of Religion or Legitimate Public Menace? Revisiting Reynolds in Light of Modern Constitutional Jurisprudence." *New York University Journal of Legislation and Public Policy.* Vol. 5, no. 1: 2001.

50 "1885 Grover Cleveland—Defense of Traditional Marriage," State of the Union History, http://www.stateoftheunionhistory.com/2015/07 /1885-grover-cleveland-defense-of.html.

51 "1885 Grover Cleveland—Defense of Traditional Marriage."

52 *Late Corporation of the Church of Jesus Christ of Latter-Day Saints et al. v. United States. Romney et al. v. Same*, 136 U.S. 1, May 19, 1890, https://www .law.cornell.edu/supremecourt/text/136/1.

53 Christine Hauser, "Utah Lowers Penalty for Polygamy, No Longer a Felony," *New York Times*, May 13, 2020, https://www.nytimes.com/2020/05/13/us/utah -bigamy-law.html.

54 Rose McDermott and Jonathan Cowden, "Polygyny and Violence Against Women," *Emory Law Journal* 64, no. 6 (2015): 1767–1814: 1781.

55 Joseph Henrich, Robert Boyd, and Peter J. Richerson, "The Puzzle of Monogamous Marriage," *Philosophical Transactions of the Royal Society B Biological Sciences* 367, no. 1589 (March 2012): 657–69: 658.

56 Henrich, Boyd, and Richerson, "The Puzzle of Monogamous Marriage," 660.

57 Amanda Marcotte, "The Real Crime Wave That Fox News Is Ignoring: Domestic Violence Has Increased Drastically," *Salon*, December 23, 2021, https://www.salon.com/2021/12/23/the-real-wave-that-fox-news-is-ignoring -domestic-violence-has-increased-drastically/.

58 William J. Cromie, "Marriage Lowers Testosterone," *Harvard Gazette*, August 22, 2002, https://news.harvard.edu/gazette/story/2002/08/marriage-lowers -testosterone/.

59 Rick Sarre, Andrew Day, Ben Livings, and Catia Malvaso, "Men Are More Likely to Commit Violent Crimes: Why Is This So and How Do We Change It?" *The Conversation*, March 25, 2021, https://theconversation.com/men -are-more-likely-to-commit-violent-crimes-why-is-this-so-and-how-do-we -change-it-157331.

60 Richard Wilkinson and Kate Pickett, *The Spirit Level: Why Greater Equality Makes Society Stronger*, (New York: Bloomsbury Press, Kindle Edition, 2010), 205.

61 Pablo Fajnzylber, Daniel Lederman, and Norman Loayza. "Inequality and Violent Crime." *The Journal of Law and Economics* 45, no. 1 (2002): 1–39.

62 https://www.economist.com/graphic-detail/2018/06/07/the-stark-relationship -between-income-inequality-and-crime.

63 B. De Courson and D. Nettle, "Why Do Inequality and Deprivation Produce High Crime and Low Trust?" *Sci Rep* 11 (2021), 1937.

64 Kristen Ghodsee and Mitchell A. Orenstein, *Taking Stock of Shock: Social Consequences of the 1989 Revolutions* (London and New York: Oxford University Press, 2021).

65 United Nations, "Global Study on Homicide: 2019 Edition," https://www .unodc.org/unodc/en/data-and-analysis/global-study-on-homicide.html.

66 Rebecca Traister, *All the Single Ladies* (New York: Simon & Schuster, 2016).

Chapter 7: You and Me and Baby Makes Misery

1 Plato, *Republic*, Book V, 457d.

2 Plato, *Republic*, Book V, 460e.

3 Plato, *Republic*, Book V, 461c.

4 Cited in Ellen G. Millender, "Spartan Women," in *A Companion to Sparta*, ed. Anton Powell (Hoboken, NJ: Wiley-Blackwell, 2017).

5 Cited in Millender, "Spartan Women."

6 Willi Braun, "Celibacy in the Greco-Roman World," in *Celibacy and Religious Traditions* (New York: Oxford University Press, 2007), 21–34; Jordan Reece Tayeh, "Blood, Lead, and Tears: The Cult of Cybele as a Means of Addressing Ancient Roman Issues of Fertility," Decentes, August 28, 2020, https://web.sas .upenn.edu/discentes/2020/08/28/blood-lead-and-tears-the-cult-of-cybele-as-a -means-of-addressing-ancient-roman-issues-of-fertility/.

7 George Tanabe Jr. *Religions of Japan in Practice* (Princeton, NJ: Princeton University Press, 1999).

8 1 Corinthians 7: 28 (New International Version).

9 1 Corinthians 7: 32–35 (New International Version).

10 1 Corinthians 7: 8–9 (New International Version).

11 Thomas More, *Utopia* (1516) Project Gutenberg, https://www.gutenberg.org /ebooks/2130.

12 More, *Utopia*.

13 William Godwin, *Enquiry Concerning Political Justice* (1793), Online Library of Liberty, https://oll.libertyfund.org/title/godwin-an-enquiry-concerning -political-justice-vol-i.

14 Clare Goldberg Moses, "Equality and Difference in Historical Perspective: A Comparative Examination of the Feminisms of the French Revolutionaries

and the Utopian Socialists," in *Rebel Daughters: Women and the French Revolution*, ed. Sara Melzer and Leslie Rabine (New York: Oxford University Press, 1992), 231–53.

15 Moses, "Equality and Difference in Historical Perspective."

16 Karl Marx and Friedrich Engels, *The Communist Manifesto*, Project Gutenberg, https://www.gutenberg.org/ebooks/61.

17 Vladimir Lenin, "August Bebel," in *Lenin Collected Works: Volume 19* (Moscow: Progress Publishers, 1977), 295–301.

18 Jürgen Schmidt, *August Bebel: Social Democracy and the Founding of the Labour Movement* (London: I. B. Tauris, 2020).

19 August Bebel, *My Life* (Chicago: University of Chicago Press, 1973), 258–59; full PDF available at: Libcom.org: https://libcom.org/article/my-life.

20 Bebel, *My Life*, 258–59.

21 August Bebel, *Woman Under Socialism*, Project Gutenberg, https://www .gutenberg.org/ebooks/30646.

22 Bebel, *Woman Under Socialism*.

23 Samuel Clowes Huneke, "Gay Liberation Behind the Iron Curtain," *Boston Review*, April 18, 2019, https://bostonreview.net/articles/gay-liberation-behind -iron-curtain/.

24 Daniel De Leon, "Translator's Preface," in Bebel, *Women Under Socialism*, vi.

25 Alexandra Kollontai, "The Social Basis of the Women's Question" (1909), in Estelle B. Friedman, *The Essential Feminist Reader* (New York: Modern Library, 2007), 178.

26 Wendy Goldman, *Women, the State and Revolution: Soviet Family Policy and Social Life, 1917–1936* (Cambridge, UK: Cambridge University Press, 1993).

27 As quoted in Goldman, *Women, the State and Revolution*, 187.

28 Alexandra Kollontai, "Theses on Communist Morality in the Sphere of Marital Relations" (1921), in Alexandra Kollontai, *Selected Writings* (London: Allison & Busby, 1977).

29 Isabel de Palencia, *Alexandra Kollontay: Ambassadress from Russia* (London: Longmans, Green, 1947), 138.

30 Sheila Fitzpatrick, "Sex and Revolution: An Examination of Literary and Statistical Data on the Mores of Soviet Students in the 1920s," *Journal of Modern History* 50, no. 2 (June 1978): 252–78.

31 Raphael Rashid, "Happy Alone: The Young South Koreans Embracing Single Life," *The Guardian*, February 5, 2022, https://www.theguardian.com/world /2022/feb/05/happy-alone-the-young-south-koreans-embracing-single-life.

32 Motoko Rich, "Craving Freedom, Japan's Women Opt Out of Marriage," *New York Times*, August 3, 2019, https://www.nytimes.com/2019/08/03 /world/asia/japan-single-women-marriage.html.

33 Maria Bucur, *The Century of Women: How Women Have Transformed the World Since 1900* (Baltimore: Rowman & Littlefield, 2018).

34 See, for instance, Esther Perel, *Mating in Captivity: Reconciling the Erotic and the Domestic* (New York: Harper, 2006).

35 TallBear, "Making Love and Relations," 163.

36 Danielle Braff, "From Best Friends to Platonic Spouses," *New York Times*, May 1, 2021, https://www.nytimes.com/2021/05/01/fashion/weddings/from-best -friends-to-platonic-spouses.html.

37 Quoted in Braff, "From Best Friends to Platonic Spouses."

38 "Report to Congress on the 'Federal Employees Family Friendly Leave Act' (Public Law 103-388)," Office of Personnel Management, June 1997, https:// www.opm.gov/policy-data-oversight/pay-leave/reference-materials/reports/federal -employees-family-friendly-leave-act/.

39 "Families First Coronavirus Response Act: Employee Paid Leave Rights," US Department of Labor, https://www.dol.gov/agencies/whd/pandemic/ffcra -employee-paid-leave; "Families First Coronavirus Response Act: Questions and Answers, 63—When Am I Eligible for Paid Sick Leave to Care For Someone Who Is Subject to a Quarantine or Isolation Order?" US Department of Labor, https://www.dol.gov/agencies/whd/pandemic/ffcra-questions/#63.

40 Ciara Muldowney, "UK: Caregivers Will Be Entitled to One Week of Unpaid Leave," SHRM, October 29, 2021, https://www.shrm.org/resourcesandtools/hr -topics/global-hr/pages/uk-caregivers-one-week-unpaid-leave.aspx.

41 "Healing of Love," Tamera, https://www.tamera.org/healing-of-love/.

42 "The Ethics of Free Love," Tamera, https://www.tamera.org/the-ethics-of-free -love/.

43 D. Waters, "Taking a Godson," *Journals of the Royal Asiatic Society Hong Kong Branch* 33 (1993): 215–16.

44 "Adopting Stepchildren," Family Lives, https://www.familylives.org.uk /advice/your-family/stepfamilies/stepfamilies-legal-information/adopting -stepchildren/.

45 Jessica Hamzelou, "Exclusive: World's First Baby Born with New '3 Parent' Technique," *New Scientist*, September 27, 2016, https://www.newscientist .com/article/2107219-exclusive-worlds-first-baby-born-with-new-3-parent -technique/.

46 Rob Stein, "Clinic Claims Success in Making Babies with 3 Parents' DNA," *National Public Radio*, June 6, 2018, https://www.npr.org/sections/health-shots /2018/06/06/615909572/inside-the-ukrainian-clinic-making-3-parent-babies -for-women-who-are-infertile.

47 "About Us," Modamily, https://www.modamily.com/about-us.

48 Daniela Cutas, "On Triparenting. Is Having Three Committed Parents Better

Than Having Only Two?" *Journal of Medical Ethics* 37, no. 12 (August 2011): 735–38.

49 Angela Chen, "The Rise of the Three-Parent Family," *The Atlantic*, September 2020, https://www.theatlantic.com/family/archive/2020/09/how -build-three-parent-family-david-jay/616421/.

50 "Relative or Stepchild Adoption," NI Direct, https://www.nidirect.gov.uk/articles /relative-or-stepchild-adoption.

51 Julia Marsh, "Historic Ruling Grants 'Tri-Custody' to Trio Who Had Threesome," *New York Post*, March 10, 2017, https://nypost.com/2017/03/10/historic-ruling -grants-custody-to-dad-and-mom-and-mom/.

52 Faith Karimi, "Three Dads, a Baby and the Legal Battle to Get Their Names Added to a Birth Certificate," *CNN*, March 6, 2021, https://www.cnn.com /2021/03/06/us/throuple-three-dads-and-baby-trnd/index.html.

53 Cutas, "On Triparenting."

54 Gavin Nobes and Georgia Panagiotaki, "The Cinderella Effect: Are Stepfathers Dangerous?" *The Conversation*, September 24, 2018, https://theconversation .com/the-cinderella-effect-are-stepfathers-dangerous-103707.

55 Kalle Grill, "How Many Parents Should There Be in a Family?" *Journal of Applied Philosophy* 37, no. 3 (July 2020): 467–84.

56 Kalle Grill, "How Many Parents Should There Be in a Family?"

57 Anca Gheaus, "More Co-Parents, Fewer Children: Multiparenting and Sustainable Population," *Essays in Philosophy* 20, no. 1 (January 2019): 1–21: 13.

58 David Autor, David Dorn, and Gordon Hanson, "When Work Disappears: Manufacturing Decline and the Falling Marriage Market Value of Young Men," *American Economic Review: Insights* 1, no. 2 (September 2019): 161–78.

59 "Healthy Marriage and Relationship Education for Adults," Office of Family Assistance, US Department of Health and Human Services, https://www .acf.hhs.gov/ofa/programs/healthy-marriage-responsible-fatherhood/healthy -marriage.

60 Gheaus, "More Co-Parents, Fewer Children."

Chapter 8: The *Star Trek* Game Plan

1 Chris Klimek, "'Star Trek' at 50: How the Sci-Fi TV Show Changed Every-thing, *Rolling Stone*, September 8, 2016, https://www.rollingstone.com/tv/tv -news/star-trek-at-50-how-the-sci-fi-tv-show-changed-everything-104127/.

2 Sarah Pruitt, "8 Ways the Original 'Star Trek' Made History," *History*, September 8, 2016, updated November 2, 2021, https://www.history.com/news /8-ways-the-original-star-trek-made-history.

3 Michael McCarrick, "How Long It Would Take to Watch All of Star Trek (Yes, ALL of It)," *CBR*, Janaury 21, 2021, https://www.cbr.com/star-trek-every-tv -episode-movie/.

4 The FedCon website: https://www.fedcon.de/en/.

5 Duncan Barrett, "We Lived Long and Prospered! How Star Trek Saved Fans' Lives," *The Guardian*, November 13, 2019, https://www.theguardian.com/tv -and-radio/2019/nov/13/how-star-trek-saved-fans-lives.

6 David Graeber and David Wengrow, *The Dawn of Everything: A New History of Humanity* (New York: Farrar, Straus and Giroux, 2021), 9.

7 "Our Mission," Institute for Family Studies, https://ifstudies.org/about/our -mission.

8 "Our Mission," Institute for Family Studies.

9 Davina Cooper, *Everyday Utopias: The Conceptual Life of Promising Spaces* (Durham, NC: Duke University Press, 2014), 34.

10 Eduardo Galeano, "Window on Utopia," in Eduardo Galeano, *Walking Words*, trans. M. Fried (New York: W. W. Norton, 1997), 326.

11 C. R. Snyder, "Hope Theory: Rainbows in the Mind," *Psychological Inquiry* 13, no. 4 (2002): 249–75.

12 M. Rahimipour, N. Shahgholian, and M. Yazdani, "Effect of Hope Therapy on Depression, Anxiety, and Stress Among the Patients Undergoing Hemodialysis," *Iranian Journal of Nursing and Midwifery Research* 20, no. 6 (November– December 2015): 694–99.

13 C. Gawrilow, K. Morgenroth, R. Schultz, G. Oettingen, and P. M. Gollwitzer, "Mental Contrasting with Implementation Intentions Enhances Self-Regulation of Goal Pursuit in Schoolchildren at Risk for ADHD," *Motivation and Emotion* 37, no. 1 (March 2012): 134–45.

14 Cooper, *Everyday Utopias*, 31.

15 See for instance: Robert McCrum, "The 100 Best Novels: No. 56—Brave New World by Aldous Huxley (1932)," *The Guardian*, October 13, 2014, https:// www.theguardian.com/books/2014/oct/13/100-best-novels-brave-new-world -aldous-huxley; "100 Best Novels," Modern Library, https://www.modern library.com/top-100/100-best-novels/.

16 "A Teacher's Guide to Brave New World," http://files.harpercollins.com/Harper Academic/BraveNewWorld_TeachingGuide_final.pdf (see page 3).

17 Alana Domingo, "How to Teach Brave New World," Prestwick House, https://www.prestwickhouse.com/blog/post/2019/06/how-to-teach-brave-new -world.

18 Aldous Huxley, *Brave New World* (New York: Harper Perennial Classics, 1998), 117.

19 Huxley, *Brave New World*, 12–13.

20 Huxley, *Brave New World*, 166.

21 Huxley, *Brave New World*, 200.

22 Dorian Lynskey, "Nothing but the Truth: The Legacy of George Orwell's Nineteen Eighty-Four," *The Guardian*, May 19, 2019, https://www.theguardian .com/books/2019/may/19/legacy-george-orwell-nineteen-eighty-four.

23 George Orwell, *1984* (New York: Plume, 1983), 183.

24 Orwell, *1984*, 183.

25 Orwell, *1984*, 276.

26 Ben Blatt, "Why Do So Many Schools Try to Ban *The Giver?*" *Slate*, August 14, 2014, https://slate.com/culture/2014/08/the-giver-banned-why-do-so-many -parents-try-to-remove-lois-lowrys-book-from-schools.html.

27 "Top 100 Chapter Book Poll Results," *School Library Journal*, July 7, 2012, https://web.archive.org/web/20120713031015/http://blog.schoollibraryjournal .com/afuse8production/2012/07/07/top-100-chapter-book-poll-results/.

28 Sheila O'Malley, "The Giver," Roger Ebert, August 15, 2014, https://www .rogerebert.com/reviews/the-giver-2014.

29 Mark Fisher, *Capitalist Realism: Is There No Alternative?* (Chicago: Zero Books, 2009), 33.

30 Mitchell Kalpakgian, "The Ideological Attack on the Family in Orwell's 1984 and Huxley's Brave New World," *Faith & Reason: The Journal of Christendom College* 26, no. 4 (Winter 2001): https://media.christendom.edu/wp-content/uploads/2016 /09/Mitchell-Kalpakgian-An-Ideologial-Attack-on-the-Family.pdf.

31 Jeane J. Kirkpatrick, "Dictatorships & Double Standards," *The Commentary*, November 1979, https://www.commentary.org/articles/jeane-kirkpatrick /dictatorships-double-standards/.

32 Kirkpatrick, "Dictatorships & Double Standards."

33 Thomas Hobbes, *Leviathan*, Project Gutenberg, https://www.gutenberg.org/ebooks /3207.

34 Richard Allen Chapman, "Leviathan Writ Small: Thomas Hobbes on the Family," *The American Political Science Review* 69, no. 1 (1975): 76–90, https://doi.org/10.2307/1957886.

35 Slavoj Žižek, *The Year of Dreaming Dangerously* (New York: Verson Books, 2012); "Expanding the Floor of the Cage: Noam Chomsky Interviewed by David Barsamian," *Z Magazine*, April 1997, https://chomsky.info/199704__/.

36 Graeber and Wengrow, *The Dawn of Everything*, 502.

37 Chloe Meley, "Should You Join a Commune in 2021? TikTok Says Yes!" *i-D Vice*, January 28, 2021, https://i-d.vice.com/en_uk/article/v7mqm9/should-you -join-a-commune-in-2021-tiktok-says-yes.

38 Antonio Gramsci, *Prison Notebooks* (New York: Columbia University Press, 2011).

39 Ryan Grim, "The Elephant in the Zoom," *The Intercept*. June 14, 2022, https://www.youtube.com/watch?v=n1xp50ZM_wk.

40 Kathi Weeks, *The Problem with Work: Feminism, Marxism, Antiwork Politics, and Postwork Imaginaries* (Durham, NC: Duke University Press, 2011).

41 Holly Jean Buck, *After Geoengineering: Climate Tragedy, Repair, and Restoration* (London and New York: Verso Books, 2019).

42 Howard Zinn, "The Optimism of Uncertainty," *The Nation*, 2004, https://www.thenation.com/article/archive/optimism-uncertainty/.

43 Donna Haraway suggests that we should all be "making kin." See Donna Haraway, "Anthropocene, Capitalocene, Plantationocene, Chthulucene: Making Kin," *Environmental Humanities* 6 (2015): 159–65.

44 Gerda Lerner, *The Creation of Patriarchy*. New York: Oxford University Press, 1986: 228.

45 Rutger Bregman, *Humankind: A Hopeful History*. New York: Little Brown, 2019.

46 Thomas Hardy, January 1, 1902, quoted in Florence Emily Hardy, *The Life of Thomas Hardy* (Stansted: Wordsworth Editions, 2007), 319.

47 "United Federation of Planets," Memory Alpha, https://memory-alpha.fandom.com/wiki/United_Federation_of_Planets.

48 "Starfleet," Memory Alpha, https://memory-alpha.fandom.com/wiki/Starfleet.

49 "All Is Possible (Episode)," Memory Alpha, https://memory-alpha.fandom.com/wiki/All_Is_Possible_(episode).

50 Thomas Richards, *The Meaning of Star Trek* (New York: Doubleday, 1997).

Selected Suggestions for Further Reading

For specific references discussed in the text, please refer to the endnotes. Below I list some general books, in alphabetical order, to acquaint you with just a glimpse of the voluminous literature on utopias and utopianism that pay specific attention to the domestic sphere, as well as a few relevant novels. Although by no means an exhaustive list, these suggestions will hopefully inspire readers to explore the many fascinating texts that can help us flex our cognitive capacities for hope.

Chapter One

Bastani, Aaron. *Fully Automated Luxury Communism: A Manifesto*. New York: Verso Books, 2019.

Beik, Doris, and Paul Beik. *Flora Tristan: Utopian Feminist, Her Travel Diaries and Personal Crusade*. Bloomington: Indiana University Press, 1993.

Bogdanov, Alexander. *Red Star: The First Bolshevik Utopia*. Bloomington: Indiana University Press, 1984.

Bregman, Rutger. *Utopia for Realists: How We Can Build the Ideal World*. New York: Back Bay Books, 2016.

Callenbach, Ernest. *Ecotopia: The Notebooks and Reports of William Weston*. Berkeley: Banyan Tree Books, 2014.

Campanella, Tommaso. *The City of the Sun*. Project Gutenberg, https://www.gutenberg.org/ebooks/2816.

Claeys, Gregory. *Searching for Utopia: The History of an Idea*. London: Thames & Hudson, 2011.

Claeys, Gregory, and Lyman Tower Sargent. *The Utopia Reader*, 2nd ed. New York: New York University Press, 2017.

Diamandis, Peter H., and Steven Kotler. *Abundance: The Future Is Better Than You Think*. New York: Free Press, 2012.

Dijkstra, Sandra. *Flora Tristan: Feminism in the Age of George Sand*. New York: Verso Books, 2019.

Graeber, David, and David Wengrow. *The Dawn of Everything: A New History of Humanity*. New York: Farrar, Straus and Giroux, 2021.

Green, Toby. *Thomas More's Magician: A Novel Account of Utopia in Mexico*. London: Weidenfeld & Nicolson, 2004.

Kahneman, Daniel. *Thinking Fast and Slow*. New York: Farrar, Straus and Giroux, 2013.

Le Guin, Ursula K. *The Dispossessed: A Novel*. New York: Harper Perennial Modern Classics, 2014.

Lepore, Jill. *The Secret History of Wonder Woman*. London: Vintage, 2015.

Lerner, Gerda. *The Creation of Patriarchy*. Oxford: Oxford University Press, 1997.

Levitas, Ruth. *The Concept of Utopia*. Syracuse, NY: Syracuse University Press, 1990.

Mannheim, Karl. *Ideology and Utopia: An Introduction to the Sociology of Knowledge*. Mansfield Center, CT: Martino, 2015.

Manuel, Frank E., and Fritzie P. Manuel. *Utopian Thought in the Western World*. Cambridge, MA: Belknap Press, 1979.

Monti, James. *The King's Good Servant but God's First: The Life and Writings of Saint Thomas More*. San Francisco: Ignatius Press, 1997.

More, Thomas. *Utopia*. Project Gutenberg, https://www.gutenberg.org/ebooks/2130.

Morris, William. *News from Nowhere; Or, An Epoch of Rest*. Project Gutenberg, https://www.gutenberg.org/ebooks/3261.

Piercy, Marge. *Woman on the Edge of Time: A Novel*. New York: Ballantine Books, 1997.

Piketty, Thomas. *A Brief History of Equality*. Cambridge, MA: Belknap Press, 2022.

———. *Capital and Ideology*. Cambridge, MA: Belknap Press, 2020.

———. *Capital in the Twenty-First Century*. Cambridge, MA: Belknap Press, 2014.

Plato. *The Republic*. Project Gutenberg, https://www.gutenberg.org/ebooks/1497.

Shaer, Roland, Gregory Claeys, and Lyman Tower Sargent, eds. *Utopia: The Search for the Ideal Society in the Western World*. New York: Oxford University Press and the New York Public Library, 2000.

Sunstein, Cass. *The World According to Star Wars*. New York: Dey Street Books, 2019.

WaiHong, Choo. *The Kingdom of Women: Life, Love and Death in China's Hidden Mountains*. London: Tauris Parke, 2020.

Zamalin, Alex. *Black Utopia: The History of an Idea from Black Nationalism to Afrofuturism*. New York: Columbia University Press, 2019.

Zamyatin, Yevgeny. *We*. New York: Penguin Books, 1993.

Zhong, Yushan. *Balancing Men and Women's Power and Status: Parental Roles and Children's Socialization in Mosuo Matrilineal Families*. Berlin: VDM Verlag Dr. Müller, 2011.

Chapter Two

Alekseyeva, Anna. *Everyday Soviet Utopias: Planning, Design, and the Aesthetics of Developed Socialism*. New York, Routledge, 2020.

Beecher, Jonathan. *The Utopian Vision of Charles Fourier*. Columbia, MO: University of Missouri Press, 1983.

Bradley, Keith. *Discovering the Roman Family: Studies in Roman Social History*. Oxford, UK: Oxford University Press, 1991.

Clark, James. *The Dissolution of the Monasteries: A New History*. New Haven, CT: Yale University Press, 2021.

Cleaver, Naomi, and Amy Frearson. *All Together Now: The Co-Living and Co-Working Revolution*. London: RIBA, 2021.

Dixon, Suzanne. *The Roman Family*. Baltimore: Johns Hopkins University Press, 1992.

Dove, Caroline. *Radical Housing: Designing Multi-Generational and Co-Living Housing for All*. London: RIBA, 2020.

Doyle, Michael. *The Ministers' War: John W. Mears, the Oneida Community, and the Crusade for Public Morality*. Syracuse, NY: Syracuse University Press, 2018.

Durrett, Charles, and Kathryn McCamant. *Creating Cohousing: Building Sustainable Communities*. Gabriola Island, BC: New Society Publishers, 2011.

Fourier, Charles. *Fourier: The Theory of the Four Movements*, ed. Gareth Stedman Jones and Ian Patterson. Cambridge, UK: Cambridge University Press, 2008.

Hillis, Faith. *Utopia's Discontents: Russian Émigrés and the Quest for Freedom, 1830s–1930s*. London and New York: Oxford University Press, 2021.

Hodder, Ian, and Christina Tsoraki, eds. *Communities at Work: The Making of Çatalhöyük*. Ankara, Turkey: British Institute of Archaeology at Ankara, 2022.

Hodder, Ian. *Çatalhöyük Excavations: The 2009–2017 Seasons* (Çatalhöyük Research Project Series). Ankara, Turkey: British Institute of Archaeology at Ankara, 2022.

Kern, Leslie. *The Feminist City: Claiming Space in a Man-Made World*. New York: Verso Books, 2020.

Klaw, Spencer. *Without Sin: The Life and Death of the Oneida Community*. London: Viking Adult, 1993.

Lions-Patacchini, Christian. *Jean-Baptiste André Godin et le familistère de Guise: Ethique et pratique*. Aix-en-Provence, France: PU Aix-Marseille, 2012.

McCamant, Kathryn, and Charles Durrett. *Cohousing: A Contemporary Approach to Housing Ourselves*. Berkeley: Ten Speed Press, 1994.

Noyes, Pierrepont B. *My Father's House: An Oneida Boyhood*. New York: Farrar & Rinehart, 1937, https://archive.org/details/myfathershouse0000unse.

Owen, Robert. *A New View of Society: And Other Writings*. Lagos, Nigeria: Origami Books, 2019.

Peters, Greg. *The Story of Monasticism: Retrieving an Ancient Tradition for Contemporary Spirituality*. Ada, MI: Baker Academic, 2015.

Rubin, Eli. *Amnesiopolis: Modernity, Space, and Memory in East Germany*. London and New York: Oxford University Press, 2016.

Simons, Walter. *Cities of Ladies: Beguine Communities in the Medieval Low Countries*. Philadelphia: University of Pennsylvania Press, 2003.

Stanek, Lukasz. *Architecture in Global Socialism: Eastern Europe, West Africa, and the Middle East in the Cold War*. Princeton, NJ: Princeton University Press, 2020.

Stierli, Martino. *Toward a Concrete Utopia: Architecture in Yugoslavia, 1948–1980*. New York: Museum of Modern Art, 2018.

Swan, Laura. *The Wisdom of the Beguines: The Forgotten Story of a Medieval Women's Movement*. Katonah, NY: BlueBridge, 2016.

Wayland-Smith, Ellen. *Oneida: From Free Love Utopia to the Well-Set Table*. New York: Picador, 2016.

Wonderley, Anthony. *Oneida Utopia: A Community Searching for Human Happiness and Prosperity*. Ithaca, NY: Cornell University Press, 2017.

Chapter Three

Abramitzsky, Ran. *The Mystery of the Kibbutz: Egalitarian Principles in a Capitalist World*. Princeton, NJ: Princeton University Press, 2018.

Calhoun, Ada. *Why We Can't Sleep: Women's New Midlife Crisis*. New York: Grove Press, 2020.

Caroli, Dorena. *Day Nurseries & Childcare in Europe, 1800–1939*. London: Palgrave Macmillan, 2016.

Clements, Barbara Evans. *Bolshevik Feminist: The Life of Aleksandra Kollontai*. Bloomington: Indiana University Press, 1979.

Crittendon, Anne. *The Price of Motherhood: Why the Most Important Job in the World Is Still the Least Valued*. New York: Picador, 2010.

Douglas, Susan. *The Mommy Myth: The Idealization of Motherhood and How It Has Undermined All Women*. New York: Free Press, 2005.

Engels, Friedrich. *The Conditions of the Working-Class in England*. Project Gutenberg, https://www.gutenberg.org/ebooks/17306.

Engels, Friedrich, and Karl Marx. *The Communist Manifesto*. Project Gutenberg, https://www.gutenberg.org/ebooks/61.

Farnsworth, Beatrice. *Aleksandra Kollontai: Socialism, Feminism and the Bolshevik Revolution*. Palo Alto, CA: Stanford University Press, 1980.

Heilbroner, Robert L. *The Worldly Philosophers: The Lives, Times and Ideas of The Great Economic Thinkers.* New York: Touchstone, 1999.

hooks, bell. *Feminist Theory: From Margin to Center.* New York: Routledge, 2014.

Kirschenbaum, Lisa. *Small Comrades: Revolutionizing Childhood in Soviet Russia, 1917–1932.* New York: Routledge, 2000.

Klaw, Spencer. *Without Sin: The Life and Death of the Oneida Community.* New York: Viking Adult, 1993.

McClellan, Josie. *Love in the Time of Communism: Intimacy and Sexuality in the GDR.* Cambridge, UK: Cambridge University Press, 2011.

Michel, Sonya. *Children's Interests/Mothers' Rights: The Shaping of America`s Child Care Policy.* New Haven, CT: Yale University Press, 1999.

Noyes, Pierrepont. *My Father's House: An Oneida Boyhood.* New York: Rinehart, 1937, and Archive.org, https://archive.org/details/myfathers house0000unse.

Porter, Cathy. *Alexandra Kollontai: A Biography.* Chicago: Haymarket Books, 2014.

Qualls, Karl D. *Stalin's Niños: Educating Spanish Civil War Refugee Children in the Soviet Union: 1937–1951.* Toronto: University of Toronto Press, 2020.

Robertson, Constance Noyes. *Oneida Community: An Autobiography.* Syracuse, NY: Syracuse University Press, 1970.

Valenti, Jessica. *Why Have Kids? A New Mom Explores the Truth About Parenting and Happiness.* New York: New Harvest, 2012.

Warner, Judith. *Perfect Madness: Motherhood in the Age of Anxiety.* New York: Riverhead, 2006.

Wonderley, Anthony. *Oneida Utopia: A Community Searching for Human Happiness and Prosperity.* Ithaca, NY: Cornell University Press, 2017.

Chapter Four

Bjerk, Paul. *Building a Peaceful Nation: Julius Nyerere and the Establishment of Sovereignty in Tanzania, 1960–1964.* Rochester, NY: University of Rochester Press, 2015.

———. *Julius Nyerere.* Athens: Ohio University Press, 2017.

Bowles, Samuel, and Herbert Gintis. *Schooling in Capitalist America: Educational Reform and the Contradictions of Economic Life.* Chicago: Haymarket Books, 2011.

Cengage Learning Gale. *A Study Guide for A Study Guide to Kurt Vonnegut's Harrison Bergeron.* Detroit: Gale Study Guides, 2017.

Fitzpatrick, Sheila. *The Commisariat of Enlightenment: Soviet Organization of Education and the Arts under Lunacharsky.* Cambridge, UK: Cambridge University Press, 1970.

Freire, Paolo. *Pedagogy of the Oppressed*. New York: Penguin, 2017.

Lave, Jean, and Etienne Wegner. *Situated Learning: Legitimate Peripheral Participation*. Cambridge, UK: Cambridge University Press, 1991.

Makarenko, Anton. *Makarenko, His Life and Work: Articles, Talks and Reminiscences*. Honolulu: University Press of the Pacific, 2004.

McNeal, Robert H. *Bride of the Revolution: Krupskaya and Lenin*. Ann Arbor: University of Michigan Press, 1972.

Mill, John Stuart. *Autobiography*. Project Gutenberg, https://www.gutenberg.org/ebooks/10378.

———. *Principles of Political Economy*. Project Gutenberg, https://www.gutenberg.org/ebooks/30107.

Nyerere, Julius K. *Freedom and Socialism / Uhuru Na Ujamaa: A Selection from Writings and Speeches, 1965–1967*. Oxford, UK: Oxford University Press, 1968.

———. *Ujamaa: Essays on Socialism*. Oxford, UK: Oxford University Press, 1971.

Pratt, Cranford. *The Critical Phase in Tanzania: Nyerere and the Emergence of a Socialist Strategy*. Cambridge, UK: Cambridge University Press, 2009.

Vonnegut, Kurt. *Welcome to the Monkey House*. New York: Dial Press, 1998.

Willis, Paul. *Learning to Labor: How Working Class Kids Get Working Class Jobs*. New York: Columbia University Press, 1981.

Chapter Five

Bakunin, Mikhail. *God and the State*. Project Gutenberg, https://www.gutenberg.org/ebooks/36568.

Barber, Malcom. *The Cathars*. New York: Routledge, 2013.

Birnbaum, Juliana, and Louis Fox. *Sustainable Revolution: Permaculture in Ecovillages, Urban Farms, and Communities Worldwide*. Berkeley: North Atlantic Books, 2014.

Brockett, L. P. *The Bogomils of Bulgaria and Bosnia: Or, The Early Protestants of the East—an Attempt to Restore Some Lost Leaves of Protestant History*. Philadelphia: American Baptist Publications Society, 2017.

Coston, Michael. *The Cathars and the Albigensian Crusade*. Manchester, UK: Manchester University Press, 1997.

Engels, Friedrich. *The Origin of the Family, Private Property, and the State*. Project Gutenberg, https://www.gutenberg.org/ebooks/33111.

———. *Socialism, Utopian and Scientific*. Project Gutenberg, https://www.gutenberg.org/ebooks/39257.

Ginsburg, Christian D. *The Essenes: Their History and Doctrines*. New Orleans: Cornerstone, 2018.

Godwin, William. *An Enquiry Concerning Political Justice*. Oxford, UK: Oxford University Press, 2013.

Gritch, Eric. *Thomas Müntzer: A Tragedy of Errors*. Minneapolis: Augsburg Fortress, 2000.

Kinkade, Kathleen. *A Walden Two Experiment: The First Five Years of Twin Oaks Community*. New York: William Morrow, 1974.

Kropotkin, Peter. *The Conquest of Bread*, edited with an introduction by Paul Avrich. New York: New York University Press, 1972.

———. *The Conquest of Bread*. Project Gutenberg, https://www.gutenberg.org/ebooks /23428.

———. *Mutual Aid: A Factor of Evolution*. Project Gutenberg, https://www .gutenberg.org/ebooks/4341.

Litfin, Karen T. *Ecovillages: Lessons for Sustainable Community*. Indianapolis: Polity, 2013.

Morris, Brian. *Kropotkin: The Politics of Community*. Oakland: PM Press, 2018.

Odell, Jenny. *How to Do Nothing: Resisting the Attention Economy*. New York: Melville House, 2019.

O'Shea, Stephen. *The Perfect Heresy: The Revolutionary Life and Death of the Medieval Cathars*. London: Walker Books, 2000.

Proudhon, Pierre-Joseph. *System of Economical Contradictions; Or, The Philosophy of Misery* (1846). Project Gutenberg, https://www.gutenberg.org/ebooks/444.

———. *What Is Property? An Inquiry into the Principle of Right and of Government* (1840). Project Gutenberg, https://www.gutenberg.org/ebooks /360.

Skinner, B. F. *Walden Two*. Indianapolis: Hackett, 2005.

Stein, Stephen J. *The Shaker Experience in America: A History of the United Society of Believers*. New Haven, CT: Yale University Press, 1994.

Strober, Clare. *Another Life Is Possible: Insights from 100 Years of Life Together*. Walden, NY: Plough, 2000.

Sumption, Jonathan. *The Albigensian Crusade*. London: Faber & Faber, 2000.

Varzonovtseva, Milena. *The Secret Books of the Bogomils*. Saarbrücken, Germany: VDM Verlag, 2008.

Wilson, Laura. *Hutterites of Montana*. New Haven, CT: Yale University Press, 2000.

Chapter Six

Bancroft, Lundy. *Why Does He Do That?: Inside the Minds of Angry and Controlling Men*. New York: Berkley Books, 2003.

Bancroft, Lundy, and Jay G. Silverman. *The Batterer as Parent: Addressing the Impact of Domestic Violence on Family Dynamics*. Thousand Oaks, CA: Sage, 2002.

Chapais, Bernard. *Primeval Kinship: How Pair-Bonding Gave Birth to Human Society*. Cambridge, MA: Harvard University Press, 2010.

Dixon, Patricia. *We Want for Our Sisters What We Want for Ourselves: African American Women Who Practice Polygyny/Polygamy by Consent*. Winter Park, FL: Nuvo Development, 2021.

Givens, Terry L. *People of Paradox: A History of Mormon Culture*. Oxford, UK: Oxford University Press, 2007.

Hrdy, Sandra Blaffer. *Mother and Others: The Evolutionary Origins of Mutual Understanding*. Cambridge, MA: Belknap Press, 2009.

———. *The Woman That Never Evolved*. Cambridge, MA: Harvard University Press, 1999.

Kauth, Michael R. *The Evolution of Human Pair-Bonding, Friendship, and Sexual Attraction*. London: Routledge, 2020.

Koenig, Walter D., and Janis L. Dickinson, eds. *Cooperative Breeding in Vertebrates: Studies of Ecology, Evolution, and Behavior*. Cambridge, UK: Cambridge University Press, 2018.

Ryan, Christopher, and Cacilda Jetha. *Sex at Dawn: How We Mate, Why We Stray, and What It Means for Modern Relationships*. New York: Harper Perennial, 2011.

Smith, George. *Nauvoo Polygamy: ". . . But We Called It Celestial Marriage."* Salt Lake City: Signature Books, 2011.

Snyder, Rachel Louise. *No Visible Bruises: What We Don't Know About Domestic Violence Can Kill Us*. London: Bloomsbury, 2019.

Weir, Alison. *The Six Wives of Henry VIII*. New York: Grove, 1992.

Chapter Seven

Bebel, August. *Aus meinem Lebem—Erster Teil* (1910). Project Gutenberg, https://www.gutenberg.org/ebooks/12267.

———. *Charles Fourier: Sein Leben und Seine Theorien* (1890). Project Gutenberg, https://www.gutenberg.org/ebooks/19596.

———. *Woman and Socialism* (1879). Project Gutenberg, https://www.gutenberg.org/ebooks/47244.

Brenner, Johanna. *Women and the Politics of Class*. New York: Monthly Review Press, 2000.

Bucur, Maria. *The Century of Women: How Women Have Transformed the World Since 1900*. Baltimore: Rowman & Littlefield, 2018.

Cerankowski, Karli June, and Megan Milks, eds. *Asexualities*. London: Routledge, 2016.

Conly, Sarah. *One Child: Do We Have a Right to More?* New York: Oxford University Press, 2015.

Cooper, Melinda. *Family Values: Between Neoliberalism and the New Social Conservatism*. Princeton, NJ: Zone Books, 2017.

Fern, Jessica. *Polysecure: Attachment, Trauma and Consensual Nonmonogamy*. Portland: Thorntree Press, 2020.

Firestone, Shulamith. *The Dialectic of Sex: The Case for Feminist Revolution*. New York: Farrar, Straus and Giroux, 2003.

Foster, Lawrence. *Religion and Sexuality: The Shakers, the Mormons, and the Oneida Community*. Champaign: University of Illinois Press, 1984.

Goldman, Emma. *Anarchism and Other Essays* (1910). Project Gutenberg, https://www.gutenberg.org/ebooks/2162.

Goldman, Emma. *Marriage and Love* (1911). Project Gutenberg, https://www.gutenberg.org/files/20715/20715-h/20715-h.htm.

Haraway, Donna. *Staying with the Trouble: Making Kin in the Chthulucene*. Durham, NC: Duke University Press, 2016.

Holmstrom, Nancy, ed. *The Socialist Feminist Project: A Contemporary Reader in Theory and Politics*. New York: Monthly Review Press, 2002.

Jenkins, Ian. *Three Dads and a Baby: Adventures in Modern Parenting*. Jersey City, NJ: Cleis Press, 2021.

Kollontai, Alexandra. *Selected Writings*. New York: W. W. Norton, 1980.

Lewis, Sophie. *Full Surrogacy Now: Feminism Against Family*. London: Verso Books, 2021.

Moses, Claire G. *French Feminism in the 19th Century*. Albany: State University of New York Press, 1985.

Perel, Esther. *Mating in Captivity: Reconciling the Erotic and the Domestic*. New York: Harper, 2006.

Pilbeam, Pamela M. *Saint-Simonians in Nineteenth-Century France: From Free Love to Algeria*. London: Palgrave Macmillan, 2014.

Powell, Anton, ed. *A Companion to Sparta*. Hoboken, NJ: Wiley-Blackwell, 2017.

TallBear, Kim. "Identity Is a Poor Substitute for Relating: Genetic Ancestry, Critical Polyamory, Property, and Relations." *Critical Indigenous Studies Handbook*. London, Routledge, 2020, 467–78.

Yalom, Marilyn. *A History of the Wife*. New York: Harper Perennial, 2002.

Chapter Eight

Bellamy, Edward. *Looking Backward*. Mineola, NY: Dover, 1996.

Bergman, Carla, and Nick Montgomery. *Joyful Militancy: Building Thriving Resistance in Toxic Times*. Chicago: AK Press, 2017.

Bloch, Ernst. *The Principle of Hope, Vol. 1*. Cambridge, MA: MIT Press, 1995.

———. *The Principle of Hope, Vol. 2*. Cambridge, MA: MIT Press, 1995.

———. *The Principle of Hope, Vol. 3*. Cambridge, MA: MIT Press, 1995.

———. *The Spirit of Utopia*. Palo Alto, CA: Stanford University Press, 2000.

Bregman, Rutger. *Humankind: A Hopeful History*. New York: Little Brown, 2019.

Buck, Holly Jean. *After Geoengineering: Climate Tragedy, Repair, and Restoration*. London and New York: Verso Books, 2019.

Butler, Samuel. *Erewhon*. New York: Penguin Classics, 1985.

Claeys, Gregory. *Dystopia: A Natural History*. Oxford, UK: Oxford University Press, 2017.

Cooper, Davina. *Everyday Utopias: The Conceptual Life of Promising Spaces*. Durham, NC: Duke University Press, 2014.

Gilman, Charlotte Perkins. *Herland*. Mineola, NY: Dover, 1998.

Gross, Edward, and Mark A. Altman. *The Fifty-Year Mission: The First 25 Years*. New York: St. Martin's Press, 2016.

Huxley, Aldous. *Brave New World*. New York: Harper Perennial, 1998.

———. *Island: A Novel*. New York: Harper Perennial, 2009.

Li, Ju Chen. *Flowers in the Mirror*, trans. Lin Tai-Yi. New York: Ishi Press, 2015.

Lowry, Lois. *The Giver*. New York: Clarion Books, 1993.

Montgomery, Nick, and Carla Bergman. *Joyful Militancy: Building Thriving Resistance in Toxic Times*. Oakland, CA: AK Press, 2017.

Morris, William. *News from Nowhere*. Mineola, NY: Dover, 2004.

Oettinger, Gabrielle. *Rethinking Positive Thinking: Inside the New Science of Motivation*. New York: Current, 2014.

Orwell, George. *1984*. London: Signet Classic, 1961.

Richards, Thomas. *The Meaning of Star Trek*. New York: Doubleday, 1997.

Saadia, Manu. *Trekonomics: The Economics of Star Trek*. San Francisco: Pipertext, 2016.

Snyder, C. R. *Psychology of Hope: You Can Get Here from There*. New York: Free Press, 2003.

Solnit, Rebecca. *Hope in the Dark: Untold Histories, Wild Possibilities*. Chicago: Haymarket Books, 2016.

Soper, Kate. *Post-Growth Living: For an Alternative Hedonism*. New York: Verso Books, 2020.

Weeks, Kathi. *The Problem with Work: Feminism, Marxism, Antiwork Politics, and Postwork Imaginaries*. Durham, NC: Duke University Press, 2011.

Wells, H. G. *A Modern Utopia*. Project Gutenberg, https://www.gutenberg.org/ebooks/6424.

———. *Men Like Gods*. Mineola, NY: Dover, 2016.

———. *The First Men in the Moon*. Project Gutenberg, https://www.gutenberg.org/ebooks/1013.

List of Figures

Index

Page numbers in *italics* refer to illustrations.

About the Author

KRISTEN R. GHODSEE is Professor and Chair of Russian and East European Studies as well as a Member of the Graduate Group in Anthropology at the University of Pennsylvania. Her articles and essays have been translated into more than twenty-five languages and have appeared in publications such as the *New York Times*, the *Washington Post*, *Ms. Magazine*, *Dissent*, *Foreign Affairs*, *Jacobin*, the *Baffler*, the *New Republic*, *Quartz*, *NBC Think*, the *Lancet*, *Project Syndicate*, *Le Monde Diplomatique*, and *Die Tageszeitung*. She is the author of eleven books, including *Why Women Have Better Sex Under Socialism: And Other Arguments for Economic Independence*, which has been translated into fourteen languages.

Ghodsee has held residential research fellowships at the Institute for Advanced Study (IAS) in Princeton, New Jersey; the Radcliffe Institute for Advanced Study at Harvard University; the Woodrow Wilson International Center for Scholars in Washington, DC; the Aleksanteri Institute of the University of Helsinki in Finland; the Center for History at Sciences Po in Paris, France, as well as the Freiburg Institute for Advanced Studies (FRIAS), the Imre Kertész Kolleg of the Friedrich-Schiller-Universität, and the Max Planck Institute for Demographic Research in Germany. In 2012, Ghodsee was awarded a John Simon Guggenheim Fellowship for her work in Anthropology and Cultural Studies. She is a consummate lover of basset hounds, an avid collector of manual typewriters, and, if forced to pick one at gunpoint, would choose Picard over Kirk.